# POLAR BEARS
## and other
# SCARES

Adventures of a Freelance Writer

RON TRUMAN

◆ FriesenPress

Suite 300 – 990 Fort St
Victoria, BC, V8V 3K2
Canada

www.friesenpress.com

**Copyright © 2016 by Ron Truman**
First Edition — 2016

All rights reserved.

No part of this publication may be reproduced, stored in a retrieval system or transmitted in any form or by any means, electronic, mechanical, photocopying, and recording or otherwise (except for brief passages for review purposes) without written permission from the FriesenPress.

ISBN
978-1-4602-8523-7 (Hardcover)
978-1-4602-8524-4 (Paperback)
978-1-4602-8525-1 (eBook)

*1. BIOGRAPHY & AUTOBIOGRAPHY, PERSONAL MEMOIRS*

Distributed to the trade by The Ingram Book Company

*Dedication*

This book is dedicated to my wife Elaine, my granddaughter Sophia and my grandson Edward Jacob—who might otherwise remain innocent of the fact that I led an interesting life before they met me.

## *Thank You Notes*

Special thanks go to Orland French, my editor, who guided me through the process of writing a book, pulling me up short when I was being too outrageous. He encouraged me to write brightly and organize the content effectively.

I am much indebted to Dr. Bill Brummitt, a retired anesthesiologist (who knows when something is putting people to sleep). He read every word as I wrote this memoir and made numerous excellent suggestions for improvement of the text.

Other friends and acquaintances have read chapters from the book, offering advice on some of the content and catching many typographical errors and grammatical inconsistencies at early stages. This group includes Elaine Truman (who read it all), Lois Brummitt, and Lois Vaughan.

Shirley Teasdale, who freelanced to *The Globe and Mail* at the same time I did and who gave me invaluable help at critical stages of my career after I left the paper, reviewed several of the early chapters in the book.

Many women who read the memoir as a work in progress cautioned me about judgements that were overly harsh and statements that came across as insensitive—ranging from mildly offensive to downright pig ignorant. Knowing what is good for me, I usually took their advice.

Greg Smith, formerly an editor at *The Toronto Star* and now a croquet-playing friend, reviewed some material at my request. I wanted his opinion on some difficult passages.

Catherine Farley, another croquet friend and retired graphic artist, designed the cover and used her photo shopping skills to improve the cover photo.

Because I wrote for many years on cardiovascular disease, I used that work history as an excuse to include my personal heart and stroke experiences in my memoir as Section V. The number of medical professionals who read (or were given the opportunity to read) this section of the work is lengthy. Listed in alphabetical order they are: Dr. Bill Brummitt, Dr. Charles Gordon, Dr. Curry Grant, Dr. Heather Ross, and Dr. Frank Silver. Four of the doctors had treated me as a patient and I learned not to expect detailed suggestions from them. I appreciate their taking time to read my account of my cardiovascular troubles and my perception of their treatment of me. Dr. Brummitt, who never had me as a patient, provided much detailed feedback, information and direction.

Finally, I would like to thank Audrey Bradshaw RN, the nurse in the stroke rehabilitation program at Belleville General Hospital. She suggested that since I had written so much on cardiovascular disease and seemed to be recovering well from my strokes, that I should write the story. When I found myself unable to start with stroke, I turned the project into my memoirs, dealing with the horrors of stroke when they came up far into my story.

# TABLE OF CONTENTS

*Dedication*
*Thank You Notes*

**SECTION I**     IX

1. A Mittyesque Nightmare Memoirs of Ron Truman    1

2. The Truman Heritage— My Unfinished Book    7

**SECTION II ADVENTURES IN FREELANCE WRITING**    17
*Going Where Others Wouldn't*

3. There are Pieces of My Face Hanging on Those Trees    19
*Covering adventure and blood sports for The Globe and Mail's Recreation Section 1976-1983*

4. Women and Children First!    36
*New topics for stories present themselves The Thursday Section: Recreation, Women's Issues, Science and Medicine 1980-1983*

5. Look Who`s Still Alive    47
*Photography and Adventure 1976-2015*

6. Polar Bears Scare Me Shitless    56
*The years with Landmarks Magazine 1984-1987*

**SECTION III COMMUNICATIONS CONSULTING**    71
*Good Writing Was My Forte*

7. Two Wimps in the Wilderness    73
*Leading tours of Ontario for visiting journalists 1983*

8. Nobody Died at Three Mile Island    81
*Crisis communications 1984-1991*

9. And h'it's in h'English!!    98
*More crisis communications 1992-2007*

10. Speech Writing    106
*You saved my ass 1983-2007*

| | |
|---|---|
| 11. Combatting Preservationist Balderdash<br>*Saving all kinds of things in the wilderness 1983-1995* | 118 |
| 12. Thin Skins for Cree Women<br>*Native issues 1986-2005* | 129 |
| **SECTION IV TECHNOLOGY AND ENERGY**<br>*Buoyed up by an erbium-doped amplifier* | 145 |
| 13. Digital Revolution and Building Energy Management<br>*Writing about technology 1983-1995* | 147 |
| 14. Rent-seeking in the Sun<br>*Permits for the world's biggest solar farm and other energy scams* | 163 |
| **SECTION V CARDIOVASCULAR ADVENTURES**<br>*The Miracles of Medicine* | 181 |
| 15. Recovery from Cardiomyopathy and Heart Failure<br>*Getting tired was my first clue* | 183 |
| 16. Stopping a Stroke in Progress<br>*My life and the squeaky toy* | 197 |
| 17. Now You Know What It Feels Like to be a Woman<br>*Dealing with the furies unleashed by stroke* | 208 |
| 18. SSRIs—Serenity Now!<br>*Crying on the outside* | 219 |
| **EPILOGUE** | 225 |
| 19. There are Lives That are Erring and Aimless,<br>and Deaths That Just Hang by a Hair | 226 |
| *Index* | |

# SECTION I

# 1.
# A Mittyesque Nightmare
# Memoirs of Ron Truman

As I neared my 30th birthday, I was off on the wrong start in life. In a misguided attempt to become an academic, I had spent eight years in university. I had an undemanding job that paid well, owned a four-bedroom house, two cars, and was debt – and mortgage-free. Set for life? Yes, but an unbearable life. Every sunrise for the rest of my days was going to bring more of the same—working at an underwhelming job and enduring card games, golf, or curling as pastimes. I was primed for a life of quiet desperation with booze to dull the pain—a fate worse than death.

A middle age like Walter Mitty's seemed to be my future. Mitty was the protagonist in James Thurber's famous short story, *The Secret Life of Walter Mitty*, a pathetic, middle-aged man who frittered away his life running trivial errands. His only excitement was daydreaming about being a navy commander, a pilot, a surgeon, a sharpshooter, and a military hero.

Thurber's story is one of the *New Yorker's* most celebrated features, originally published in 1939 and still on their website. It was made into movies in 1947 and again in 2013. Why? It strikes a chord with men who have adventure in their blood; men who want to do something with their lives—and didn't or haven't yet had the chance.

During the writing of this memoir, the working title was *Ta-pocketa, Pocketa*, a reference to the words that Thurber used to represent the sounds of the imaginary engines, medical devices and flamethrowers that accompanied Mitty's elaborate fantasies. I changed the title at the last minute because most people didn't seem to know about Walter Mitty. A title that required explanation isn't a good one.

But it was the Walter Mitty story that inspired my writing career. Mitty's fate was my worst nightmare. My ability to write offered an escape from a pedestrian career and a tedious life.

How do you make a living as a writer? The great Canadian novel? A non-starter for someone with my short attention span. So I began my writing career freelancing feature articles to newspapers. A twin-lens camera shoved into my hands in a small-town newsroom led me to discover an aptitude for photography.

Excitement, adventure and innovation immediately flooded into my life. While in my 30s, I tagged polar bears, chased sturgeon in the Hudson Bay watershed, did Single and Twin Otter landings directly on the Arctic tundra, dealt with medical innovation, underwater archaeology, Himalayan expeditions and an emerging technology known as digital switching. For Canada's national newspaper, I paddled white water, climbed ice, went to avalanche schools and skied off the back of mountains. I was *The Globe and Mail's* last hunting writer and the only shooting sports writer who regularly contributed articles on women's issues, children, science, and sail racing. I freelanced more than 500 feature articles and about the same number of photographs to *The Globe and Mail*. I had a pseudonym used when I had more than one article in a single issue of a geographic magazine and wrote regular columns in two competing hunting and fishing magazines. As a tourism writing guide, I led a famous British author and a London toff from *The Guardian* on a memorable adventure tour in northern Ontario. Life was good, perhaps seeming a bit risky at times, but I was being paid to live fantasies come to life.

After my 40th birthday, everything changed. I stopped doing things that were hazardous. Why? A sudden decline in hormones?[1] Had life become worth staying alive for? But despite personal changes and the changes in newspaper and magazine markets, I still sought excitement. Danger? Meh. Not so much.

Fortunately, my clients had discovered I felt at home in crisis situations, calmly dealing with the unexpected and reacting placidly to outrage, deceit and subterfuge. My relatives had prepared me well. The family motto should be "Never EVER Tell the Truth." Many of my kin—most of those I knew well anyway—were profoundly alcoholic or extraordinarily dysfunctional (often both) as well as bright enough to keep track of their tangled web of lies. After decades of surviving them, hurling me into the turmoil of a nuclear accident, a terrorist attack or an animal rights outrage was like throwing Br'er Rabbit into a briar patch. It was where I felt most at home. Compared to enduring a family gathering, managing information flow in a crisis was relatively stress-free.

At the peak of my crisis management career, I acted as Ontario's Director of Emergency Information in preparation for terrorist attack and nuclear accident in Exercises TransBord III and Darlington '89. Trained in crisis communications, I participated in many real-life events, including the Ottawa meeting of the parties to the Convention on International Trade in Endangered Species (CITES) and the Golden Lake land claim involving Algonquin Provincial Park. Crisis communications was an exciting addition to an often-heavy workload of writing and consulting.

I frittered away most of my 50s. Burnt out, I left Toronto for eastern Ontario, and then spent a year in Australia. With no suitable steady work in small town eastern Ontario for someone the locals regarded as

---

1   I believe hormones drove my behaviour. Until I heard of dopamine, I blamed my antics on testosterone. But high-testosterone men are basically thrill-seeking. High-dopamine men seek risk. (Those who are high in both are prime candidates for a Darwin Award for eliminating themselves from the gene pool.) I was never one to get tattoos, ride motorcycles or go bald. So I suspect I was dopamine-driven. At maturity, Mother Nature, who is a catastrophic bitch, started shutting down my production of all hormones in preparation for shutting me down as a living organism. But there is hope for the hormonally challenged. We now have testosterone replacement therapy. The world might be a better place for old men if we had dopamine replacement therapy as well.

a "Toronto All-Star," I began a book-length project before attempting a return to newspaper freelancing. On the morning I boarded the plane for Australia, the *National Post* printed two of my feature stories. A flash in the pan, they were my last two articles in the *Post*.

On return from Down Under, I was back at Queen's Park, brought in to handle speech writing and news releases for difficult tourism projects, including a 100-event summer tour by Tim Hudak, then a young tourism minister laying the groundwork to become Leader of the Opposition and (he hoped) Premier of Ontario.

Real crises—9/11 and SARS—devastated the Ontario tourism industry, creating an overwhelming demand for communications. I was a wordsmith and communications advisor through these crises, no longer a decision-maker but thriving in an environment with levels of stress that meant instant burnout for many others. At the culmination of this work, I was hired to produce the communiqué at the Federal-Provincial Conference on SARS—given only a few hours to negotiate and write, I came up with a news release that 10 provinces, two territories, and the federal government endorsed.

At the age of 60, I was client-less and contract-less. A new government in Ontario dispensed with all the consultants. I took on oddball assignments and jobs. Then an unexpected phone call looking for communications help came from a company building the world's largest solar farm in Sarnia. Many energy experts regard wind and solar schemes as basically fraudulent, rent-seeking operations—but the idea of becoming rich was seductive as I neared retirement. I shut down my corporation and became a solar company employee with stock options and a fancy title—Director of Project Development.

Bad things began happening. Financial crisis finished the solar company. A falling out with upper levels in the company ensured that I would not survive restructuring. A polio-type virus attacked, leaving me with catastrophic heart failure. In 2008, I became a patient of the director of heart transplant at Toronto General Hospital. It's good to have a renowned cardiologist; it's not so good to be a patient in the Heart Function Clinic—the name is a euphemism for Heart F*cked Clinic.

But things got better. The solar industry began a well-deserved worldwide crashing and burning. I made an unpredicted and unexpected complete recovery from heart failure—on drug and exercise therapy alone. No surgery, although I came within a whisker of an implanted cardiac defibrillator (ICD).

Life was good for me by my late 60s. Comfortably retired and wintering in Florida, I was active in cycling and sport, producing a photo-filled croquet newsletter. Much of my work was in a collection held jointly by the Ontario Archives and the Public Archives of Canada, described in a thank-you letter from a federal committee in Ottawa as having "national and historic significance." I began referring to myself (at home only and very much tongue-in-cheek) as a "national treasure." While this amused and annoyed my wife, it helped me to convince myself that I had nothing left to accomplish and was finally retired.

But danger, challenge and excitement weren't finished with me.

My 70th year started disastrously. On January 1, 2014 I woke up paralyzed on my entire right side. Only grunts came out when I tried to speak and I was having trouble breathing.

I knew—all too well—what was happening. I had been one of the first to write on stroke back in the late 1970s when stroke victims were often hidden away and stroke rehabilitation was a novel idea. In the 1980s, I spent several years working on communications for what had been the Heart Foundation as it transformed itself into the Heart <u>and</u> <u>Stroke</u> Foundation.

That New Year's morning I underwent procedures that were unheard of 30 years earlier. An innovative interventional radiologist reached up into my brain from my groin and actually vacuumed the clot out of my brainstem. Then he cleaned things up with clot-busting drugs. I was still on the table in the cardiac studio when I recovered my ability to move and speak.

Stroke rehabilitation, I feared, was going to be a slow and uncertain process, beginning with learning to stand up again, then to walk. I never imagined that six months to the day I was taken off a Florida croquet court by ambulance that I would step onto a croquet court in a Canadian championship and win my first two games. A complete recovery from massive stroke would be a nice addition to a lifetime that already contained a considerable share of excitement, innovation and challenge.

This memoir is my personal remembrance of interesting and important events from four decades, grouped under subject headings in loosely chronological order. No doubt I remember some things differently from how they actually happened. My excuse is that I often found myself in situations where no one understood what was going on. My other excuse is, of course, old age.

# 2.
# The Truman Heritage—My Unfinished Book

I had little understanding of what it meant to be a Truman until I began writing a book on the first Truman born in Canada—aviator George Truman.

Orville Wright would have gone to the Dayton airport to meet my uncle George Truman in December 1947, but Wright's failing heart prevented him from leaving his house. So Orville never saw the aircraft Truman was flying around the world—a 1940s version of the Wright Flyer, a fabric-covered airframe powered by a four-cylinder engine. The historic meeting of aviation pioneers took place in Wright's living room. The inventor who put man in the air with powered flight chatted with the first man to take that original aviation technology to its limit with a circumnavigation of the globe. They talked airplanes and flying. Newspaper reporters listened and took pictures. Truman's Piper PA-12 was actually smaller than the Wright Flyer. Its engine, producing 100 horsepower, was more powerful.

Wright, aware of the significance of the Truman accomplishment, had asked for the meeting, phoning Van Nuys airport in California when Truman arrived near the end of his circumnavigation. He invited the Piper PA-12 flight to swing by Dayton *en route* to the Teterboro NJ airport where the round-the-world flight had begun. The meeting was Wright's last formal interview; he died a few weeks later. When the Smithsonian Air and Space Museum opened in the 1970s, both the Wright Flyer and a PA-12 from the round-the-world flight were on prominent display.

In 2015, you would have to do some searching in the Smithsonian aviation museums to find memorabilia from George Truman's round-the-world flight. The Piper PA-12 was taken off display and put in storage in Suitland for restoration. For years, a bronze plaque on the wall of the round-the-world section of the main museum was the only celebration of the greatest Truman aviation accomplishment. That is now gone. When the Smithsonian's Steven F. Udvar-Hazy Center opened at Dulles airport in DC, the restored PA-12 was hanging from the ceiling, where it can still be viewed, along with a lackadaisical description of the flight.

The world may have forgotten about the incredible journey taken by a Truman, but I was aware of it. I knew I had an uncle who was famous; I didn't know any living relative who had met him although he was supposed to have phoned our house before taking off on a long distance flight from Hamilton, Ontario to deliver a snowball to Miami, Florida. As the 50th anniversary of the flight approached, I decided to write a book about the only circumnavigation of the world in light aircraft with 100-horsepower engines. I have yet to complete the book, but the research for it has taken me to places I never imagined and allowed me to meet people I did not know were relatives—a journey of personal discovery.

A dusty box in the state archives in St. Paul, Minnesota held one of the keys to deeper understanding of my Truman heritage. The box, unopened for decades, contained mid-19th century divorce proceedings from a Minnesota county court. Divorce was rare in the 1860s, so the box contained only a handful of documents. The records of each case were tied up with faded red ribbon holding the documents together. One packet of documents was 10 times as big as the others in the box. Without hesitating, I reached for it. Sure enough, the covering parchment was inscribed "Truman vs. Truman."

My great-great grandfather, Charles Truman, was a character. I already knew that from his Civil War and pension records. Suspected of being a bigamist when he reached retirement age early in the 20th century, he had more than one woman laying claim to a share of his pension from his service with the Minnesota Volunteers. His veterans' medical records suggested a severe drinking problem. There was no mention of military honors, but there was an account of his desertion and subsequent trial, in which he was simply chastised and sent back to his unit, probably because he had joined the army and deserted when he was still too young to enlist.

I thought he had been killed in the Civil War. From the 1860s on, the Minnesota Trumans actively peddled the myth that Charles was deceased. I was curious whether he had died from disease or had been killed in action, so I requested his war records from the National Archives in Washington, DC. Pension records proved that my branch of the Truman family was lying through their teeth. Charles actually lived into his 90s, started a second family, and was given a veteran's burial in the 1930s. The divorce proceedings stored in St. Paul gave a truer picture of what happened at the end of the Civil War.

Depositions from his ex-wife and his neighbors portrayed Charles as a bad actor who despised his wife and pulled all kinds of unseemly tricks before deserting her with an infant son (my great grandfather). He vamoosed to Iowa and was never heard from again. He and memory of him were banished from my branch of the Truman family for more than a century. We Canadian Trumans are the descendants of the only child of his first marriage. That Truman, born in the 1860s in Red Wing, Minnesota, was forced to flee north to Saskatchewan for a new homestead when a severe drought in South Dakota dried up his first attempt to be a wheat farmer.

Charles' spirit lives on: not all the apples fall miles away from the tree and in every generation someone like Charles seems to appear in the Truman family and proceeds to live his life exactly as he pleases. The unfinished book I have tucked away is based on a true story of a Truman who lived a wild life seeking adventure and fame. George Truman was one of the Truman early adopters of the technology of flight and a true believer in the potential of celebrity.

George was born in Fairlight Saskatchewan and when his mother died he was dumped in a Manitoba orphanage at the age of seven; his father promptly decamped to Los Angeles, California with a redhead from a nearby farm. George moved to Hollywood CA as a teenager. He was 40 years old when he eventually found the 15 minutes of fame he sought. In his younger days, he was a high-board diving state champion, a motorcycle hill-climbing competitor good enough to be pictured in *Sports Illustrated* magazine, coach of movie stars who wanted to do their own stunts and drinking buddies with the likes of Bing Crosby and Marlene Dietrich.

*The author poses with the Piper "Cub" that George Truman flew around the world in 1947. The plane has been restored to flying condition and is in the Piper Museum in Lock Haven Pennsylvania. The Piper in the Smithsonian is the other plane from the flight and was actually the second 100-horsepower plane to make the circumnavigation, taking off and landing after George's. The planes are actually PA-12S.*
*– photo by Elaine Truman*

In 1947 George was accompanied by a wingman flying an identical PA-12. Newsreels show George taking off first and landing first on the round-the-world flight. There is no doubt he was the first man to fly a 100-horsepower aircraft around the world. His wingman is the only other pilot to accomplish the same feat, just a few seconds after George did it. The plane displayed in the Smithsonian is the one flown by the wingman, and George always maintained the museum had the wrong plane. The one flown by George has been restored and it is flown out of the Piper Museum in Lock Haven, Pennsylvania.

It should have been easy to write the book. *National Geographic* visited every major destination where George landed about the same time, as the world was reopening after the Second World War. Photos are available of what George saw. Newsreels caught him in many destinations.

Newspapers reported arrivals and departures, doing feature stories on the flight and the pilots.

The anecdotes were appealing. He received personal congratulations from Orville Wright in Dayton and President Harry S Truman in the Oval Office. Before going into the congratulatory meeting with President Truman, George was sternly warned not to ask the president about any possible family relationship. Of course, the president's first unscripted question to George was "How do you think we're related?" George replied that his family was "from the other side of the blanket." [2]

*Saskatchewan farm boy George Truman had 15 minutes of fame after flying around the world in a Piper PA-12. George is on the right. President Harry S Truman center. On the left is Cliff Evans, George's wingman. December 1947*
*– Photo by Harris and Ewing*

---

2   George may have been wrong. Ancestors of both Harry and George arrived on the Mary and John, the first ship to reach Boston Harbor in the Great Migration of 1630. A single congregation from Crewkerne in Somerset made up the passengers on the ship. George's ancestor was the deacon, the civic leader of the group; Harry's was only an elder.

Among those who fly Piper airplanes, George has not been forgotten. A flying instructor I interviewed over the phone was still furious with George 50 years later. In 1947, she had been doing circuits and bumps (repeated landings and takeoffs with a student) at an Alaska air force base, when her plane nearly collided in mid-air with George's round-the-world Piper. George was flying against the flow of traffic and not watching where he was going, violating the most basic of safety rules on a training base. She landed and while chewing him out for what he had done, found out "Truman had been on the base for a few hours celebrating his crossing of the Pacific when a film crew asked him to take the plane back up because they didn't have good footage of the Piper landing. He was flying drunk as a skunk."

*Colliers Magazine* assigned a writer to publicize the adventure. But George and his wingman, according to the disappointed scribe, saw nothing but their instruments as they flew round the world. He interviewed the pilots on their return to New York and failed to get enough color to write a story. They remembered aviation issues but little else.

After failing to find a publisher for my first attempt to write the story, I decided that someday I would write the book as historical fiction, making up what they had seen to make the book more interesting.

Researching the book on George gave me an opportunity to learn about my ancestry and gave me abundant excuses for my behavioral and personality quirks. I tracked one branch of Truman ancestry back to Normandy in the 1500s. Being religious non-conformists (naturally) they moved to southern England in the mid-1500s. Being religious non-conformists (naturally) they were on the first ship to arrive at the Massachusetts Colony in the Great Migration of 1630. Being religious non-conformists (naturally), they lasted in Boston for only a few years before starting one of the first westward migrations in colonial history to get away from Puritan theocrats who had the upper hand in Beantown.

They left places where they didn't fit in or that didn't suit their desire for individual freedom of thought and action. They didn't always leave quietly or peacefully. By colonizing Connecticut, they started the Pequot War in 1637 and by invading Pennsylvania, started two of the Pennamite wars in the 1700s.

It is a military ancestry. One forefather's records of his participation in the French and Indian Wars are stored at Fort Ticonderoga in New York. Three ancestral grandfathers fought in the same Connecticut regiment in the Revolutionary War. More recently my own grandfather and two of his sons served in the Canadian forces during World War Two. I tried to join the military when I was only 16—but in university and eligible to enlist in a program for university students called the Regular Officer Training Program.

Not all my ancestors were militaristic or adventuresome. Some, unfortunately, were not. In the last couple of centuries, for which there are reasonable documents, Truman males seem to come in two varieties, two distinct morphs.

George, his grandfather Charles Truman, one of his older brothers, and his grandson are representatives of one Truman morph. George's grandfather Charles did exactly what he felt like doing, the law and social convention be damned. One of George's brothers, too old to throw in an orphanage in 1915, joined the Royal Flying Corps in Winnipeg in World War One (probably lying about his age) and washed out after crashing too many planes. He later became one of the first motorcycle cops in Minnesota, and was killed breaking up a street fight in Red Wing. Rumor is he died engaged in a favorite pastime—wading into melees and beating up on everybody. George's eldest grandson died in a helicopter crash in the Korean DMZ and is buried in the US Marine cemetery in San Diego, California. The Viking ancestry speaks loudly in these men's lives.[3]

At the other end of the spectrum you find another Truman morph. Those who seem completely lacking in the right stuff. A typical example was one Truman who was cashiered out of pilot training in World War Two, not because he crashed too many planes, but because he was afraid to take the controls of the plane he was supposed to be learning to fly. He drank and smoked himself to death in young middle age. It's not hard to find other Trumans with a life history similar to his. All too common. The other kind of males with the Truman name often live hen-pecked

---

3   Truman military history from the 17th to the 20th centuries in North America resolves the 1960s peacenik question—"What if they held a war and nobody showed up?" The answer being—"The question is moot if there is a Truman anywhere nearby."

lives, controlled by women they made the mistake of marrying. Any adventure in their lives is Mittyesque daydreaming.

And the women they have married! There are Truman divorce records dating back to the mid-19th century. Noting the number of Trumans who have had second wives, it seems like gross understatement to say Trumans often don't marry well the first time. How bad can it get? My great-great grandfather decided he was better off "dead" than wed. And the situation seems not to have improved since the 1860s. A first wives club made up of selected historical Mrs. Trumans could terrify a freight train—make it want to jump the tracks and hide somewhere down a dirt road.[4] But what can you do if you come from the shallow end of the Truman gene pool and, through no fault of your own, are hereditarily prone to marrying a girl just like the girl who did her best to drive dear old dad to drink and an early grave?

Genealogical research confirms that alcohol is another multi-generational Truman curse. Even those with exciting lives can turn into drunks. Trumans at the hopeless end of the Mitty spectrum may find their quiet desperation more tolerable in an alcoholic blur. A Viking ancestry is probably a genetic cause of alcohol problems. Personally, I rarely touched alcohol before I was 30 because of alcoholism in my family and became a teetotaler before the age of 60, again because of a family history of alcoholism.

In 1997 I re-established contact between the two branches of the family. There had been little or no contact between the Canadian Trumans[5] and the U.S. Trumans since 1947, when George, on an Edmonton stopover on his way round the world, phoned his brother who was living on the Canadian prairies. That brother was my grandfather. How he fits into the constellation of Trumans is a puzzle. I saw him only a few times. He died

---

4   This metaphor is borrowed from Fred Reed's web blog, "Fred on Everything."

5   An 1890s drought in South Dakota bankrupted my great grandfather and led him to take a land grant in Saskatchewan where he lived for nearly 20 years, prospering when the Great War created demand for wheat. My great grandmother died in Saskatchewan in 1915 and was buried in her home town of Lake City, Minnesota. My GGF migrated to Los Angeles with a new redheaded wife. One son ended up in an orphanage, one stayed in Manitoba for a while and one married the redhead on the neighbouring farm, starting the Canadian branch of the family.

when I was 16. He was definitely a drinker. Like many of my ancestors, he was military, albeit briefly. He was over 40 when he joined the Canadian army in World War Two and although he didn't get overseas, Ottawa records show he served honorably.

My Grandpa Truman was regarded as a wrong-headed dreamer. I can distinctly remember other family members ridiculing him in 1955 for holding forth on his belief that someday cars would have devices that would keep track of where you were and give you spoken instructions telling you where to turn. Who would ever believe that nonsense the silly old fool was spouting? (I often think of that incident when I am fed up with Silicon Sally's nagging from the GPS in a vehicle I am driving.) Military records portray Grandpa Truman as a bold, confident man. That's when he was away from the house. Maybe his life would have been different if he hadn't hooked up with a redheaded girl from the Saskatchewan farm next door and started a family when he was still a teenager.

While using the Internet to research the book, I found where George retired, at 65 still a flying instructor giving USAF combat pilots their basic flight training. I tracked down his last address and stopped in at his place near Tucson, Arizona in 1997, more than 20 years after his death. His widow and his twin daughters were in the living room when I walked in. His widow beamed. "He's back," she murmured. The twins groaned and moaned something to each other that sounded to me like, "Oh God! NO! He's b-a-a-a-ck."

Having known George in person, they could see the Truman Y-chromosome marching down the generations. I had only photos of George and some movie clips to go by. I didn't see any strong resemblance until I had a flight in George's plane, the one in the Piper Museum. Afterwards, I had my photo taken with the airplane replicating the pose George had used when last photographed with the same Piper PA-12. We were both in our mid-50s when the photos were taken. Then I could see the similarity.

I'd like to finish the book as an historical novel. George Truman deserves a bigger place in the history of aviation. But he was born in Saskatchewan, the only Truman of his generation to be born in Canada. As a result, I believe he isn't considered to be part of the pantheon of

American aviation celebrities. The Smithsonian's blurb on him is full of errors and he's been ignored in books in which he should be featured. And there's a Zeitgeist problem—in a feminized world there's minimal demand for books about adventurous men. Now if George had been a transgendered lesbian, publishers and producers would be pounding at my door, demanding completion of the book and offering movie rights.

Researching the book about George Truman had an impact on me.

By the time I was in my 70th year and starting my memoirs, I was aware that a lot of things I had done in my life were inexplicable. Quite frankly, I thought there was no excuse for me and some of my antics. After finding out about my ancestors—their wars, their women, their wanderlust, their occasional wonderful accomplishment—I realized I had a perfectly valid excuse. It's genetic.

# SECTION II
# Adventures in Freelance Writing

*Going Where Others Wouldn't*

My reputation as an adventurous freelancer originated in a realization that if you were going to sell a story to a major newspaper, you'd better do features that regular staffers would avoid. What reporter would accept an assignment that involved floating upside-down and backwards through turbulent rapids, bouncing his head off rocks on the river bottom—cold, wet and concussed all at the same time? I gravitated to stories on topics like white-water kayaking, backcountry skiing and ice climbing, not because I enjoyed thrilling discomfort, but because the stories would sell.

As a freelancer, I had to find my own stories and sell them to newspapers and magazines. Working on spec and submitting finished features to the editors in the hopes that they would buy them, I was completely independent. After a brief apprenticeship with local papers in eastern Ontario, *The Globe and Mail* became my market of choice. Primarily a feature writer rather than a news reporter, I sought to write stories that ranged from about 1500 words to a full page. Starting out writing on adventure sports, hunting, and shooting, I soon began selling features on sailing, medicine, science, literacy, children's issues and women's issues. I sold 530 stories to the national newspaper, most of them in the five years between 1978 and 1982.

I had to learn photography. Snapshots with Brownie box cameras and Kodak Instamatics were the best I could do when I began. Editors wanted more professional art to illustrate my stories. That meant learning the intricacies of using reflex cameras with manual settings as well as developing the skills to shoot black and white film and color transparencies. Eventually, I became proficient enough to have a two-page photo spread in *The Globe and Mail* and sell color transparencies to geographic magazines.

In the 1980s, working for magazines, I had regular opinion columns in *Outdoor Canada* and *The Angler and Hunter in Ontario*—small-circulation publications targeting the hook-and-bullet crowd. I became the most-published author in *Landmarks*, a geographic magazine published by the Ontario Ministry of Natural Resources. Landmarks provided my greatest adventures. Tagging polar bears, playing with snapping turtles during their breeding season, flying into the Arctic watershed to do research on sturgeon, and hunting moose in northwestern Ontario were included in my escapades.

After the early 1990s, I rarely contributed freelance features to newspapers or magazines. Changes in the publishing world had turned selling to them into a losing proposition.

# 3.
# There are Pieces of My Face Hanging on Those Trees

*Covering adventure and blood sports for The Globe and Mail's Recreation Section 1976-1983*

The signs on the mountain road were covered with snow, so much light, fluffy powder that they resembled white lollipops made of dandelion thistledown. Their diamond shapes and the occasional glimpse of yellow visible through their snowball coating made it clear they were warning signs intended for automobile traffic—but what were they warning drivers about? When my curiosity got the better of me, I stopped the station wagon, got out, slammed the door, walked up to a sign, and brushed the snow from it. The chilling warning read: **No Stopping. Avalanche Zone.**

I tiptoed back to the rental vehicle, pulled the door closed as silently as possible. Slipping the vehicle into gear, I crept away, hoping that I wasn't making a noise that might trigger a slide and snuff my career as a skiing writer for *The Globe and Mail*. I was at the apex of that part of my career. I was in British Columbia, the guest of the provincial government, skiing premier B.C. resorts and welcomed as the writer/photographer from the national newspaper.

My original plans for a writing career never included becoming the skiing writer reviewing Blackcomb and Whistler, Red Mountain and Whitewater, all downhill skiing destinations. I didn't even own a pair of downhill skis when I started as a freelance feature writer in the mid-1970s at *The Globe and Mail*. My chosen beat was more offbeat. I covered minor recreational sports and pastimes that changed with the season: cross-country skiing in winter, fishing in the spring, sailing in the summer and hunting in the fall.

*My personal sailing was limited to small boats—sailboards and lasers—things that would go fast.*

Cross-country skiing was my winter pursuit of choice, replacing jogging whenever there was enough snow on the ground to go ski touring on waxed boards. My entertainment for a winter evening could be going to a gentle slope, skiing up it, then turning around and sliding back down. And repeat for an hour or so until I was pooped. I got my start in newspapers writing about skiing, mostly about where to ski. Early in my writing career, I even had a skiing column syndicated in several local papers.

By the late 1970s cross-country skiing was a mature sport, having peaked in popularity and entered its decline. When I started freelancing to *The Globe and Mail*, it never even crossed my mind that I would become their cross-country writer. I was behind the wave in cross-country's popularity and the paper had already printed regular articles on the topic, somewhat didactic, written by a staffer.

But my feature stories on cross-country skiing, accompanied by pictures, soon pushed the competition aside at the paper. I skied with the blind, with the antiquated in master's competitions, with famous skiers like Booty Griffiths of Red Mountain, with telemark skiers who swooped down the hills in a crouched posture with one knee almost touching the snow, on carpets, with backcountry skiers in the Cascades, with rifle-carrying skiers training for the Olympic sport of biathlon, and in the Canadian Ski Marathon (CSM), a 100-mile loppet (race) from Lachute, Quebec to Ottawa.

Cross-country skiing has its moments of exhilaration and fear on downhill runs, but it's mostly boring—just plugging along on skis sometimes referred to as torture sticks. Fascinating people were attracted to the pastime and I always approached feature writing with one basic principle—people are interested in people. I would sprinkle my articles with what editors called color: the blind skier who pulled her tuque down over her face when wind-driven hail was hurting her cheeks and lips, the six-year-old boy who skied all day in the CSM, always anxious to check under the next bridge for trolls, the one-armed man who could keep up with others going uphill . . .

Jackrabbit Johannsen, the patron saint of cross-country skiing in Canada, was still alive, over 100 years old. He was a regular at the CSM and still feisty. Young women soon learned to stay out of his reach at press receptions and he bemoaned the fact that he could no longer chop wood until he worked up a sweat. He provided one of my favorite anecdotes about cross-country. He visited the Gold Courier du Bois camp at the CSM, the place where skiers who set out to ski the entire 100-mile route slept out overnight in the snow. First he pointed out that one of the skiers had his boots too close to the campfire and was about to set his feet on fire. Then he launched into a tirade that the gold skiers were wimps. I still have a reel-to-reel audiotape of that harangue. Jackrabbit didn't intend to leave them laughing, but they were amused with his opinions.

That night, before he was taken back to the Chateau Montebello by his daughter, who escorted him everywhere, I asked him about ski lifts and the growing popularity of downhill skiing. Jackrabbit said, "There's nothing wrong with ski lifts. But the way to use them is taking the lift to the top of the hill and keeping going." I agreed with that sentiment, but as a writer who could ski, I was pushed into the downhill skiing field.

There were two markets for downhill skiing writing at the *Globe and Mail*—the Travel Section and the Recreation Section. The Recreation Section often required skiing with interesting people, the ones I fondly called "the crazies." The Travel Section expected you to stay in the best accommodation and eat at the finest resort restaurants. It's tough work but someone has to do it. *Globe and Mail* travel editors turned a blind eye to accepting of freebies by skiing freelancers.

The original call from the travel editor was a surprise. There was a lot of competition to write skiing for his section, but scuttlebutt reached him that I was heading to Atikokan in December to go winter moose hunting for a geographic magazine. He wanted to know if I would take an extra day *en route* and go skiing in Thunder Bay. He liked the story he got from me. From then on I was part of the in-group at the Travel Section. It seemed that everything I submitted got printed.

*On assignment. Skiing Big White Ski Resort in British Columbia and writing bumf about snow ghosts.*

Most of my skiing was in the east. The Ontario Ski Resorts Association went out of their way to cultivate me, providing a skiing pass and inviting me to receptions. I skied most destinations in relatively flat Ontario as well as a number in Quebec, an eastern Canadian destination with hills. Quebec did not nurture me—they didn't need publicity for their skiing.

Killington in Vermont was my favorite eastern skiing destination. My initial article about Killington covered the entire front page of *The Globe and Mail* travel section, featuring my favorite lodge and bloviating about the variety of the skiing experiences available at the huge resort. I hadn't interviewed the lodge owners or the resort management before I did the yarn; I simply wrote it off the top of my head. So the people in Killington were stunned and delighted at the free publicity they had in the national paper in one of their important markets. Three months after the article appeared, I showed up at Killington for a week of skiing and got the warmest of receptions. From that time on, anything I wanted at Killington was mine for the asking.

Crafting ordinary travel articles on downhill skiing was like writing tourism bumf—everything seemed a bit hyped up. But skiing with the notorious and the loonies could get interesting. The cream of the crazies are found in the Canadian west, where mountains are big, powder is deep and skiing headwalls, avalanche hazards and tunneling through cornices are all in the realm of the possible. There were plenty of eccentrics known to me as budgies—backcountry types who avoided ski lifts and fed on a mixture of seeds and nuts known as gorp.

BC Tourism facilitated a tour of their resorts, meeting me at the Vancouver airport with a rental car for my use, lift ticket passes and free accommodation everywhere.

At Whistler, the management paired me up with Diamond Jim McConkey, who had come to the resort in 1968 to head up the ski school. He was hard to keep up with, skiing with wide, sweeping turns on long, fast skis. The stories he told provided more color than I ever could use and he showed me fascinating pictures of the early days, including a shot that showed a line of skiers holding naked women upside-down in the snow. I've seen thousands of skiing pictures, but that one sticks in my mind after more than 30 years. They all must have been members of the Whistler's famous UIC Ski Team, named for the Unemployment

Insurance Commission benefits that supported them, and unable to afford ski clothing.

Compared to some of the resorts I skied in the east, Whistler in the early 1980s seemed a bit primitive. Signage wasn't up to my standards—too often I misread signs and got on the wrong trail carrying 20 or 30 pounds of camera equipment, and found myself on slopes I had trouble handling. Some lifts had no safety bars. One bitterly cold day there was a rumor that a skier had become hypothermic, slid out of the chair and off the lift. But it had been far wilder in the past.

Diamond Jim told stories of Whistler when logs still lay helter-skelter on the slopes and skiing season did not begin until there was enough snow to cover the old downed timber. He related frankly scary tales of antique ski lifts. The one thing that had not changed was the snow. Close to the Pacific Ocean, snow was plentiful but moisture-filled and skiers referred to it as "cement powder."

I left Whistler, headed to the BC Interior, where the moisture had been sucked out of the snow by higher altitudes. The powder was deep and dry. Heli-skiing, already well covered in many publications, did not appeal to me as original enough for story material for *The Globe and Mail*. Real backcountry adventure beckoned.

Equipped with a pair of hybrid cross-country/downhill skis, I took Jackrabbit's advice and took a ski lift to the top of Red Mountain in Castlegar, then kept going. My guide and I skied off the back, down to the saddle between Red and Mt. Kirkup, put climbing skins on our skis to work our way uphill to the top of Kirkup. From there we locked our heels into the ski bindings, turning them into downhill skis and skied the unbroken snow of the backcountry down to civilization.

That was my first experience with an avalanche beeper. You keep the radio-type device near your head. If you were suffocating in the snow whoever was urgently digging you out wouldn't go for your rear end first. It was serious business. We did several dry runs finding each other with the beeps.

Moments after starting down from the top of Kirkup, I was in trouble. After making a turn, I found myself hanging upside-down in a tree. I couldn't believe my situation; couldn't extricate myself. My guide dug me out and complementing the practical lesson I had just endured, gave me the theory behind tree wells. Conifers shed snow and there can be a cone of empty space and tree branches in the snow. Never make a turn or a stop when you see a treetop poking out of the snow. It might not be a sapling, but a full-size tree and a trap for the unwary.

It was a real relief to reach the car left waiting for us at the bottom. Six hours on skis on un-groomed terrain and breakable crust was an endurance test. Exhausted and filled with new respect for Jackrabbit, I resolved to be reluctant about skiing off-piste again, no matter where I could sell the story.

Next destination, an avalanche school in the Kootenays. The school's owner, while an eccentric of the kind often found in ski country, was anything but crazy. Tony Salway was an English-born mountain-lover and climber. He had a legitimate Ph.D. in avalanche studies and was a veteran of avalanche control in the Rogers Pass. He showed films explaining the phenomenon, something that people are familiar with in miniature when the wet snow slumps on the front windshield of their car. He talked about how snow crystals change as they get older and are covered by new layers of snow.

He also showed entertaining and scary films of avalanches taking out trees and skiers making cuts across the slope that started snow sliding behind them. The next day, on a mountain tour, he dug a snow pit, demonstrating how to evaluate avalanche danger. Down a few feet in the snow pit he found a layer of snow that had metamorphosed into ball bearing shapes. He touched the stratum and little balls of snow rolled out. "She's ready to go," he said, looking up the steep slope. I was relieved to get in his modified snow cat and get out of there. I had my story and pictures. Didn't need the additional excitement of even a little avalanche.

A visit to Whitewater resort was the highlight of the B.C. trip and the venue for my best Recreation Section ski story ever. Whitewater is a small resort. Located in a box canyon near Nelson, B.C., it sucks high-altitude precipitation—falling as the driest and lightest of powder snow.

My discovery that the road into the resort ran through an avalanche zone whetted my appetite for skiing the resort. I knew I had struck skiing writer gold when I was in the Whitewater cafeteria doing a preliminary interview with my guide. He talked of cornice jumping, digging through cliff-top snow overhangs to start a run. He'd been caught in avalanches.

Ron Truman | 25

He said, "Don't even try to make swimming motions; it's like you've been thrown into a clothes drier. You don't know which way is up." He skied powder so deep that it flowed over his head and wore a snorkel to keep from inhaling it. "You can't see where you're going. You can't see where you've been. So you just point your skis down the hill and set up a rhythm," he advised me.

I was sorry I didn't have my miniature magnet with me to find out if he already had a metal plate in his head. I figured I had a genuine crazy on my hands and a great story even before we went outside to put on our skis. Then it got better. The chairlift passed over a heavily treed area on the way up to barren high altitude slopes. Unsure if the conifer-covered lower section was skiable, I asked, "Is that Whitewater's glades run?" He nodded affirmatively and what he said became Quote of the Day on the front page of *The Globe and Mail*, "There's a lot of pieces of my face hanging from those trees."

Winter only seems to last forever. Most of the snow in Canada does eventually melt and people get bored with skiing in late winter. Much of the outdoor-loving population looks forward to spring and one of the first signs of it is the Toronto Sportsmen's Show each March. Today's Sportsmen's Show is a pale shadow of the weeklong extravaganza that occupied many buildings on the CNE grounds 30 to 40 years ago.

For many years, the first springtime story I freelanced to the Recreation Section was a review of that year's Sportsmen's Show. Written on the opening weekend and published Wednesday mid-show, it would give a boost to the show's attendance for the last five days. My feature would often emphasize the Ministry of Natural Resources display, which would include caged living wildlife native to the province. The Press Room gave access to show guests, who one year included the actor who played Radar O'Reilly in M✳A✳S✳H. He was a dog lover, who participated in the canine part of the show.

The show's press preview night provided interesting experiences. One year, an acquaintance took up the offer to wrestle a bear. He got up after grappling with an ugly, toothless bruin. He dusted himself off, then confided in me that it wasn't so bad—he'd slept with women who weren't as good looking and smelled worse. Knowing his reputation, I believed him.

Go to the Sportsmen's Show today and you won't find wrestling bears or caged wolves. People's interests and attitudes have changed. Big breweries are no longer sponsors of season-long big fish contests. Tourism marketing boards only reluctantly give limited support to what they regard as hook-and-bullet operations. Everything is eco-friendly. I liked the old days when you could go home from the show with new equipment and new ideas and wait for the weather to warm up so you could do something that might not be eco-friendly but could be exciting.

Eventually the ice goes out and fishing seasons open. Springtime at the Recreation Section meant coverage of the rainbow run up creeks and rivers to spawn, trout fishing, walleye angling and then bass season as summer began. For a number of years, my seasonal routine was the same. In early April, fisheries biologists made predictions on how good or poor the fishing season would be. At the end of April I would cover the pandemonium of trout opening day on the Ganaraska River, banks jammed shoulder-to-shoulder with rainbow anglers. I'd do my fishing with the kids at stocked trout ponds north of Port Hope.

The first Saturday in May would find me on the Bay of Quinte, reporting on pike and walleye fishing that started a week ahead of most southern Ontario seasons. Then bass season opened. Once I spent a cold, late summer weekend on the St. Lawrence River to report on a tournament involving the most frustrating and fruitless of water-flogging pastimes— angling for the legendary muskie, a fighting cousin to the pike. We all got skunked.

Personally, I found catching fish about as appealing as eating fish— something I usually did only out of a sense of obligation. If I needed a fishing story for the Recreation Section, I'd just as soon write about fly-tiers, lure manufacturers, creek rehabilitation or world casting championships rather than actual angling.

Working with game wardens in enforcement led to excitement for me. One mid-May, I went to the Kawarthas where I met a conservation officer (CO) to patrol the walleye opener. About an hour before legal fishing time we approached a houseboat anchored in a channel. Hearing a splash we thought was suspicious, we boarded the boat and took a look for fish that had been illegally caught and kept. Finding nothing, we motored downstream and in the ambient light as midnight got closer, we could see anglers fishing from a second boat. As we approached, the anglers surmised we were on patrol. Having started fishing before legal time, they reeled in furiously. Suddenly, one angler's rod bent over double. By this time, we had lights glaring on the suspect boat and the CO ordered the angler to keep reeling.

The angler discovered he had not caught a fish, but had snagged a stringer of six fish. The boats were now gunwale to gunwale. The angler sputtered that he had not caught any fish and that the stringer was not his. The CO said gruffly, "A million people would never believe that story." Then, after a long pause in which he took the stringer of fish away from the angler, added, "But I will." We released our hold on the other boat, and, trying to suppress our laughter at the angler's surprised reaction, we motored back upstream to charge the anglers on the houseboat with fishing out of season. As we surmised, the splash we had heard near the houseboat was them throwing the stringer away. They admitted the fish were theirs and were charged.

Today, what used to be called enforcement is now called, politically correctly, compliance. I trust that name change has not spoiled the cat-and-mouse game that the conservation officers enjoy.

My yearly story cycle turned to boating coverage as living outdoors became tolerable. There would be a few stories needed about getting boats ready to launch, then features on sail touring and on using the canals for recreation. But as the season wore on, sailing competition of various classes of boats would provide material for stories in *The Globe and Mail*, either in the recreation or sports sections.

CORK, the Canadian Olympic Regatta in Kingston, was an annual event after the 1976 Olympics. The Laser Worlds, Tornado Worlds and Shark Worlds took place in Canada in my years with the paper. In pre-Internet days, filing stories was often rushed. Races ended a few hours to a few minutes before *The Globe and Mail*'s deadline. You had to write quickly and then dictate your story over the telephone before deadline. The last regattas were usually over before the summer ended, but racing sailors would sometimes be sharing the water with waterfowl hunters late in September in the first days of fall.

Fall brought hunting seasons. *The Globe and Mail* was the only Toronto paper that made a concerted effort to cover the outdoors and topics of concern to non-urbanites. *The Star* and *The Sun* had outdoor columnists who gave hit-and-miss coverage to hunting, sometimes highly opinionated.

Bob Rife, who edited the Recreation Section, did a thorough job. He had worked in Sudbury and had connections with outdoors people. He would get three or more pages in the Sports Section every Wednesday, well supported by advertisers who used his pages to market their lodges and expeditions. Rife depended on freelancers and would coach those he thought had talent and direct them to stories he wanted to print. It was a big break for me when I submitted a story about duck hunting in the icy waters of December to *The Globe and Mail*. It ended up on his desk. Bob took me in hand and soon I regarded myself as the leading freelancer in his section. I was flattered to be featured by him in one of the "Globe and Mail, Well Written, Well Read" ads.

Rife turned me into a writer on hunting, going into deer hunting camps, carrying a camera instead of a gun on water fowling expeditions and upland game jaunts, even using dogs to push rabbits into the open. More important, Bob made me wrap my head around the complexities of deer and moose management and selective harvesting.

*With my first shotgun and first duck. Photo taken in Penhold, Alberta in September 1956. At 11 years of age, I was big enough to shoot a 12-gauge shotgun although the recoil bothered me.*

Perhaps the best move I made in the writing part of my career was my first interview when preparing a multi-part series on deer management in Ontario. I made an appointment with Doug Roseborough, Director of the Ontario Ministry of Natural Resources' Wildlife Branch. I didn't say, as many hunting writers would, "I am writing a series on deer for *The Globe and Mail*; I'm going to tell you how deer should be managed." Instead, my opening statement was, "I know a deer when I see one, but that's about the limit of my expertise. Can I get your help in a series I am supposed to write?"

Doug's answer was a smile from ear to ear.[6] My reputation grew rapidly as a writer who listened and did not have strong opinions to influence his articles. Wildlife biologists, who had often chosen their career path because they preferred dealing with animals to dealing with people, liked getting a story to me first. It was their best chance of getting it written right.

At a time when modern environmentalism was birthing and anti-hunting was becoming a significant factor in Ontario, identifying as a hunting writer was not always beneficial. Some people and organizations would have nothing to do with me. Unless I was with a hunting crowd, I would usually not mention it. But writing on hunting was non-controversial, compared to writing on trapping.

At the time, the fur industry believed that trapping could be made acceptable to the public by creating more humane traps and by emphasizing the fact that trappers were often nice people who were making a living. I wrote articles featuring a pet beaver owned by Ralph Bice, a trapper who was a member of the Order of Canada. I covered Ontario's efforts to develop an instant-kill trap. My usual newspaper articles seldom attracted a letter-to-the-editor but anything on trapping could bring forth a stream of vitriol.

Guns were also controversial. At the specific request of Recreation Editor Bob Rife, I began writing on guns and the shooting sports. I had owned guns ever since duck hunting season opened prior to my 12th birthday in the late 1950s. My present that year, given to me a few months

---

6 Doug Roseborough and I became consulting partners after he retired and I left the newspaper.

early, was a 12-gauge shotgun. I still have a photo of myself, holding the gadwall that was the first duck I shot. I was a large boy, but the kick of that 12-gauge bruised my shoulder, so I didn't shoot much the first season. I hunted duck and upland game while in high school, resuming after I finished university. I quit hunting in my 30s when writing about hunting and getting some good photos of the hunt conflicted with shooting game. You can't do them all well on the same outing.

Attitudes towards guns were remarkably different in the 1970s than they were in the early 1960s. On opening day of duck hunting season in 1960, I rode my pedal bike to the nearest pond. With no time to go home after the sunrise shoot, I biked directly to school, put my bike in the rack, my shotgun in my locker and went to class. When the intercom crackled with the message that I was to report to the principal's office, I thought I was in trouble for being late. No. The principal had seen me arrive at school with a shotgun. He closed the door to his office and said, "Are you ever lucky to be able to hunt when opening day falls mid-week. I had to go straight to work." We had a relaxed discussion about hunting prospects for the coming season.

By the late 1970s, when I began writing on guns and shooting for *The Globe and Mail's* Recreation Section, public attitudes were troublesome for the shooters. I wrote stories about all kinds of shooting sports—trap, skeet, rapid-fire pistol, Olympic pistol, running boar, silhouette, running rat, and black powder. Shooting is a head game that requires absolute concentration and attracts many dedicated and thoughtful participants. Most of them worried about public misunderstanding of their pastime.

When the federal government introduced Bill C-51 that would force gun owners to purchase Firearms Acquisition Certificates (FACs), gun owners regarded it as the first step on the slippery slope to registering all firearms, then disarming of the population. The editors of *The Globe and Mail* showed their bias by indicating every intention of letting a controversial bill become law without properly covering the opposition to it. Bob Rife assigned me to cover Bill C-51 so gun owners and sportsmen would not be totally ignored.

I was familiar with guns, having grown up in the Prairies and spent some of my university years in Texas, where my father was Canadian Military Attaché at U.S. Air Training Command. I believed that an armed society was a polite society. I owned and used guns but I paid more attention to the care and feeding of my cross-country skis than to practicing with my firearms. Definitely I had no aversion to guns. I had antipathies to the increasing role government played in everyday life.

Covering the gun laws turned into a personal and professional nightmare. In London, Ontario, the municipal police decided to give a psychological test to anyone applying for a Firearms Acquisition Certificate (FAC), something clearly not anticipated in the legislation. The Chief Provincial Firearms Officer (CPFO) did not seem to be dealing properly with this extra-legal situation. I interviewed him and his right hand man, then wrote news items which made some contradictions in their stories evident. Seeing this in *The Globe and Mail* did not please them and led to my most famous complaint, "You quoted me accurately, word for word, and made me look like a fool."

Then I made a mistake. Instructed to send someone in to apply for an FAC and refuse the psychological test, I asked the Ontario Federation of Anglers and Hunters for a London-based volunteer. I got a report back that my volunteer got his FAC after refusing the psychological test. Then editorial staff at *The Globe and Mail* got involved. I was told that my volunteer had actually taken the psychological test and that I should have sent a lawyer in to do the job properly. Where was a freelancer going to find and finance a lawyer to do that job? It seemed to me that my reputation was being damaged and that I had no business as a freelancer getting into investigative reporting, taking police departments and federal cabinet ministers to task, as much fun as that was. I resolved to stick to feature writing. I also decided that visiting London, risking being stopped for some traffic offence, was something I didn't need to do. So I tried to let the furor die down quietly and get on with pleasurable freelancing. That didn't work.

Usually I went to the Toronto Sportsmen's Show the weekend it opened so I could feature it in the Recreation Section. That year, the Chief Provincial Firearms Officer's office had a display with the CPFO's second-in-command manning the booth. He recognized me as the person who had interviewed him. It wasn't too difficult as I was wearing a media badge with my name and newspaper on it. I regarded his subsequent treatment of me as downright threatening. As a matter of fact, I thought I was going to be torn limb from limb or beaten to a pulp right in the show.

I went back to *The Globe and Mail* newsroom and told Rife what had happened. He told me to sit down and write the incident up as a news story, referring to myself in the third person. In half an hour, he had my story on his computer system. He made a few minor edits, then picked up his phone and dialed OPP headquarters. He identified himself and his newspaper and asked to speak to the Commissioner of the OPP, the head of the provincial police. When the top cop was on the line, he read him the story. Then he offered the commissioner a stark choice. Did he want to see the story on the front page of the next day's *Globe and Mail* or did he want to resolve the issue in a different way? When Rife hung up, he assured me he was satisfied with how the commissioner was going to deal with the issue. I was never given the details, but I always imagined my antagonist soon found himself on his way to someplace like Rainy River—far, far away.

The story doesn't end there. A few months later, I got word that the CPFO wanted to talk to me in his office. I can't remember why I didn't refuse the invitation but I ended up at OPP Headquarters for a late afternoon appointment. The workday ended and the building was pretty well deserted before I was ushered into a meeting with him and his new deputy.

That heel-cooling time gave me pause to think of stories I heard in Texas as a teenager, with people disliked by the cops turning up dead. One notorious individual apparently committed a very serious and thorough act of suicide in police custody, stabbing himself 17 times in his back and tying himself up with chain before drowning himself with a millstone around his neck. My memory of the Sportsmen's Show confrontation with was still fresh. As I went into the meeting, I had some trepidation.

The conversation was unbelievably cooperative, with me (fallaciously reputed to have a difficult personality) admitting that there could be misinterpretations of what had gone down and giving assurances that I would be more careful in the future—much, much more careful. In a deserted building with two men who probably didn't like me very much, I knew what I wanted—nothing more than to get the hell out of there.

Dealing with the gun laws has to be the most unpleasant episode in my time at *The Globe and Mail*. Nobody, it seemed, told the truth. Every answer was evasive. All too many people were looking to find fault with what you had written if it wasn't supportive of more and more onerous gun control. Stories were killed, including one involving an Olympic shooting coach who had been clearly targeted by police. But coverage of the shooting sports continued to the very end of my stint at *The Globe and Mail*. One of my last stories for the Recreation Section was about a shooter who target-shot with a super-accurate .50 caliber muzzle-loader used in buffalo-hunting days.

By 1980, Rife's mentoring had turned me into a passable *Globe* hand. I had no formal journalism training, only a natural aptitude for writing that had kept me afloat through eight years of university. Rife would explain what he was doing with his edits and emphasize the proper use of color in newspaper writing. His teaching methods weren't always pleasant. Early in my days with his section, my phone rang in the middle of the night. It was Rife, editing my contribution to that week's section. He read me a sentence. "Whose opinion is that?" he demanded. I had to admit that it was mine. That wasn't permissible. Several expletives followed, ending with, "Who do you think you are—Pierre Berton? When I want your opinion, I'll ask for it." Rife slammed down his phone. After that, I was careful to make certain everything I wrote was properly attributed.

But the Recreation Section was clearly doomed. Bob Rife would be the last Recreation editor; I would be the last hunting and shooting writer for *The Globe and Mail*. A new mentality, urban and metrosexual, was pervading the newspaper. Hunting, wildlife management, the outdoors and adventure were no longer considered important enough to deserve regular coverage. In late 1980, the Recreation Section, Women's Section, Medical and Science pages were merged into the Thursday Section.

I was absolutely delighted with the merger. With a rapacious appetite for bylines, I constantly sought editors who wanted my stories. I had been stuck in the Sports Department, which limited my horizons. Unexpectedly, my home at the paper was moved out of the physical isolation of sports across the hall into the newsroom and I was being edited by greater numbers of the people I wanted to work for.

One of the other contributors to the Recreation Section saw the forced merger of the Recreation Section and the Women's Section as incontrovertible evidence that the girlymen were taking over *The Globe and Mail*. The amalgamation was an unhappy one. Six months later, Recreation was back in the Sports Section. A few years later, following a recession that cut into newspaper advertising revenues, the Recreation section closed.

Today, the newspaper I was once so proud to write for seems to have degenerated into a pulp version of *Cosmopolitan* for women whose main concerns in life are wrinkles, wattles and their fading allure. Perhaps the editors of the famous old Grey Lady of Canadian papers have learned that sex sells even if their political bias, the "soft, left sludge"[7] they peddle as news and shrieking feminist irrationality passing for opinion doesn't attract subscribers and is beginning to repel advertisers. I think *The Globe and Mail* hit its semi-sweet spot in the years I was a regular contributor and is doomed to decrepitude and decay under its current editorial direction.

---

7   A nice turn of phrase that is attributed to Conrad Black at the time he started the *National Post*.

# 4.
# Women and Children First!

*New topics for stories present themselves
The Thursday Section: Recreation, Women's
Issues, Science and Medicine 1980-1983*

Dozens of wilderness guides—bronzed, muscular, most of them bearded—gathered in Toronto. You could tell from the look of them that they could easily portage a canoe 10 miles over hill and dale, set up a comfortable camp on a barren rock and find wild edibles anywhere. These were obviously men you could trust with your life and safety in the great outdoors.

Testosterone and anger were boiling over in the room at this stormy meeting of the Ontario Wilderness Guides Association (OWGA).[8] The fierce debate and furor were over certification (i.e. provincial regulation) of guides. Some OWGA members were deliberately disrupting proceedings. One of them, a climbing specialist who was an actor in the off-season, used his considerable theatrical skills to antagonize those who favored regulation. Tempers flared.

There seemed to be only one bit of humor in the room, a few chuckles. I was the butt of the joke. That day's issue of *The Globe and Mail* was being passed around. Each guide would glance at the paper, snicker, and give me a sidelong glance before passing it on. The source of amusement

---

[8] The OWGA was formed after 13 canoeists drowned in Lake Temiskaming in 1978. The organization attempted to set standards for leaders of wilderness expeditions. It had a short and stormy history.

was on Page 15, which had a story and photo with my byline and the headline "Mother winning fight for her daughter's future." It was my heartstring-tugging story of an aphasic nine-year old and her mother's long struggle to find treatment for her. Somehow that didn't fit with the OWGA members' preconceptions about a writer most of them knew, a guy they identified with adventure, the shooting sports and hunting.

My reputation had become problematic. Many of the editors at *The Globe and Mail* had the same perception of me. They didn't expect the hook-and-bullet writer to produce sensitive stories on other issues, no matter how hungry he was for bylines. That changed in October 1980 when the Thursday Section was born. *The Globe and Mail*'s Recreation Section was merged with the Women's pages, Medicine pages and Science pages to become a brand new section of the paper. It was an ill-fated management maneuver lasting less than six months before Recreation was back in the sports pages.[9]

After nearly three years of regular contributions to the Recreation Section I had written stories on almost all of the customary topics: angling, hunting, trapping, shooting, skiing, sailing, climbing and oddball pastimes. I was truly in the groove as a feature writer on those topics but also stuck in a rut. It was starting to feel like same shit, different week. Repetitious if not boring.

In the new Thursday section, a rotating group of editors handled my recreation stories, getting to know me and my capabilities better. They liked what they could get from me. After two months in the Thursday Section, the editors began handing me plum assignments, beginning with a full-page review of Huntsville's luxury Deerhurst Inn for a new

---

9   It was a brief reprieve for the Recreation Section which was probably already marked for execution in an increasingly metrosexual and urban paper. Editor Bob Rife recalls being informed by a senior editor that there was no place for Recreation in *The Globe and Mail*. The section closed in 1985, an important milestone in the decline of what was once a great newspaper.

section called *On the Move*.[10] When Recreation moved back to Sports, I was well established in the Thursday section.

By July 1981, I seemed to be one of the *Thursday Section's* main writers, with a full page on a retired couple who lived on a 36-foot yacht, another on restored mills, a full front page on women and sailing, and another full front page on bright children in summer camp. I was getting more space in the paper than some staff writers. A few let me know to my face how much they resented it. In the early days of the merger of sections they weren't pleased to have me around because they expected I was a rowdy, rifle-toting, carnivorous caveman. They liked it even less when I turned out to be a well-educated, sophisticated competitor who quietly set about eating their lunch.

One of my first stories on women's issues was about Linda Sweet, an extremely provocative woman featured in the Thursday Section. A Grade Two teacher and a championship keelboat racer in the Shark class, she would do her best to provoke other skippers as she passed them. When her boat pulled into the lead, she would put on a large, flowered hat and wiggle her rear end at the yacht being left behind. It was a purely tactical maneuver. She believed that if the skipper she out-maneuvered lost his cool because he had been passed by a woman, it might help her win the race.

Linda's story provoked *The Globe and Mail* into revealing its hand when it came to killing stories, something that is usually well covered up in the news business. My story's lead paragraph detailed Linda's multi-year unsuccessful attempts to join a yacht club in Toronto. Apparently the membership of yacht clubs was fearful that women who joined could bring male bimbos as guests, spoiling the club's atmosphere. (Female bimbos brought as guests did not pose the same problem.)

Somebody downstairs in production did not want to see that in print. Why? Because he didn't want women in yacht clubs? Because he didn't

---

10 Word reached me that editor-in-chief Richard Doyle described my feature on Deerhurst as the "worst piece of fluff ever printed by the *Globe and Mail*." Being a money writer and a byline-seeker, I failed to take insult. Besides, I had thoroughly enjoyed the freebie weekend in Huntsville. Poor Senator Dic would be spinning in his grave if he saw the post-modern ordure and soft left sludge that today's editors regard as suitable feature material.

want exposure of the fact that yacht clubs traditionally discriminated against women? Nobody ever told me who objected or why. But whoever it was came within an inch of killing the feature.

The story was sent for printing and in mid-afternoon on Wednesday (almost at the very last minute for the Thursday paper) I got a frantic call from my editor, Vivian Smith. She had been told that the banning of females at yacht clubs simply wasn't true. She was shocked and appalled when I "laughed in (her) face" at the accusation. Vivian wasn't pleased or convinced by my affirmation that my information was correct. I suggested she phone the Canadian Yachting Association for confirmation. A while later, she called me back to say the story was correct and was going to print. We never discussed it again, but I finally had proof that *The Globe and Mail* killed stories that contained information they didn't want to see printed.[11] I have always said: the bias in the media isn't necessarily in what is printed; the bias most often is in what doesn't get printed and you don't get to read.

Other women's section stories that I wrote included one about a young kayaking champion who feared the weightlifting regime needed to make her strong enough to compete would turn her into the Incredible Hulk. Another featured a serious ice climber whose husband was a non-climber and stayed home to watch their children. The increasing number of women sailing skippers was grist for my mill. Women in paintball competitions were also the subject of one of my features. When I heard that two women were starting a women's hunting and fishing club, I was all over the story like ugly on an ape. My personal niche in the Thursday section seemed to be high-testosterone girly stuff. I had it all to myself.

I also wrote about interactions between women and wildlife, relations that I often considered to be more emotional than realistic. One was a major feature on a woman who ran an owl rehabilitation center. Another was on a woman who was a successful amateur whale researcher. She imitated the work with chimpanzees done by Jane Goodall and was inspired to study whales by Farley Mowat's book *A Whale for the Killing*.

---

11  When I was writing on gun laws, I had the feeling that some of my stories were not treated fairly and some features and news items were killed as being opposed to the laws being enacted federally. Support for restrictions on firearms was widespread at the paper.

That was more like it: stories about real women, real women's issues. All produced by a writer with enough hypocrisy to hide his cynicism and the skill to do it.

Stories about children ran into communications difficulties. I like kids and wrote a number of major features about them. But successful feature writing starts with good interviewing skills, knowing how to ask leading questions and watching carefully for the non-verbal indicators that tell an important truth is being revealed. Those verities become the core of a story interesting enough to sell and should be expressed in good quotes from the person being interviewed. One of the hardest parts of writing about children is that they can be remarkably inarticulate. Sometimes the most leading of questions fails to keep them on topic.

My only full front-page story on children was about a camp for bright kids. Thursday Section senior editor Terry Christian handed that idea to me. It turned into a good yarn about the summer camp and the Association for Bright Children. I identified with precocious children and being bored in school, so I knew what to listen for when the kids told me their stories.

When writing about children, one of my main themes was development of language skills. As word processors began finding their way into schools in the 1980s, I wrote about the impact of the use of computers in developing children's writing skills.

Most of my stories were about children with communications problems. As a result of my writing on stroke (see Section V of this memoir) I became aware of aphasia, a disruption of the ability to understand language or speak. Realizing that my local School for the Deaf was being transformed into a center for aphasic children, I wrote up the school and had a continuing series on aphasic children. It was a topic that appealed to parents who had worries about their child's language development. Most of the interviewing was not of children but of parents telling the story of how they finally realized their child was aphasic and about the hoops they had to jump through before they were able to get help.

The Thursday Section also brought the science section within easy reach. The Recreation Section covered science only as it related to wildlife and fisheries management. Since the paper's science editor was attached to the new Thursday Section, I had the opportunity to branch out into writing about archaeology.

My involvement with underwater archaeology started with a threat of violence at a cross-country skiing event. An angry skier headed towards me where I was shooting pictures at the bottom of Section 7 of the Canadian Ski Marathon (CSM) in Quebec. The section ended with a long run down a steep hill. Tired skiers were falling regularly. This skier had crashed. He was carrying a broken ski and when he reached my position, he offered to punch my lights out for taking advantage of others' misfortune to get a picture.

I explained that I was covering the CSM for *The Globe and Mail* and that any pictures used would simply be good national publicity for the marathon. Besides, I had an extra pair of skis on my car roof rack and would let him exchange his broken skis for the ones on my car. He immediately calmed down, switched skis and agreed to meet me at the Chateau Montebello that evening to return my skis. There was little time to talk, but before he left to resume his trek, he said, "Have I got a story for you!"

He did. In spades. He was an Ottawa-based archaeologist specializing in underwater exploration and he gave me story leads that provided front-page stories on underwater archeology. The first one was significant. Shortly after Columbus arrived in the Caribbean, Basque whalers from the Bay of Biscay established a whaling station on the mainland just across the Strait of Belle Isle from the settlement the Vikings created at 500 years earlier at L'Anse au Meadow in Vinland (Newfoundland).

Divers working in the frigid and murky waters of Red Bay found a whaling vessel that sank in 1565, loaded with barrels of whale oil and ready to cross the Atlantic. They discovered the ship in 1977, following a lead provided by an archivist who had discovered a centuries-old insurance claim on the sunken ship. By 1982, archaeologists were ready to talk publicly about the find—one of great historical significance, the earliest European ship found in Canada.

I broke the story on the front page of *The Globe and Mail*. The next year, when work resumed at the Red Bay site, I had another front-page story. The archaeologists found 70 skeletons of healthy young men who had probably drowned over the years in Red Bay. They phoned me from their diving raft to announce the discovery of four more ships from Spain. My pursuit of watery archaeology led me to features on the Hamilton and Scourge, two War of 1812 warships sunk in western Lake Ontario, and another on an 1812 gunboat in the St. Lawrence River. I also wrote on the difficulty of preserving material that had been underwater for centuries and tended to deteriorate when exposed to the air. I had features on organization known as Preserve Our Wrecks (POW) and on the opening of a Great Lakes marine museum in Kingston.

The archaeologists turned out to be great fun to work with. Many of them spent their working days underwater in diving suits that had hot water running through them to keep them from getting hypothermia. In the era before zebra mussels increased the water clarity in some lakes, they sometimes did their work exploring by feel in near-zero visibility. At professional meetings, they were rambunctious and gossipy. They had dirt on people like Jacques Cousteau and would tell unprintable stories about some incidents. They knew how to party.

Eventually I was invited to Ottawa where archeological conservationists were going to examine a 400-year-old compass that the Basque whalers had used to find their way across the Atlantic. The compass wasn't impressive, looking like a brownish grapefruit soaking in water and mud. But the experience of examining it had a big impact on me. Here was something that adventurous men had used to guide themselves into the unknown. I could relate to that.

**Remains of a Spanish compass, ca. 1565.** Found during the archaeological excavation between 1978 and 1985 at Red Bay Harbour, Labrador.
Courtesy of the Department of Canadian Heritage, Parks Canada, Federal Archaelogy. ©Her Majesty the Queen in Right of Canada. Reproduced with the permission of the Minister of Public Works and Government Services, Canada. Larger Version (35 kb)

**16th century Spanish compass in case.** An artist's reconstruction of the compass found at Red Bay Harbour, Labrador.
Illustration by Duleepa Wijayawardhana. Based upon a Carol Pillar sketch courtesy of Parks Canada from James A. Tuck and Robert Grenier, *Red Bay, Labrador: World Whaling Capital A. D. 1550-1600* (St. John's, Newfoundland: Atlantic Archaelogy Ltd., ©1989) 30.

*One of the highlights of my time writing about underwater archaeology was being invited to a conservation institute in Ottawa to witness the opening of a compass that had been drowned and unseen for more than 400 years. My photos make it look like an ancient grapefruit covered with mud. This page is from Parks Canada. But I was there watching when the compass that guided Basque whalers across the Atlantic was revealed.*

Writing on underwater archaeology was both the apex and the end of my brief career as a freelance journalist for national papers. I had started as a feature writer doing stories most other reporters would avoid. I had progressed to increasingly difficult and significant topics, to stories that actually informed people and didn't just entertain them. With underwater archaeology, I was into historically significant stuff, including stories on the first ships to be sunk in North America and the ships sunk in Lake Ontario in the War of 1812.

Archaeologists had filled me in on all kinds of information that I was unable to use in stories at the time. I would have eventually used all that information in the *Globe* but the deep recession of the early 1980s devastated my market. The sale of *The Globe and Mail* to the legendarily cheap Thomson empire finally destroyed it. The penny dropped for me that the end had truly come when I was grossly underpaid for a page one archeology story in 1983—Canadian science on the front page of the national paper. The *ne plus ultra* for a freelancer. I finally understood that selling stories and photos to the *Globe* was no way to make a living and never would be again. I have memories of walking around to my favorite editors, saying goodbye and telling them I was off to seek my fortune.

After that I would only contribute to *The Globe and Mail* if I stumbled on something interesting. I sold them fewer than three dozen stories in the years after my last front page story on Spanish galleons in Labrador. I considered taking up freelancing to national papers again in 1998, when I was about to leave for a year in Australia and began writing for the National Post. On the day I left YYZ on the first leg of my journey Down Under, the copy of the *National Post* the stewardess dropped in my lap had two stories by me in it. Once I reached Australia, the *Post* seemed to lose interest completely.

But my years of newspaper freelancing in the 1970s and 1980s had established my reputation. For decades, my phone would ring and people would offer me unlikely projects because they had read my stuff in the paper. They thought if anyone would be capable of helping them,

Ron Truman | 43

it might be me. By 1983 I was well-positioned to have a good writing, consulting and public relations career. I was off to seek my fortune and more excitement. I would find it by working for a geographic magazine, drifting into crisis communications and getting continuing opportunities to do interesting writing assignments.

My last Globe and Mail article was an obituary. When my mentor died in 1998 I wrote him up in *The Globe and Mail*'s *Lives Lived* column. It read:

> Take just one step beyond the place where the pavement ends in Ontario, and you walk with the spirit and legacy of J. Douglas Roseborough.
>
> Go, for example, on an interpretive hike in Algonquin Park. In the early 1950s, shortly after graduating from the University of Toronto, Doug was involved in setting up the first interpretive program introducing city folk to the mysteries of the park's tamed wilderness.
>
> Push through the tangle of greenery to cast a fly to wary brook trout hiding deep in a shady pool in a southern Ontario stream and you'll need a fishing license because of Doug. He introduced Ontario's first angling license in the early 1970s.
>
> Out in the boondocks, where the year's highlight is a week in a moose or deer camp, with its unparalleled camaraderie, the red-gold glow of sunrise through the forest, and the ear-splitting crack of a high-powered rifle, Doug's legacy — in the form of a lottery tag — had better be in your pocket along with your license. He introduced selective harvest systems designed to keep deer and moose populations healthy.
>
> And anywhere electricity flows in Ontario, fish and wildlife will forever be in debt to Doug. It was his relentless pressure that forced Ontario Hydro to acknowledge the environmental effects of damming the rivers and to start hiring biologists to deal with the impacts.

For most of his career in the Ontario government, Doug was a high-level administrator: Director of Fisheries Branch, Director of Wildlife Research, Wildlife Branch Director. He served in a time of dramatic change, through the 1960s and 1970s, when people recognized how modern society was affecting the environment and sometimes threatening the balance of the ecosystem, a brief era when conservation issues were important to society at large. Many of the policies and programs he introduced or shaped are the framework for today's fish and wildlife programs.

Natural resources issues were highly controversial, with anti-hunters battling hunters, preservationists taking on conservationists, animal-rights activists challenging trappers, and tree-huggers spitting passive-aggressive fury at the forest industry. Doug met the challenges head-on. "Get the lawyers out of this room," he once told a group dealing with a crisis, "They'll just tell us what we can't do. We're here to find out what we can do."

He was as formidable in his personal life as in his professional life, for biology influenced his attitudes. He was a naturalist, something of a sociobiologist, and definitely a testosterone-fueled organism. A birder, he would identify each bird by its song. He believed in dominance, a pecking order. When a pet dog got out of line, Doug disciplined it by fighting it wolf-style. The battle ended with the dog on its back, quivering in submission, with Doug snarling over the animal, his teeth just inches from his dog's exposed throat. Thereafter, the dog was well behaved and sub-dominant. Then there was the famous incident in Algonquin Park when Doug stepped into a wildlife research enclosure holding a young bull moose. The bull normally allowed researchers to wander freely in its pen. But not Doug. It began preparing for battle. Doug chose not to fight, but acknowledged the compliment; as he told the story, the moral was that there was room for only one alpha male in a pen that small.

After he retired, he returned to his urban Toronto roots. His focus shifted from the flora and fauna of the Canadian Shield's Precambrian granite to fundraising and sport at North Toronto's Granite Club. He spent the last hour of his life winning a tennis game at his club.

To the extent that Doug was successful in improving the way we treat our environment and manage our resources, Ontario's woodland animals, the fish swimming in the lakes, and even the very rocks themselves will continue to celebrate his life and work long after the humans who attended his memorial are gone.

*The Globe and Mail* itself may soon be needing an obituary, victim of technological change and the unwillingness of the public to pay good money for the Orwellian dullness of its political correctness, the shrillness of its feminist columnists and the triviality of its petty intellectuals—its refusal to come to terms with reality. I'll volunteer to write that obit.

Early in the 21st century, *The Globe and Mail* was forced by the *Robertson v Thomson* class action lawsuit to cough up millions of dollars for 25 years of unpaid-for digitizing of freelancers' articles and making them available to paying customers. All freelancers had to submit a claim based on the material digitized by the paper. With the incentive to do an actual count of my contributions, I found in my few years with the paper I managed to produce more than 530 feature articles, which constituted a substantial claim.

# 5.
# Look Who's Still Alive

*Photography and Adventure 1976-2015*

The model put her arms akimbo and leaned forward slightly to dangle her bare breasts at the most attractive and perky angle. Dark-haired, thirty-ish, and far from being a rousing beauty, she was a real professional, holding herself completely motionless for minutes. Meanwhile, the students in the advanced photography class adjusted the barn doors on the studio lights to create exactly the artsy image they were seeking—rim lighting or whatever. Their goal was to please the instructor and get a good mark or to create a memento for themselves.

I had a different agenda. Off to one side, loading rolls of 36 into my camera, I was shooting a few frames, then rewinding each film cassette. I would listen carefully for the camera's take-up reel to release the tail of the roll without winding it all the way back into the cassette. I would repeat the process with a new roll of film.

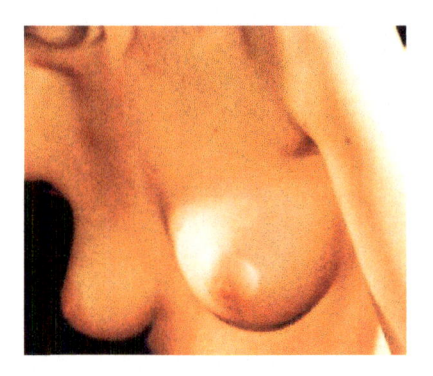

*Evidence of a gratuitous attempt to curry favor with darkroom staff at The Globe and Mail. They resented souping the large amount of film shot by an amateur attempting to compete with professionals. I contrived to have the first few frames of the occasional roll of Tri-X have off-topic pics that might provide my critics with a little amusement and soften their attitudes. It seemed to work.*

Each roll of high-speed (ASA 400) black and white film I took out of my Canon F-1 still had 30 or more frames of unexposed film and the tail hanging out so I could readily reload it. Later, in the field, when I reloaded that roll, I would cover the objective lens to prevent double-exposure of the photos I had taken in class, bang off a few frames, then continue with the shoot. The end result would be a roll of Kodak Tri X that was mostly pictures illustrating whatever story I was covering. The first few frames were pictures of boobs—shot with a long lens to exclude identifying features like faces or location.

I never turned the pictures in as part of the coursework. I knew I was going to fail the course, same as I had flunked all previous photography courses. I didn't even develop the film. My goal was to improve my popularity in *The Globe and Mail*'s photo department. In my first years freelancing to the national paper, the photographers and lab technicians at the paper tended to regard me as a rank amateur. They treated me like an unwelcome pest. I would show up in photo department with a handful of film, only to be ignored for what seemed forever when I desperately wanted to dump my film for processing and start writing my story at one of the computer terminals.

The darkroom technicians, especially one that I nicknamed "microscope eyes" for his ability to find the tiniest flaws in my photos, gave me the impression I increased their workload by shooting too much film. They would have to develop all my exposed rolls and make contact sheets. Where a real pro could get a good picture shooting one roll of 36, I would shoot five or six rolls hoping that one of my hundreds of exposures would produce something of G&M quality. I was a lot of work for the photo department.

Behind the desk in the photo department I had noticed a whole series of "oops" photos pinned to a hanging cabinet that ran the length of the room at ceiling level. Water polo players, figure skaters and other attractive women were pictured in wardrobe malfunctions—in photos taken for the G&M by their pros but, of course, never published. That gave me the idea for the boob pictures. The lab technicians were all visual types and seeing bare breasts on my film might amuse them.

It worked. I took some teasing about shooting pictures in no-tell motels. I told the truth about my photo course and hinted that there would be more cassettes of Tri-X from me with a few salacious frames at the start of the roll. They had something to look forward to, a promise of future titillation. It was an icebreaker for me with the darkroom staff, an important step in being accepted and having supporters in the photo department. I desperately needed friends because there was no getting around the fact that I truly was a rank amateur with a camera in my hands.

I never expected to become a photographer and my meteoric rise in the field surprised me. In July 1976, the first picture I ever took with a real camera (with f-stops and shutter speeds) appeared on page one of the *Trentonian*, a small-city paper that published every other weekday. A few weeks later I had a picture on page one of *The Globe and Mail*—the first of 500 photos I would sell to the national paper in my brief newspaper freelancing career. Soon I became a regular in *The Globe and Mail*, not because my pictures were exceptionally good but because I was a two-way man, capable of creating the art required for my own stories. And because of my predilection for risk-taking.

I learned photography in on-the-job training at the *Trentonian* and the *Picton Gazette* and took basic photography courses from John Peterson, who taught photojournalism at Loyalist College. John had been head of the photo department at *The Toronto Star* and gave me valuable tips on shooting for the big papers. He failed me because I sold my pictures before turning them in as assignments.

In the late 1970s, photography was complex and film-based. Black and white pictures required use of fast film—Ilford HP5 or Kodak Tri-X, fragile media that had to be protected from light and heat, loaded and unloaded carefully and painstakingly developed. Cameras, the 35 mm Canon F-1s favored by news photographers at the G&M, were totally manual—the photographer set the aperture, shutter speed and focus for each exposure.

You had to know what you were doing. Lenses used by pros were fixed focal length—I carried 200mm, 100mm and 28mm lenses in my kit. Most of the time, two F-1s dangled around my neck, one with a wide-angle lens and one with a telephoto lens. As the situation changed, I would switch cameras rather than fumble around changing lenses. I used one of Canon's original motor drives on my F-1, an add-on with a long handle and a separate battery pack holding 10 AA batteries.

F-1s last forever and are reputed to be so durable you can pound nails with them, then continue taking pictures. But they are heavy, with the bodies alone weighing more than two pounds and requiring many accessories. For a writer who did a lot of skiing, climbing and other backcountry assignments, a camera bag with two F-1s and their peripherals was a heavy burden. I sometimes added more than four pounds to that load by carrying a medium-format Mamiya C330 with a huge flash, known as a potato-masher because of its size and shape.

The Mamiya reflected my lack of confidence. It shot 120 film, producing a negative that was 2¼ inches from corner to corner, huge compared to 35mm negatives. Good pictures on a contact sheet of 120 negatives seemed to jump right out at you while you had to use a magnifying glass to examine contact sheets of 35mm negatives. I was convinced that pictures taken with 2¼ film were easier to sell. Good pictures were immediately obvious on a contact sheet.

Small newspapers, unlike the big-city dailies, had not fully adopted the 35mm Single Lens Reflex (SLR) camera as a standard in the late 1970s. Many papers were using medium-format film in twin-lens reflex cameras. News photographers held their cameras at waist level, looking down at a screen that showed the image about to be captured. When the photographer finished a roll of black and white film, he rewound it, then put an adhesive band on to hold it in place on its spool. I carried a blackout bag that would hold my camera and allow me to put both hands into it (like a woman's fur muff for hand warming in winter) to ensure no light would spoil my film. Photographers learned to change rolls by feel and sound. Developing film was a tricky process carried out in complete darkness—transferring the film to another spool of metal or plastic and putting it into a cylinder where liquid chemicals would bring out the images.

Some small papers required reporters to develop their own film and print their own pictures. The bigger the news organization, the easier it was to get your pictures ready for the paper. At the G&M, photo technicians put a leader on the tail of your film, held the cassette up against a slot in a developing machine which took the film in and pumped it out as a finished negative. Prints were on plasticized paper. If the picture was urgent, you could walk in with a roll of exposed film and less than half an hour later, walk out with prints. In the 1970s, that was almost miraculous.

My skill as a photographer increased steadily over the newspaper freelancing years. I carried a camera daily and, for me, film was free. I could shoot as much as I wanted. By the early 1980s, my photos were good enough that I had a two-page photo feature in *The Globe and Mail*, one of the paper's rare pictorial spreads.

I would take risks to get good pictures. I lashed myself to a cliff and took pictures of a rock climber going over me. I hung upside-down from the rigging of a brigantine sailboat to get a picture of a terrified youngster trying to climb to the yardarm. In a cave, I had a row of spelunkers holding their breath so that the condensation of the moisture they were emitting didn't blur the image I was making.

I would <u>appear</u> to take risks to get pictures—aka faking it. My photo of an iceboat, runner in the air, looked for all the world like a speeding craft was on the verge of running over me. Actually, the boat was stock-still with its brakes on. The pilot raised the runner by pulling in the mainsail sheet. In other assignments in which I could not (or would not) get close enough to the action to get decent shots—things like ice climbing or motorcycle racing—I would give a camera to a participant or official and ask him to take pictures for me.

I learned how to take T&A (tits and ass) shots that would sell. One of my favorites is of a woman walking over me in snowshoes—I discovered that slender women could be shot from the feet up. Another choice shot is that of a pneumatic young woman hauling her dinghy out of the water at the Laser Worlds in Kingston. It took me a while to talk someone into shedding her wetsuit and hauling her boat up the ramp while wearing a bathing suit. Her reward—she got her picture splashed on sports pages across the country.

I suffered only one injury taking pictures for *The Globe and Mail*. At a bird sanctuary in Montreal, I was using a 200mm lens to photograph a chicken stalking a squirrel. The young chicken had imprinted on a golden eagle. Thinking it was an eagle, the chick went after the squirrel fully intending to kill and eat it—unable to fly, the chick chased its prey on foot. I wanted a photo that would say: carnivorous chicken. My guide at the sanctuary blurted, "Watch Out!" I looked up from the camera viewfinder to see a golden eagle with a six-foot wingspan almost upon me. The eagle was allowed a short flight path along a clothesline wire that kept her close to the ground. It was already terrifyingly close to me, talons ready to do damage to protect her baby. The demented captive eagle believed I was a threat. In the ensuing ducking and dodging, I ended up with a deep gouge over my left eye.

A growing reputation for doing hazardous things was helpful in gaining acceptance with the photographers at work. One day I walked into the photo department, with my usual handful of film cassettes, fully expecting to be ignored for a while because I had shot too much film. A group of photographers was sitting around a table, waiting for their daily assignments. One pro looked up and said, "Well, well! Look who's still alive!" There was no sarcasm in the greeting. I knew I had finally been accepted.

I began imitating pro behavior. Almost every *Globe and Mail* photographer used the same model of camera bag, a brown canvas bag with a black leather strap and lots of compartments. To keep from grabbing the wrong bag when leaving the newsroom, they added a large identifying pin, button or brooch to the front flap. I chose a huge button with the logo: NUKE THE WHALES. It spoke to my sense of humor and reflected my irreverence. It didn't appeal to some members of the growing environmentalist movement. At a conference of greenies, a typically humorless individual challenged me about the button. I tried to explain it was a combination of No Nukes and Save the Whales, boiled down to three words that would fit on a button. I don't think she bought my story.

After leaving *The Globe and Mail*, I shot less black and white film every year. It became difficult to find film processors who would develop it, even though I needed B&W prints for some newsletters I was doing. Eventually I discovered film that could be developed by the C-41 process used for color print film. It didn't give the quality demanded by first-line publications, but it would pass for my purposes.

When I began working for geographic magazines, I had to learn some of the intricacies of shooting color transparency film (color slides), re-educating myself to shoot Kodachrome 64 and Ektachrome 64, slow slide films demanding long exposure times. Bright, sunny days were best for these films and I had trouble in less-than-ideal situations. One assignment for the magazine had to be shot over four specific days in November that turned out to be heavily overcast and rainy. None of my pictures were useable, so the editors solved the problem by hiring a watercolor artist to render my photos into paintings.

My willingness to go into the wilderness and do things that other photographers would not do led to my being the most-published author in one geographic publication. I had to invent a pseudonym for issues of the magazine that contained more than one of my articles. Unfortunately the publication was killed after only a few years. The Ontario Provincial Archives is the only place I know where you can find a complete collection of issues of *Landmarks* magazine.

My last hooray in *Globe and Mail* photography was done for the NDP government's Green Workplace in the mid-1990s. The Dippers, on their way out, wanted to reach the business community with the message that offices could be run in a more environmentally friendly way—recycling more, reducing paper and energy use.

What better way than to put a full-color 16-page insert into every issue of *The Globe and Mail* distributed in Ontario? After costing out the price the G&M would charge and discovering what an advertising firm

Ron Truman | 53

that would do the layout and printing of the little publication would cost, they realized that going to Toronto agencies for writing and photography would break their budget.

I got a call asking if I could do both the writing and the photography. I agreed, using the assignment as an excuse to buy a new camera outfit—a Nikon F90X, a super-sophisticated film camera known as a chip camera. I enjoyed working with the leading-edge advertising firm that handled the project and watched as the resulting product, called *Let's hear it for the stones* appeared in the national paper and vanished without a ripple. It was a reflection of the delusional thinking of the NDP.

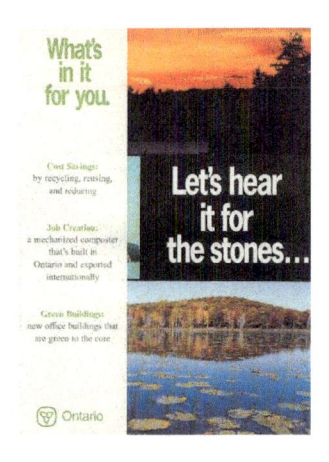

*When you want to convince office managers to make the "green-ness" of their offices a priority, how do you go about it? You put a full-color insert in every copy of The Globe and Mail. I was hired to write the text and take the pictures for this extraordinarily expensive piece of junk mail.*

There was one story in that advertorial publication that typifies for me the barking moonbat madness of those five NDP years. That was about worms in the office. You read it right—worms, red wrigglers. Instead of throwing lunch scraps in the garbage, you were supposed to have a worm box in your office and give the leftovers to the annelids, that would recycle it into the highest quality soil.

After my Green Workplace publication appeared and disappeared, I heard about office worms only once more. That was when Mike Harris and his Progressive Conservatives moved into the premier's office in 1995.

I saw a news item stating the transition team was mystified at finding a box full of worms among the things Bob Rae left behind. I knew why the worms were there. And I also know where this loony-tunes idea was pilot-tested, because I visited and photographed the site—an insane asylum in Brockville. How appropriate.

> Brockville Psychiatric Hospital's 800,000 worms will feed happily on the 200 kg of scraps and waste food that the kitchen produces daily. But first you have to create a waste stream especially for the worms. "And the word worm," says the hospital's director of materials management Jack Hewitt, "is a word you don't even use in polite society unless you happen to be going fishing."

> **Dinner is served.**

> Vermiculture uses red wrigglers, worms that can eat their weight in food every day. Brockville Psychiatric Hospital installed a large-scale vermiculture composting system. The worms can handle 275 kg of food per day.

> "They'll eat almost everything," says head gardener Dave Wilson. "The only things left in the castings when the worms are finished are little bits of plastic from the lining of milk cartons that were ground up with the food. The rest is soil that can be used as fertilizer – and we have nearly 20 hectares of lawn here to use it on; once we are getting enough castings from our vermiculture operation, we will be able to stop buying fertilizer for the lawns."

*Office worms were among the more demented topics I got to write about. Red wrigglers kept in your workplace would eat your lunch scraps, playing an important part in saving the world. Only in the batshit lunacy of the insane years of Bob Rae's NDP government in Ontario would such a topic be celebrated province-wide in a full-color insert.*

I still shoot, often trying to get exciting pictures of the sport of croquet. Very challenging. My current equipment is digital, a couple of basic Nikon Ds with vibration-reduced zoom lenses that range from 18 mm wide-angle lenses to 300mm telephotos. That's made photography fun again. Photoshopping—forget it. The technical side of photography has always bored me. I donated almost all my photographs and negatives to the archives after I retired. More than 15,000 of my images are held in the Provincial Archives in Toronto, listed in the Public Archives of Canada and officially described as a collection of "national and historic significance."

Ron Truman | 55

# 6.
# Polar Bears Scare Me Shitless

*The years with Landmarks Magazine 1984-1987*

The polar bear was belly-down on the tundra, spread-eagle with paws pointing in four directions. He was snoring softly and blinking regularly in a drug-induced coma. He wasn't going to be in a cheerful mood when we brought him out of it.

*Posing with bear biologist George Kolonoski as wildlife technicians prepare to gather data on the animal. The bear has had eye protection against bugs but the darts that put the animal to sleep have not been dug out. The helicopter that carried five people and all the equipment needed for the research is in the background.*

He had reason to be snarling when awakened. Bloodied and blindfolded, one of his teeth was missing, collected with a biologist's deft twist of a pair of pliers. He'd been rolled around, hauled up in a cargo net to be weighed, anointed with ointments—some to prevent bugs from getting in his eyes, some to ward off infection in the minor wounds created by digging out tranquillizer darts. He'd had his temperature taken the hard way.

His yellowish-white back bore a gigantic alphanumeric label the size of airplane call letters, painted on with Lady Clairol hair dye. The letter and number were damp and brownish, slowly darkening to black. This would provide temporary identification for a season or two until the fur grew out. His permanent identification number was inked on the inside of his upper lip, a new tattoo that might well have said, "I hate biologists."

*Now I lay me down to sleep. Two solid hits with darts put a large bear into dreamland until it is awoken with a drug known as an antagonist. The animal snores and blinks. The tagging team rubs grease into the eyes to keep the bugs out and puts a blindfold on the animal to guard against sun damage. Also good for hiding the startling blinking that could make me think the bear might be waking up.*

Bear behavior along the rocky Hudson Bay coastline where the tagging team had been working suggested we were making a change in the bears' attitude and ambiance. Many untagged polar bears ignored the helicopter when we flew near them—they were completely fearless. Even if they had never seen a chopper before, it wasn't going to faze them.

Bears wearing the alphanumeric branding, showing they had already encountered the tagging team, would react to the helicopter. Some ran away, others stood on their hind legs, challenging the chopper. One day nine bears, mostly big males, stood shoulder-to-shoulder in a group, as if daring the taggers to land and rumble with a whole gang.[12]

I was completely new to the procedure. Preoccupied with taking photographs with four cameras, I marveled at every step taken. This was intimate contact with an apex predator weighting more than half a ton, one of the most dangerous animals you could ever encounter.

I knew only one thing for sure: the first step in waking up the bear had to be warming up the helicopter. We'd want to get the hell out of there as quickly as possible once the bear was moving.

My camera clicked as a biologist reached into the bear's mouth, extracted his tongue and jabbed a huge hypodermic needle into its underside. I asked what the needle was for. My heart sunk when I got the answer. "That's the antagonist. It will counteract the sedative we knocked the bear out with and this big hoss will wake up," the biologist explained.

I stammered something about the desirability of being somewhere else when the bear woke up, even if the animal was a little dopey to start with. "We stay with the bear until its heart rate and respiration rate double," the bio explained. So we stayed. When we left, we hovered around for a few minutes in the helicopter, but the bear lay still. We were running out of time, so we left, with the team leader saying he'd return to the area first thing in the morning to ensure the bear was fully recovered.

This was the kind of adventure I could never afford when I was working for a newspaper. My reputation for taking on difficult assignments and turning in quality pictures and writing had led to better things. I became a freelancer for a geographic magazine with deep pockets and unlimited access to pricy items like airplanes, helicopters, remote areas and fascinating wildlife research projects.

---

12 Cinematographer Lloyd Walton was in the helicopter the day the bears circled the wagons. He captured a remarkable still photo of the event.

The polar bear tagging story, one of my most exotic adventures, was sponsored by *Landmarks*[13], a quarterly geographic magazine published by the Ontario Ministry of Natural Resources. As a writer-photographer who had empathy for hunting and wildlife management, I was a natural for the publication. They used me so often I required a pseudonym for issues in which I had more than one feature story.[14]

It was a change of pace for me. Working for *The Globe and Mail*, I was careful about running up expenses. I found my own adventures, did things on the cheap and would always accept freebies when they were offered. With *Landmarks*, I was told what they wanted. They seemed to spare no expense getting me into a location where I could do my job.

The publication was designed to promote the ministry's programs and initiatives. You got paid whether or not the story was published but political sensitivity could lead to some heavy-handed editing and even outright story-killing. For example, I spent weeks on a feature about Ontario's efforts at improving the Chinese People's Republic's (CPR's) forest fire control.

I didn't get to go to China, only to Sault Ste. Marie to interview fire-fighters who had been in the CPR training the Chinese. The story was killed after it was print-ready and illustrated with snapshots taken by Ontario foresters.

No matter how carefully I wrote it, the Chinese were so inept at fire-fighting—swatting at fires with brooms and communicating between fire fighters on the ground and spotters in the air with notes tied to rocks thrown from the planes—even the most politically correct reader would spontaneously think of the proverbial Chinese fire drill. There was fear that the CPR would not want to see anything in print that might draw attention to frequent public executions of those found guilty of starting forest fires. Severe measures apparently were required to deal with the perennial problem of fighting fires started by the burning of paper money in ancestor-worship rites.

---

13   *Landmarks* is difficult to find. The Ontario Archives in Toronto has all the issues. Internet searches fail to turn up any hits on the publication.

14   My pseudonym was Russell Valentino Franklin.

MNR top echelon staff must have seen no point in giving China bad publicity or inviting people to look into new dimensions in use of the death penalty in the CPR. When the story was killed, the efforts of top firefighters who had gone to China were never properly recognized.

Many of my Landmarks features—on urban fishing, Lake of the Woods, habitat restoration, trapping, rainbow trout, and suburban deer hunting—were fun to do but pretty routine when it came to travel and the amount of risk involved. Some were exciting.

A December moose hunt near Atikokan in a forest covered by freezing rain followed by deep snow was an outstanding hunting experience. On snowshoes and with no telescopic sights on our rifles, we tracked moose in what I called a "tinkle bell forest" filled with the music of ice-covered twigs breaking in the breeze. We found plenty of moose tracks and several bedding sites but we ran out of time before my guide was able to walk down a moose. The *raison d'être* for the story was to raise awareness of a new selective harvest system that allowed moose hunting seasons to be extended into the winter. This feature led to great photographs of a low-tech moose hunt in a picturesque environment.

A sturgeon research feature story involved interesting travel. It began with a canoe trip 50 miles from Timmins down the Kabinakagami River to a sturgeon research camp at Mamamatawa—the place where many rivers join. Despite having an outboard motor on the stern of the long canoe that took us down the river, I felt like a voyageur. The Kabi was one of the voyageurs' historic routes. The sloping riverbanks were lined with one of the last surviving stands of mature elms in Ontario. The trees were important in the days of the voyageurs, who preferred elm for the keels of their boats. The destructive elm bark beetle had not reached the area by the 1980s.

The sturgeons were as enormous and as valuable as they were unsightly, with mouths surrounded by dangling sensors used to find food. Poachers would arrive by float plane, catch fish and sell the caviar. Sturgeons were once so common in Ontario they were used as fuel in steamboats on the Great Lakes. Long-lived fish that reproduce late in life, their populations can't sustain a lot of harvesting. The fisheries research was a study of the state of one of the province's last remaining healthy sturgeon populations.

After a couple of days of catching, measuring, tagging and releasing sturgeon, we flew back to Timmins. Our canoe was lashed between the pontoons of a float plane. The journey that had taken so long by canoe on the river went by in a flash. On the way out, our pilot diverted to show us a place where a plane's tail section stuck out of the muskeg. It was all that had not been removed after a mid-air collision of two military planes and a reminder of the hazards of flying in the north.

I did a *Landmarks* story on enforcement of the Game and Fish act. I went on boat patrols, hid out in the dark waiting for poachers to spear spawning walleye below a dam, and walked the banks of a stream near Port Hope looking for people who were snagging fish rather than angling for them. We busted one individual twice—after the first time we took his illegal equipment, he returned with more only to lose that as well. And we dealt with a threatening ruffian, who promised to use his spear on people rather than fish. The only people we enforced the law on were white recreational anglers. Political correctness, even though it wasn't called that at the time, played a role.

I did stories dealing with fearsome creatures living in Ontario. Snapping turtles were as cute as the extra-terrestrial of the movie ET when they were not much bigger than a silver dollar. They grew into huge, moss-covered monsters that lived for centuries. A research lake in Algonquin Provincial Park had a multi-year program on their growth and breeding.

On my visit for *Landmarks*, I was particularly interested in a weight gain research project. Biologists were feeding and weighing turtles named Big Al and Burt Reynolds. They discovered they didn't need to throw the fish to them. If they canoed into the turtles' home bay and splashed a dead, one-pound trout in the water, Big Al or Burt would surface and gently take the fish out of the researcher's hand. I wanted a picture. On the way to the cove where the turtles resided, biologists cautioned that it could be hours rather than minutes before the turtle surfaced.

*A researcher from Guelph University holds a large male snapping turtle at a research lake in Algonquin Provincial Park in June 1987. The red paint on the turtle's shell helps identify the creature. Snappers can't withdraw their heads and legs into their shell, which makes them dangerous on land. Unable to hide in their carapaces, they are inclined to defend themselves.*

The young biologist paddling my canoe idly dangled her hand in the water. Suddenly there was an uproar that nearly tipped the flimsy craft. Burt Reynolds (the handsomest turtle in the lake) had come up under the canoe and, mistaking the hand lolling in the water for a fish, chomped down on it. The terrified biologist reacted instantly, but the turtle, realizing that the human hand was not food, released his grip just as quickly. The young woman's hand had no broken skin, even though Burt had bitten down hard enough to cause pain. After the panic subsided, we got down to work and I got plenty of pictures of a biologist feeding a snapping turtle by hand. But after my visit, things changed at the research lake—the guys were reluctant to go skinny-dipping in the cove that was home to Big Al and Burt.

The polar bear tagging expedition came in the middle of my stint with *Landmarks*. It was unforgettable—not just the bears, but also the air transportation and being presented with the worst meal ever.

I arrived in Moosonee by commercial air before transferring to the single Otter to fly up the coast to Cape Henrietta Maria. Weather delayed our start by a day. Restaurants in Moose would not accept MasterCard, only Visa. I had no cash, so I had to depend on an MNR staff residence for sleeping and dinner.

The housing was comfortable but supper was a comedy of errors. There was no beef or pork on hand and the sea trout in the freezer had spoiled. Eventually, four big men sat down to a meal of boiled celery and wild duck. One pitifully tiny duck. Worse, a big chunk of the duck's breast was missing. When the staffer who provided the duck was criticized for shooting it at too close a range and destroying much of the meat, he said, "I didn't shoot the duck. I was out walking my dog and chased off a skunk that was eating it."

I went to bed hungry. The next morning I borrowed cash and had steak and eggs at the airport restaurant.

Flying was challenging in early fall in the Hudson Bay watershed. There was enough ice on the water to make pontoons useless but not enough snow to use skis. That made it difficult to get exactly where you wanted to be on the tundra. MNR discovered they could land on elevated beach ridges in the Hudson Bay watershed. The whole area has been rising since the weight of ice was removed at the end of the last ice age. Land that once was a pebbly beach was now high and dry. As long as no logs had drifted ashore in that location thousands of years ago, an elevated beach ridge was a perfect natural landing strip.[15] The bush pilots used oversized, underinflated tires on single-engine De Havilland Otters for landing directly on the tundra.

There were three of us and a 50-gallon barrel of helicopter fuel in the single Otter, a plane with the call letters ODU. We headed up the coast of James and Hudson Bays. This was a light load for ODU, but progress was slow. We had to follow the coastline so a beach ridge would always be available for emergency landings. ODU was equipped with huge tires designed for a larger aircraft, spoiling aerodynamics and forcing us to fly at a ridiculously low airspeed. It seemed to take forever. After several hours, I noticed an empty fuel barrel washed up on the shore. I was

---

15  The beach ridges are visible on Google Earth.

relieved. This was concrete evidence that we had not flown off the end of the earth.

It was my first view of the Hudson Bay Lowlands, where trees grow only on the well-drained soil of river valleys. The rest is low and swampy, mostly muskeg with stunted bushes and lots of moss and lichens. It isn't just a dull green, khaki-colored landscape—there are a remarkable variety of colors. And the Arctic Ocean makes its own weather. While flying along the coast of James and Hudson Bays, I admired an ever-changing skyscape.

It was blowing stink by the time we could see the bear camp, nine miles inland, far enough from water to be out of normal range of wandering bears. As we got closer to the camp, we could see the gravel beach ridge used for landing was dusted with snow. A helicopter—a Bell Jet Ranger with a capacity of five—sat near the researcher's tents, its fuel dump at the far end of our ersatz landing strip. Five people stood near the tents, watching our approach.

Lloyd Walton, the cinematographer whom I was going to replace in camp, had set up his camera to film our landing. I leaned out the window of the single Otter, snapping pictures as we descended. ODU pitched and yawed in the stiff crosswind. The pilot expertly made a three-point landing but as soon as we touched down, control over the plane was impossible and we began sliding into the fuel dump. The pilot hit the throttle and the lightly loaded plane jumped back into the air. The cinematographer caught it all on film, the crazy approach, the perfect touchdown, and the reappearance of ODU out of a cloud of snow, clawing for altitude.

I thought we were immediately going to implement Plan B and head for Winisk, a trip that would take only an hour or so. We could return to land at the bear camp when weather improved. But no. The pilot, to my shock and dismay, circled for another landing attempt. I could feel my heart racing and my blood pressure going stratospheric. I took my cameras off my neck, packed them in my camera bag and put the bag at my feet, holding it down so the cameras wouldn't fly around if the second landing attempt ended with a prang.

The pilot brought ODU to ground level, brushed the wheels on the snow-covered beach, then eased back on the stick to put us in the air again. I slowly regained my calmness, feeling the heat in my face from high blood pressure draining away. After a short hop to Winisk, where we had an actual gravel runway, we called it a day. There was no discussion of the near-crash landing or the second try at landing. I figured the pilot had a fright on the first attempt and did the second approach just to calm himself down.

My original plan, to replace the cinematographer and sleep in a tent at the research camp, was canned. Everybody in camp slept with a pistol under their pillow. The instructions were to start shooting if a bear wandered into your tent; you might save somebody else's life. I wasn't going to get a chance to spend my first night in the Hudson Bay Lowlands wondering if an uninvited bear might join the pajama party. For someone with a bit of bear phobia, that was just too bad. Too, too bad. I slept in what passed for a hotel at the abandoned Royal Canadian Air Force base at the former Mid-Canada Distant Early Warning line site at Winisk.

The next morning dawned calm and clear. We took off at first light. ODU made a smooth landing at the bear camp; I deplaned and the cinematographer clambered aboard. The Otter left immediately to return the cinematographer to Moosonee and then come back to fly me to the same destination. It was going to be a long day for the pilot.

ODU headed south and five of us climbed in the helicopter to go off in search of a bear that had not been tagged. No problem finding bears—Ontario is home to one of the world's largest concentrations of polar bears. They aestivate along the shore of Hudson Bay, losing weight, fighting and loafing until the ice forms again in October. We found groups of animals but did not land in case nearby bears got curious about our chopper and decided to investigate, which potentially could ruin our whole day.

We found a bear having a nap, off by itself on an island, miles away from any other animals. We hovered over the animal, rising and falling a few feet to get his attention—no easy task. He was a large male, afraid of nothing on earth. We had to disturb him, get him up and moving to estimate his size then fill the tranquillizer darts with precisely the right amount of sedative.

"He's a big hoss," said the biologist with the shotgun, preparing two darts for him. Each dart held drug and an explosive cap that discharged on impact, injecting the hypodermic's contents into the bear's muscle.

We moved off about a mile and lightened our load for the final chase. The photographer was deemed excess weight and left to wander the shoreline. That would be me. In those days, you were not supposed to be on the ground in Polar Bear Provincial Park unarmed, but with all the camera equipment I carried, I could do no better than stay as close as possible to a heavily armed biologist.

*Standing on the shore of Hudson Bay, dumped out of the helicopter to lighten the load as the lead biologist fires darts at a polar bear.*

It was a magical interlude of waiting. The land was littered with huge snow-covered rocks, any of which could have been a bear, not a boulder. The salt water of the Arctic Ocean lapped on the shore. Long, undulating lines of snow geese and blue geese flew overhead. A peregrine falcon, one of the arctic race, folded its wings near its side to stoop; outstretched claws first, it hit a duck. There was an explosion of feathers as predator and prey collided. In the distance, the sound of the helicopter chasing the bear went ta-pocketa-pocketa.

The shooter had to dart the bear twice in the hump near its neck. No point in hitting it in the rear end; too far from the brain. The pilot and biologist followed the bear until the sedative took effect and the bear slowly lay down among the scrub willow. Then they came for the rest of us, loaded the gear and returned to the bear, landing on a little knoll a respectable distance from the snoring animal.

The drama began. Three biologists approached the bear from behind, two as point men holding riot guns at the ready. The third held a 10-foot pole, a real one made of extendable aluminum, in his left hand, a .357 magnum in his right. As soon as he could touch the bear, he began jabbing at it with the aluminum pole, watching for reaction. None came. He rapped each of the hypodermic darts hanging from the bear's hump, listening for a rattle that would indicate the percussion caps had fired on impact, giving the animal a full dose of sedative. Things sounded good and the researcher was in position to make physical contact with the animal.

There was a humorous moment. The researcher made foot contact, booting the animal in the rear end. A mini-tsunami of loose skin and fat rolled up the bear's back and broke over its ears. The biologist worked his cautious way up the bear's body until he held his cocked .357 pistol to the back of the polar bear's head, just behind the right ear. The bear didn't move and the bio sneaked his left hand around the bear's snout and parted the animal's lips. His hand disappeared into the maw and emerged holding the tongue. He gave the tongue a shake. It waggled freely, and the bio stood up, holstered the .357 and said, "He's out. Let's get to work."

The biologists gathered their data while I took pictures. I had one taken of me crouching near the bear with the expedition's team leader beside me and the helicopter in the background. That was my trophy shot. My souvenir was a clump of polar bear fur, which I still have. And, of course, the magazine article. When all the data had been gathered and entered on the reporting sheets, we boarded the chopper and left.

Timing was perfect back at the beach ridge landing strip at the camp. I went almost directly from the helicopter to ODU and began the long, slow flight back to Moosonee. ODU was late getting in from the bear camp and the last commercial flight from Moose to Timmins was full. It was the Friday before an October long weekend, Canadian Thanksgiving. The airline offered me an option. I could use my ticket to Timmins for a ride in a transport plane, provided I was willing to sit in the jump seat between the pilot and co-pilot.

There was a hitch. The plane wasn't flying directly to Timmins. First, it had to pick up a load of siding for a hospital building and fly it up to the village of Attawapiskat on the coast of James Bay. Loading the plane took hours and it was well after dark before we squeezed into the heavily loaded plane, me into a seat that folded down between the two pilots.

The severely burdened multi-engine transport roared down the gravel runway at Moose and I had an unrivalled view of the takeoff. When the last of the gravel runway disappeared underneath the plane, I could sense we hadn't left the ground. I thought I could feel the wheels still crunching gravel and concluded pessimistically that we were going to end up in a stand of evergreen trees. Suddenly we were airborne and the tops of the trees, lit up by the takeoff lights, seemed to brush the fuselage as we groaned for altitude. The flight was short and in Attawapiskat the pilot managed to bring the plane to a halt before we ran out of runway.

While everyone was busy unloading the siding, I slid a small point-and-shoot camera into my jacket pocket, and staying out of the way of the laborers, surreptitiously wandered around the aircraft. If any bits of evergreen tree had ended up caught in the transport's undercarriage, I would have photographic proof of a close call on takeoff from Moose. No such evidence. Maybe it was just a normal takeoff and my fantasy of crashing a plane at the conclusion of several days of hairy flying and landings was just a Mittyesque moment.

The Attawapiskat-Timmins flight was remarkable. After days of lumbering along in underpowered or heavily loaded aircraft, the powerful transport seemed like a fighter jet as it soared empty into the sky at the start of the 300-mile journey. It was a clear, low-humidity fall night. You could see forever. As soon as we reached cruising altitude, the lights of Moosonee, Hearst and Timmins were visible, all three twinkling in the distance. They kept the Timmins airport open until we arrived. After grabbing a few hours' sleep in a real hotel bed and a swirl in the whirlpool, I was back in the airport for a passenger jet flight to Toronto.

With time to put in before my Via Rail train left for the last stage of my journey home to eastern Ontario and anxious to see some of my photos, I went to one of the photo processing shops in the Eaton Centre.

I must have been a strange sight standing in downtown Toronto, wearing a wintery red anorak and Logan boots on a mild October day, a dirty, blue duffel bag and a brown canvas camera bag at my feet. I pressed my nose to the glass watching pictures fall out of the printing machine.

Other people waiting for their pictures noticed photographs of a polar bear sliding down the drying rack. Then they saw photos of a guy loaded down with cameras and wearing a red anorak kneeling near the bear. "Hey, that's *that* guy," said one of the onlookers, pointing me out to his friends. That was it for me. Some people get 15 minutes of fame. Some only get 15 seconds of celebrity, being recognized in public.

Personally, I was just glad to be back, celebrity or not. Bad experiences and surprise confrontations with bold-as-brass bruins in Banff in the 1950s, animals that were after food and not very aggressive, had given me a lifelong dislike for bears.[16] Polar bears were different. A bear expert told me that whenever he confronted a black bear, he could see fear and trembling in its eyes. Polar bears, even cubs, did not know the meaning of fear and would attack anything that annoyed them.

The gigantic white bears were a special case for those with a bit of bear-phobia. Weeks later, when someone mentioned he'd heard I had seemed nervous on the tundra, I fixed him with my usual calm look and said, "Nervous? I wasn't nervous. I was scared shitless."

I didn't know it at the time, but I was finished with assignments that put me at personal risk. I turned 40 a few months after the bear tagging expedition. The next spring, the phone rang and I was invited to tag caribou. I had seen caribou on the tundra and nicknamed them "crazy legs" for their running ability. I had heard stories about the problems of capturing them with rocket-launched nets. I didn't think twice before I said no.

This chapter in my life came full circle at the bush plane museum in Sault Ste. Marie in September 2014, exactly 30 years later. ODU was on display. The Otter ended its flying career upside-down in the muskeg

---

16  I have had bad reactions to bears since 1955-56 when as a pre-teenager, I camped with my family in Banff National Park. On several occasions, I wandered out of my tent in the early morning and walked right into a bear marauding in the campsite. I think I may have been traumatized by the encounters because my reactions to the presence of bears has always been disproportionate. I don't like being anywhere near bears.

north of Moosonee just a couple months after my flight in it. ODU's pilot had made a perfect emergency landing when the engine failed. The wheels sunk in the soft muskeg when the plane touched down. It flipped. No one was hurt, but ODU was damaged beyond repair.

*The de Havilland single Otter known as ODU crashed in the muskeg near Moosonee a few months after my scary incident in the plane. ODU lay tits-up on the tundra until restorers from the Canadian Bush Plane Museum gathered up the wreckage and shipped it by raid to Sault St. Marie. I visited the museum exactly 30 years after my adventures in the plane, sat in the co-pilot's seat and leaned out the window with my camera. Trying to relive a bit of the past.*

Removed in pieces and shipped by rail to the Soo, ten years later it was partially restored and put on display at the museum. When I saw it, the public had access to the cargo area, but the flight deck was closed. I explained my history with ODU to the museum staff and they allowed me to climb into the co-pilot seat that I had occupied three decades earlier. Leaving one digital camera with a museum staffer to take pictures of me, I leaned out the window of the aircraft holding a camera with a long lens on it and took a few pictures of the surrounding museum. The staffer took pictures of me. The cockpit was cramped and uncomfortable. It was hard to get a camera out the window in a proper position to take pictures.

But leaning out the window of an airplane and taking pictures was something I used to do—until I just stopped doing it. As the song puts it, "Those were the days my friend; I thought they'd never end."

They did. I guess I realized in 1984 that either the days were going to come to an end or I would. I never agreed to do anything I considered dangerous after tagging polar bears. I was through, washed up, a 40-something has-been in the field of adventure writing and photography.

# SECTION III
# Communications Consulting

*Good Writing Was My Forte*

My career as a communications consultant was based on my ability to write. Writing can bring focus to issues and situations. Often I would be invited into a chaotic situation because the participants had difficulty seeing the forest for the trees. They often didn't have the skills to communicate clearly and effectively either to each other or to the public.

My first drafts were often erroneous. But they were clear, relatively simple and focused. People who were accustomed to comprehending issues in all their complexity were sometimes surprised to see matters simplified and put into focus. They would give feedback. I would rewrite the material to incorporate their detailed and nuanced understanding of the situation with the goal of arriving at a product that was both accurate and understandable.

Many of the groups on my client list were the *bêtes noires* of the mainstream media. They included the nuclear industry, the fur industry, medical researchers who used animals for testing, as well as organizations of hunters and shooters. Facing remorseless unfairness and scrutiny, they needed clear communications that could withstand hostile treatment by the media. There was often an urgent demand for clear communications, for statements and releases that could cut though all the drivel and bias.

My career as a consultant can be plotted on a bell curve. After starting with a client as a writer, soon I would have a role making policy and devising strategy rather than just putting words to policy and strategy devised by someone else. I reached my peak in my late 40s when I functioned as a director and as a lead consultant. By the time I was in my 60s, I was usually back to being a wordsmith with less responsibility for policy or strategy.

Much of my consulting work was an outgrowth of my freelance writing for *The Globe and Mail* and *Landmarks*. People with problems that seemed intractable and with no one to turn to would recall having read an article relating to their challenge. When they tracked down the author, if it was me, they would call me out of the blue. If their business proposal was not something I could agree to immediately, I made it a policy to take as much as a day to travel to Toronto or Ottawa to check out the prospect.

Speech writing, another branch of consulting, was a real moneymaker for me. When I gave up on *The Globe and Mail*, I didn't even know that speech writing, like newswriting, was a recognized branch of the profession. My interest had always been in writing features about things that were novel and exciting. I stumbled into speech writing by accident at the Ontario Ministry of Tourism. I seemed to have an aptitude for it and soon found that if you were writing a series of remarks for one speaker, it was easy to use large sections of previous speeches as boilerplate. Sometimes, all that was required in terms of original writing was a few paragraphs that oriented the material to the interests of that day's audience.

My aptitude for crisis communications led to a great deal of consulting work. Not everyone can stay calm and continue producing meaningful news releases and statements when events are moving at breakneck speed. Even fewer will willingly throw themselves into communications involving nuclear accident or terrorist attack. I would.

Consulting has its fun side as well. It can involve simply chatting up people while roaming the Hudson Bay Lowlands or wandering fancy-free through Algonquin Provincial Park, gathering opinions from the inhabitants. And consulting has its unexpected side—babysitting a British book author and a booze-loving English aristo on an outrageously trouble-plagued tour of northern Ontario.

# 7.
# Two Wimps in the Wilderness

*Leading tours of Ontario for visiting journalists 1983*

British writer Robin Hunter Neillands and I set out seeking adventure. We didn't need to go looking for trouble; it was going to come looking for us.

Under contract to the Ontario Ministry of Tourism, I was escorting him on a tour of Ontario. He wanted something more daring than the usual Niagara Falls and Ottawa, Shaw and Stratford Festivals. He got his wish. At the end of the first day of our tour, he was sporting a head of hair that was painted half orange, the result of a paintball game gone wrong. Adding to complications, he spoke with a tony British accent, broadcasting how much out of place he was in northern Ontario every time he opened his mouth.

Our tour had been strange and exciting from the get-go. My instructions were to meet a British writer at a luxury hotel in Toronto, then head north, stopping to play paintball, stay at remote lodges, go fly-in fishing, and sail in the North Channel out of Manitoulin Island returning via Sainte Marie Among the Hurons. After seven days, I could hand him off to another tourism escort back in the city and go home for Thanksgiving.

The bellhop at Toronto's Royal York hotel, where we were supposed to kick off the tour, had an animated discussion with the desk clerk. He was waving a room key and glancing back at a scruffy individual in the lobby. That would be me.

I was dressed to rough it in the cold weather of early fall and use unconventional transportation. On a warm October day in Toronto, I was garbed in my trademark red anorak scarred with rips and indelible stains from previous expeditions, lined wool trousers and scuffed up Logan boots. I would have looked out of place among Toronto's homeless. In the lobby of one of the city's best hotels, I stuck out like a Maori in a monastery.

My luggage was two well-used duffel bags. They didn't even match. One was a light brown air force issue from World War Two and the other a dark blue one made of heavy canvas, big enough to contain some camera equipment and plenty of spare clothing, raingear and other paraphernalia. I never believed in travelling light, especially when it was cold and I was going to be around water. Never know when or how many times I might have to change clothes to ward off hypothermia.

The bellhop daintily picked up my "luggage," wrinkling his nose in distain as if he was shoveling unwrapped garbage onto his cart. He gave me a disparaging look as he invited me to follow him. His problem was that I had been assigned one of the best rooms in the Royal York, a suite on the mezzanine floor.

He unlocked the door and asked me where I wanted my luggage put. "Just throw the duffel bags in the corner," I replied. Then the bellhop noticed a boxed bottle of Crown Royal whiskey on the coffee table with a note from the hotel manager welcoming me. As he handed me the note and accepted my tip, he said, shaking his head in dismay, "I don't know who you are, sir. But around here you sure rate."

Actually, the one who rated was the journalist I was escorting, one of the best and most productive writers in the British travel industry. In 1983, I knew almost nothing about him. There was no Internet to check him out; I didn't bother to go to the library and see what he had written, blithely working blind.

The Royal York PR department was disappointed if their purpose had been to impress him. A message from him rearranged the tour start. I was to meet him the next morning in an airline layover hotel near the airport. His message implied that it had been a long, tiring flight in first class from Heathrow and that *en route* he had accepted a better invitation for a place to sleep. A stewardess about half his age was having breakfast with him when we met in the morning. I never asked for details.

Our first stop was a paintball game, a relatively new amusement at the time. By previous arrangement, my journalist was put on one of the teams. (I don't play—as a shooting sports aficionado, I don't point anything gun-like at people.) He was back at the starting point long before I expected him. A shocking sight, he had taken a paintball pellet to the head. His hair was totally orange on the right side.

The other players in the game seemed surly and uncommunicative, so I promptly got my journalist into the rental car and headed north. The story emerged. Someone on his own team shot him at close range. Why? Because he had been picking off his opponents—left, right and center. In his original career, he enlightened me, he had been an SAS commando, the first on the beach in Britain's Suez invasion. When you put him in a war-like situation, I guess old instincts must have kicked in. It was like putting an NHL player into a bantam hockey game; he dominated to the point that it spoilt the fun for others. So someone took revenge.

The orange hairdo in Northern Ontario was a red flag in a bullring. I saved two men's bacon when we stopped to gas up the car just south of the French River. They were working on a piece of logging equipment when they noticed my commando *cum* journalist, camera in hand, oohing and aahing over the colors of some scrub maple growing at the side of the filling station. He was making a bad impression.

The boys were heading over to deal with him when I pulled the car between them and my journalist and quickly got my Brit into the passenger seat. I sometimes wonder what would have become of those two northern boys if they had surprise-jumped a commando, presuming he was some orange-headed wussy who richly deserved a rough welcome to the wilderness.

That night, in a bar in Sudbury, I overheard a group of ruffians making comments about my travelling companion, his accent, and his unorthodox appearance. I went to their table, introduced myself as news editor of a hunting magazine they all read. My credibility established, I explained what I was doing in the north and informed them the guy with the funny hair and tony accent was former SAS. A bar fight with him might be easy to start but could never end well for them. That shut them up. New dimensions in babysitting.

The next day, we fished. The helicopter had no floats. Instead, the pilot put one runner on a gigantic rock in the middle of a lake. The chopper was still flying as we jumped out. The commando-journalist did it easily; I managed to break my fishing rod while deplaning. We launched a boat that was pulled up on the huge boulder for fly-in fishing clients.

After casting for an hour or so, my journalist hadn't had a bite. Relying on my fishing experience, I watched as minnows began jumping out of the water near our boat. That was an indication they were fleeing from a predator, likely a pike or a bass. I told Robin exactly where to cast his lure, just a little ahead of the pattern of surfacing minnows, promising him he would catch a fish. Indeed he immediately hooked a little hammer handle pike and was delighted as well as being impressed with my knowledge of nature.

The sailing expedition from Manitoulin Island was an unmitigated string of disasters. The liquor store in Gore Bay closed at noon. We set sail in an Aloha sloop provisioned with lots of food but only one, lonely bottle of red wine. Worse, our party had grown to five. Another Visit Ontario Program (VOP) tour had joined us for the sail.

As far as I was concerned, neither the other VOP escort nor his London-based journalist should have been allowed north of Bloor, the Toronto street that clearly demarcates the boundary of civilization. Edward Mace was travel editor of *The Observer*, the Sunday supplement to *The Guardian*. Although I didn't know it until I read his obituary years later, he was a snob who claimed to be descended from British royalty and whose best travel stories "were about the dotty, often dodgy, aristos he met at weekend house parties in stately homes" and whose ideal vacation "was to motor through the Italian lake district, preferably in a chum's Rolls-Royce." What brought him to roam round the northern colonies in an autumn chill, God only knows. All I got to know in our initial meeting was that he believed that anywhere you could not get alcohol on Wednesday afternoon was worse than any third-world hellhole on earth.

And the fifth man, the boat's skipper, was young, a recent graduate from a sailing program at community college. Not exactly the kind of seasoned sailor you would wish for when sailing the unpredictable waters of the North Channel in early fall.

We cruised 20 miles northeast to a group of uninhabited pink granite islands, barbecued steak on the boat, split the bottle of wine five ways and went to bed. We had the North Channel's favorite harbor to ourselves. It was a mild, bug-free night, so I chose to sleep in the roomy cockpit under the stars. Feeling something was wrong, I awoke before dawn. The wind at ground level was blowing one way but the clouds were scudding across the sky in a different direction. By breakfast time, it was truly blowing stink. Getting out of harbor was a challenge as more semi-submerged islands posed a hazard to navigation.

Sailing on a small triangle of jib, I took the wheel of the boat. Robin took over the trimming of the sail, and the young skipper pointed out the navigation hazards in the tricky waters. It was wild. One rogue wave was so high, it seemed to be about to break over the boat and swamp us. Caught by surprise, I let out an involuntary "O my God" that wasn't good for crew morale. The sloop pitched and yawed at the edge of control with the hull slamming on the waves.

The other VOP escort and Edward Mace, who had lost faith in me entirely as "the wild colonial who sleeps in the open air" ignored my request to stay in the cockpit. Instead, they headed down to their bunks, where they were certain to get sick. They spent hours suffering the delightful consequences of the buffeting as all the water in the North Channel did its best to get into Georgian Bay.

Once we were in calmer waters near the Canadian Yacht Charters' marina in Gore Bay, the young skipper looked through the companionway and blanched. He turned to me and invited me to take a look at the unholy mess. I took a death grip on the wheel and refused to budge.

As we neared the dock, I started the engine and furled the jib. I asked Robin to bring my duffel bags to me as I didn't want to go below and become a witness to the disarray. Inviting the young skipper to take the wheel and dock his sloop, I relaxed, leaning back on the cushioned seat, listening to the diesel go "ta-pocketa, pocketa, pocketa" as we maneuvered dead slow to the dock. We left the marina quickly, heading for the Chi-Cheemaun car ferry that would take us to Tobermory.

The tour ended quietly with a tour of the restored 17th century French mission near Midland. Black-robed re-enactors portraying Jesuits wandered the site, which had been rebuilt to its fortified state before it was abandoned and burned to the ground in the mid-1600s. The historical re-enactment was impressive. With a papal visit scheduled for the next year, Sainte-Marie among the Hurons had become a world-class tourism attraction for Roman Catholics.

The tour over, we drove back to Toronto where I handed off my journalist to another VOP escort who would take him for a continuation tour of more standard Ontario attractions—easy-peasy stuff (boring to me) like Niagara Falls and the Shaw and Stratford Festivals.

The replacement escort took me aside to ask how things had been going. My response was, "We survived" … "Just barely" … "How do you expect things are going to go when you turn two wimps loose in the wilderness?"

The tour became known as Two Wimps in the Wilderness. The other VOP escort from the North Channel adventure, who later discovered he was a natural writer, had an outstanding career in communications as a director. I believe he never trusted me after that October adventure. I unfailingly greeted him with a resounding and friendly "Howdy, Sailor!" every time we met, but he never gave me any work even though he had assignments to hand out.

I led only three tours for the VOP. I had become an escort by accident. On deciding to leave *The Globe and Mail* in the spring of 1983, I paid a visit to Shirley Teasdale, a freelancer who departed from *The Globe and Mail* before me. She was in the tourism communications branch running the *Visit Ontario Program* that brought foreign journalists to Ontario and gave them escorted tours of the province. She was leveraging publicity by encouraging travel writers to feature Ontario attractions in the media.

Niagara Falls, the Stratford Festival and Ottawa were the usual destinations for media types, who would be flown in from around the world and pampered on their tours, all-expenses paid. The escorts were a mixed bag of freelancers and staffers who developed tours and babysat the visiting journalists. Shirley had use for someone who would lead more adventurous tours of Ontario. She gave me my first contract in post-newspaper years.

My initial tour was a springtime excursion with a fishing writer who wrote for the big outdoor magazines in the US—*Sports Afield* and *Field and Stream*. He turned out to be demanding and petulant. He expected an escort to buy him everything, even chewing gum. Refusing to walk anywhere, he used taxis to travel a couple of blocks.

After spending several days with him, I realized that freebee tours were a big part of his life and that when he was home, he sustained himself by eating the fish he had caught and the game he had shot. I was glad to drop him at the airport and resisted the temptation to tell conservation officers that he was probably exporting an over-limit of smallmouth bass. Within a year, I heard he had died and wondered if some of his odd behavior was due to illness.

A summer white water tour of Ontario was more satisfying. The Madawaska Kanu Centre and OWL Rafting, both run by the Kirkoffs, a kayak championship family who know the value of good publicity, provided my vanload of travel writers with grist for their mills. They gave the journalists their fill of kayaks, canoes, rafts, hydraulics and standing waves, a variety of experiences in cold, roiling water suitable for all ages and skill levels along with first-rate tourism hospitality and meals.

*Kayaking in Claudia's roller at the Madawaska Kanu Camp. One of the tests at MKC was sitting in the hydraulic, twirling your paddle above your head and shouting "Ich bin der beste." I did a number of stories out of MKC when writing adventure sports for The Globe and Mail. I visited several times after leaving the paper, leading white water tours of Ontario and taking lessons.*

Ron Truman | 79

Shirley Teasdale, who was an accomplished travel writer in her own right, saw the VOP as providing cost-effective marketing for Ontario Tourism. It was an industry-government partnership long before the Ontario Tourism Marketing Partnership was formed. Under the VOP, the tourism industry provided free airline tickets, accommodation, and meals for visiting journalists. The tourism ministry provided organization and escorts.

Later, they tracked publications for the stories written by visiting journalists. The marketing principle was that a written story from a journalist who had already visited was about 10 times as effective as an advertisement in getting the word out to the potential market. And Ontario's tourism industry needed all the help it could get.

The government was getting good bang for its buck with VOP, although the program was open to abuse. People with connections could get a familiarization tour where they could soak up free booze and enjoy complimentary travel.

I had no doubts that almost all of the journalists I escorted were legitimately researching stories on Ontario. One young writer aroused my suspicions. He said he was a staffer for a small-town paper.

He spent much of his time stretching his leg muscles. Almost every time I gathered up the group to move on, I had to search for him. Usually he could be found in the woods leaning on a tree, lengthening his tendons. He told an anecdote about running out of stories for his local paper and filling the news hole by writing everything he knew about sumo wrestlers. And, apropos of nothing, one day he announced that sex was over-rated.

Somehow, he didn't seem to be a typical journalist—he was indifferent to news value in stories, obsessed with a strange fitness regime, and blasé about getting laid. He may have had a friend who got him on the tour—possibly a girlfriend who wanted him out of the way for a while.

By the time the touring season began the next spring, I had become the jack-of-all-trades contract writer for the tourism communications branch and was too busy to take a week off to babysit visiting journalists. Escorting visiting writers was my introduction to tourism and I worked in the tourism industry sporadically for more than 30 years as a writer and communications consultant.

# 8.
# Nobody Died at Three Mile Island

*Crisis communications 1984-1991*

Exercise TransBord III—the 1989 simulation of a terrorist attack on the Canadian-U.S. border—ended dramatically. Imaginary clouds of poison gas with a fragrance reminiscent of a field of new-mown hay drifted over an ever-growing swath of Detroit. Heavier than air, the gas hugged the ground as it spread. Like early morning fog, it collected in hollows and low places. It was invisible and motorists trying to escape the fake disaster discovered concentrated levels of poison only when they found their cars stalling as they drove through underpasses. They began coughing, their eyes and throats burning, their vision blurred. In the final hours of this three-day simulation of a terrorist attack, thousands of pretend people would die before the sun went down; others would suffer from delayed effects—breathing difficulties or heart failure.

Two days earlier, make-believe terrorists had made their move simultaneously on land and water. While one group of terrorists took hostages in a small southwestern Ontario town, others commandeered a barge loaded with 45-gallon drums of industrial chemicals. They traversed Lake St. Clair into the shipping channel that separates Detroit from Windsor. The barge was sabotaged with explosive charges; terrorists took turns holding a dead man's switch. If a sniper killed the man holding the switch, the explosives would go off, triggering disaster as the chemicals combined to create poison gas.

This fictional catastrophe took place after frenetic activity by emergency response agencies in Ontario and Michigan, coast guards from both countries, the Ontario Provincial Police, Michigan State Police, FEMA, the RCMP and FBI. They attempted to stop the terrorists and evacuate the entire area the poisonous gas might affect. At the end of the third day, when make-believe terrorists detonated the explosives, a pretend southerly wind wafted the low-hanging cloud over Detroit.

This was the scenario for TransBord III, one of the first attempts to coordinate emergency response agencies and police forces in Canada and the USA to deal with a terrorist attack. It took three years to prepare the model exercise to deal with a make-believe group known as the Joint Alliance Against Military Occupation. In 2015 suicidal terrorists, hostage taking, and mass murder of civilians are commonplace; the 1989 drill seems incredibly far-sighted. When it took place, the proposition seemed mind-boggling. A quarter-century ago, terrorist acts were infrequent and seemed to happen mostly in the Middle East, Far East and Europe, involving hijacking of commercial aircraft.

Ontario's response team gathered in the war room of Ontario Provincial Police headquarters near Lakeshore Boulevard in downtown Toronto. Phone lines hung from the ceiling, telexes chattered, uniformed police and civilian authorities roamed the floor of the room, with executives and politicians sitting on a raised platform. New developments in the imaginary crisis arrived by fax or telex, permitting communications with the situation rooms and war rooms in other capital cities.

Conflicting messages prevailed as different jurisdictions had varying methods of dealing with emergency. For example, in Ontario, declaration of a state of emergency meant you were to go home and stay put until further instructed. Across the border, when a state of emergency was declared, you were supposed to hit the road and evacuate the area. Radio stations with far-reaching signals broadcasting the alert in both jurisdictions created a massive muddle. The imaginary public knew there was big trouble brewing, but with severe communications confusion didn't know whether they were supposed to run or hide, to go to ground or head for the hills.

Nothing actually happed on the street and on the water in southwestern Ontario. There were no police actions, no SWAT or SCUBA teams to alert the public that the drill was taking place. News of the exercise leaked out and Windsor media ran with the story but it fizzled. Among my souvenirs is my badge from Exercise TransBord III. In big, block letters it reads: DIRECTOR OF EMERGENCY INFORMATION. It was my first time advising on what the Ontario government should tell the public and writing the news releases and communiqués that would be issued to the media.

In some ways my stint playing the role of Ontario's director of emergency information was the peak of my career in crisis communications. This was only role-playing in simulations. I was already doing some real-life crisis communications by 1984. And even earlier. As soon as I launched my journalism career, communications in urgent situations became part of my life. Trouble seemed to seek me out.

My first invitation to be communicator in a long-fuse-big-bang crisis situation came from hockey star Carl Brewer,[17] who maintained in the 1970s that hockey czar Alan Eagleson[18] deserved to be convicted as a fraud and a crook. But for some reason—perhaps because Eagleson was astoundingly politically well-connected and treated as a hero by the media—Brewer was prevented from communicating that to the public.

One day in 1978, I picked up the phone at my home in Eastern Ontario. Brewer had tracked me down. I quickly established that this was not a prank call by someone posing as the famous hockey player. He was the real thing. He needed help from someone skilled in communications, someone with access to the national media. He wasn't going to rest until the world knew that Eagleson had abused the trust of many National Hockey League players and went to jail for his crimes.

---

17 Carl Brewer played for a number of National Hockey League teams and was an NHL All-Star. I knew who he was in 1978 because, loath as I am to admit it, I was once a Toronto Maple Leafs fan. Brewer died in 2001.

18 Alan Eagleson was NHL players' union president and a Hockey Canada director. His name was a household word after his role in the 1972 Canada-Russia games. He was a Progressive Conservative MPP in Ontario in the 1960s and had a reputation as a major fund raiser for the PC Party. He was convicted, jailed and disbarred in the 1990s.

I thanked Brewer for the story lead but explained that I was a freelance feature writer. He needed a staff reporter—someone backed up with the researchers, the legal department and the deep pockets of a big newspaper—to take on a celebrity with the reputation and political clout of Eagleson. The most I could do would be to pass the lead on to the editors of *The Globe and Mail*. Brewer told me not to bother.

My interpretation of that situation: Brewer had already called every media contact he had and was now down to calling freelancers, the bottom of the barrel. A gutless Canadian media would not touch Eagleson. I did nothing and rarely thought about the incident for 20 years. Then the news broke that a Boston reporter, apparently with Brewer's help, had nailed Eagleson and the Eagle was convicted in both Canada and the USA.

When Eagleson went to jail, I wrote a letter to the editor of *The Globe and Mail*, chiding the paper for turning down the sports story of the century—a story that had been offered to them on a silver platter. At the time, Sports had a letters section and published my missive. I telephoned Brewer, hoping to get background information on his struggle with the media, but he wasn't interested in talking to me. I had never felt good about turning down the story and the opportunity it might have given me. It was a communications crisis in which people were refusing to communicate vital facts, a cover-up of the type I later learned some techniques for handling.

Crisis communications as a specialty became more appealing to me only after I had turned 40 and was less interested in putting myself at risk or in danger to get a story. It offered plenty of stress and lots of excitement but little objective hazard. Despite my appearance of having matured, the grey hair and all, I still had almost no compunction about rushing in where angels might fear to tread. I got plenty of invites.

Not many people get an opening in crisis communications. Many avoid stressful situations or break down quickly under pressure. I have tried to understand why I frequently got invited to participate when things got scary. The best answer I can come up with it that an unusual childhood, my physical appearance (my presence), and the ability to write quickly made me something of a natural for the field.

As an air force brat, growing up on Royal Canadian Air Force bases, I lived from airplane crash to airplane crash. My father's job was Senior Aeronautical Engineering Officer on RCAF bases in Alberta; if the cause of a crash was mechanical failure, the buck stopped with him. The stress of each incident came home with him and we all lived through it. I knew too many people killed in the crashes. When you are immersed in that kind of environment, crisis becomes just a normal part of daily life. The fact that my family was largely dysfunctional, alcoholic, and sprinkled with fanatics who were more Catholic than the pope[19] turned out to be an asset. I was family background-trained to cope with stress exacerbated by secrecy, denial, deception and distrust.

My presence—my physical appearance and the general aura I projected—contributed to my crisis communications career. Some people look like Central Casting sent them to play a role. In crisis communications, that would be me. At Emergency Planning Ontario, I heard myself referred to as "The Iceman" because I seemed to be totally unflappable. A young woman who worked on 9/11 with me (and disliked me) compared me to Hannibal Lecter in *Silence of the Lambs* for what she considered my uncanny calmness.

My wife is appalled by my anecdote about entering the washroom in a sergeant's mess. Three NCOs already at the urinals noticed me and

---

19 This Catholic cliché truly does apply to some of my family. Among my first and second cousins you can find the RC bishop of Miami, a papal legate, and Jesuits in the Philippines along with an assortment of everyday priests and nuns. One great aunt, who was excommunicated with bell, book and candle after marrying her divorced first cousin, actually won a decades-long passive-aggressive battle with the Church. Banned from taking communion, she went to mass every day to stand at the back. She raised a priest and a nun among her children. On her 50$^{th}$ wedding anniversary, she was de-excommunicated. The pope could take no more and threw in the towel, admitting the Church had been wrong. My aunt's bitter struggle with another branch of North American Catholicism—the Irish Catholic Matriarchy—continued on for decades. Fought viciously with backbiting hypocrisy among sisters, it was a true cage match, a battle to the death with no surrender. She won only by outliving all her siblings and becoming matriarch herself. She was the last matriarch of her line, which had its North American origins in the 1800s with Irish men leaving women in charge of their entire brood when they went off to work on the railway. Men left at home were destined for the priesthood. Women ruled the roost. An increasingly atomistic society, declining birth rates and enhanced employment opportunities for the Irish seem to have doomed the matriarchic tradition.

immediately changed hands to salute, presuming I was a visiting general. In crisis communications training, my group put me forward as their spokesman. When I was in my 40s and 50s, I came across as authoritative, perfect for crisis communications in the 1980s and early 1990s. In today's world, I am exactly the person you would not want as ~~spokesman~~ spokesperson—but back in the day …

I was fast and speed is vital in crises. A communications crisis is defined as a situation in which events are outpacing your ability to communicate and you appear to be losing control. My quickness in writing speeches, news releases and backgrounders proved invaluable in advancing my crisis communications career.

Much of my work in crisis communications was created by the depredations of post-1970s environmentalism—widespread public adoption of radical and irrational beliefs regarding the fragility of ecosystems, the wrongness of using animals for meat, fur or research, the need to severely restrict land use and the danger of nuclear energy.

Like the carnival game Whack-a-Mole, every time one environmentalist scare dissipated, another would pop up. Sometimes the scare would simply disappear.[20] Sometimes it would be replaced by the exact opposite of the first phenomenon. For example, the fears of a new ice age brought on by cold winters in the 1970s were transformed into panic in the late 1980s about an overheating planet. But each scare was primarily a public relations battle that had to be fought with communications.

Modern environmentalism reached maturity with emotional reactions to the Atlantic seal hunt in the 1960s and early 1970s, the founding

---

20 Whatever happened to acid rain? It was promoted as the environmental disaster of the 20th century, killing all the fish in the lakes, affecting the growth of vegetables, destroying the tourism industry. The media got into the act, to the point that the U.S. Department of Justice branded a National Film Board "documentary" *Acid from Heaven* as foreign propaganda. When a limited agreement was negotiated between the U.S. and Canada on emissions of sulphur dioxide, the issue swirled down the memory hole. It was simply forgotten. Decades later, I had a chance meeting in Florida with the head of the U.S. scientific delegation negotiating the agreement. His point of view was that acid rain was a limited threat to a few lakes in the high Adirondacks but little else. As far as he was concerned the Canadian position had been determined by Quebec Hydro and its desire to limit American ability to produce electricity with coal-burning generating stations thus building their market for hydraulic generation of electricity.

of Greenpeace in 1971, and the establishment of Earth Day on the anniversary of Lenin's birthday in 1971. The movement evolved into ever-broadening attacks on hunting, trapping, logging, guns and even medical research involving animals. The media came on board slowly but by the 1980s it was hard to find reporters who were not on some environmentalist-type bandwagon.

On my first visit to *The Globe and Mail* newsroom in 1977 Earle Gill on the national desk asked me if I would be interested in becoming environmental reporter for the paper. The paper didn't have one. I wasn't interested. Later the paper hired Michael Keating for the job. Environmental coverage grew in all newspapers through the next two decades with all major newspapers working themselves into an uproarious furor about global warming in the 1990s. Then it began to fade. By early in the 21$^{st}$ century, the *New York Times* had an environmental desk with two editors and seven reporters, a desk that was dismantled in early 2013 as many of the myths promoted by the environmentalist movement began to be seen primarily as hyping "the-sky-is-falling" panics with little basis in reality and "solutions" that often only made things worse.[21]

In the last decades of the 20$^{th}$ century, the religion of contemporary environmentalism caused many social and economic changes. At first it affected mainly resource-dependent people like sealers and trappers. Then it started affecting people who enjoyed hunting, fishing and park use as recreation. I got into the communications end of the business with the recreationists, who recognized quickly that the myths being perpetrated and the lies being told were going to spoil their fun. Only later did I get into working for the resource users. Eventually I was doing crisis communications on an international level.

Anti-hunting sentiments on the part of environmentalist movement caused a low-key, slowly developing crisis that gave me an entrée to crisis communications. The Ontario Federation of Anglers and Hunters (OFAH) had a communications problem in the 1980s. With the closing of the Recreation Section at *The Globe and Mail*, the media usually ignored the

---

21 The reduced seal hunt, for example, is currently often linked to an ensuing overpopulation of seals, the collapse of the Atlantic cod fishery and attracting increased numbers of seal-eating great white sharks near the beaches that were the locale for the movie *Jaws*, affecting summer tourism industry in the area.

OFAH. If a reporter (almost guaranteed to be a left-wing dilettante with no experience with guns and hunting) showed up at one of the annual conventions, the result was too frequently negative publicity, often about guns or hunting. Legitimate news about the annual convention appeared weeks later in the OFAH house publication, the *Angler and Hunter* magazine. As the news editor for the magazine, I wrote that summary.

**Angler &Hunter**
ONTARIO'S WILDLIFE MAGAZINE

P.O. BOX 1541
PETERBOROUGH
ONTARIO K9J 7H7
(705) 748-3891

**RON TRUMAN**
ASSOCIATE EDITOR

In the mid-1980s, the OFAH started putting my annual convention writing efforts on something of a crisis communications footing—trying to communicate as quickly as events happened. I began writing media releases and backgrounders while the annual conference was in progress. I would write OFAH reactions to speeches given by politicians addressing the conference. (More than once I crafted a news release reacting to a minister's speech that I had written—talk about playing both sides.)

The trick was to be fast. At the end of three-day conferences, selected OFAH members were given copies of the releases and asked to deliver them in person to local media all over the province. That tactic, the OFAH executive hoped, would bypass major news organizations that ignored or disparaged the OFAH. This continued until the OFAH shut down its magazine in the early 1990s and I stopped attending annual conventions.

If wildlife federations were having difficulties in the 1980s, the very existence of Canada's fur industry was threatened. Greenpeace attacks on the seal hunt in the 1970s had a dramatic effect. The attacks, designed to make money for the new "green" organizations, were pure emotionalism almost completely lacking in a scientific basis[22]. Baby seals and blood on the ice can mobilize certain demographic groups and the politicians of the European Economic Community (EEC) into frenzied action.

The loss of market for seal pelts was having a dramatic effect on the economy of some of the least fortunate groups in Canada. In 1983 the EEC banned import of the skins of young harp and hooded seal pups. That same year the federal government funded the Fur Institute of Canada (FIC) to incorporate the work of a federal-provincial wildlife committee on humane trapping and to deal with the public relations crisis brought on by the growth of the modern environmental movement in the last quarter of the 20th century.

My mentor Doug Roseborough was on the board of directors of the Fur Institute. He brought me into the battle against animal rights activism. The two of us often travelled together and attended the same meetings. The FIC was on its second executive director: Kirk Smith, a journalist and filmmaker who had been director of the Sealers Association in Newfoundland. Smith had a tough job. He had to hold together a group of trappers, fur farmers, native representatives and wildlife biologists that made up his board. At the same time, he was fighting a pro-fur battle in two very different theatres of war, Europe and North America.

The development of humane traps was a primary goal of the FIC, which was a successor to a federal-provincial effort to improve trapping. Modern environmentalism had transformed the controversy from one over humane treatment of wild animals into a controversy over whether we should be trapping animals at all. Emerging animal rights extremism insisted that we could not use any animals at all (even as pampered pets) and took outrageous action to advance their point of view.

The FIC efforts in Europe depended on Native spokesmen defending their way of life and didn`t involve me. But the FIC had two broad North American initiatives that kept me busy. One was designed to improve public attitudes towards fur through media relations, public relations and education. The other was building alliances with various other animal

---

22 Jacques Cousteau, the publicity-seeking SCUBA diver and defender of the oceans, supported the seal hunt as a legitimate activity and not threatening the extinction of marine mammals. Other celebrities lined up to condemn the hunt, visiting the ice floes to publicize their opinions.

user groups so that the opponents of the fur industry could be fought as opposing farming, zoos, and animal-based medical research.

I produced the annual report for the FIC, attended meetings of the Ontario Trappers Association in North Bay, toured the humane trapping research facility at the Alberta Environmental Centre, and I was active enough in opposing the Toronto Humane Society for its animal rights activism that I was condemned by name at the society's annual meeting.

Usually I was out of the public eye, preparing material issued by the FIC or scripting words for other people. When the FIC hired Alan Herscovici,[23] author of the 1985 book *Second Nature: the animal rights controversy*, to go on a national tour of newsrooms, I prepared his material. To each meeting with an editorial board, he took a three-ring binder full of information, including his talking points. I had produced it in the hopes that if left behind in the newsroom, it would be useful in raising awareness of animal rights activism.

I attended a speech given by Paul Watson of the Sea Shepherd Society at Guelph University. I expected Watson would get a rough reception at a school known for its training of farmers and veterinarians. Surprisingly the animal rights activist was cheered when he announced his ultimate goal was to reduce the population of humans on the globe to a few hundred thousand. Academics are incredibly stupid or naive. My tape recorder malfunctioned, so I visited *The Globe and Mail*, where I was still a familiar enough face to get into the newsroom unchallenged. I borrowed the audiotape made by the reporter who had attended the speech. Without letting him know that I thought the press was being a useful idiot and a megaphone for animal rights nonsense, I acquired a tape the FIC could use in attacking animal rights advocates.

---

23 Alan Herscovici, at the time of writing this memoir, is with the Fur Council of Canada. He is an excellent spokesman for the fur industry with a friendly television presence and a charming manner of engaging in debate. His book, which was published by the CBC (believe it or not) in 1985, is listed and reviewed on Amazon but not available today. Alan's main theme has always been that the fur industry is environmentally friendly, which is probably true but will probably never make any difference to a public that reacts emotionally to trapping and captivity. Alan also got a lot of dirt on animal rights activism.

Another major effort for me was production of a short video designed for use in schools. I wrote the script positioning the fur industry as an appropriate use of animals. After the script was approved, I was given photos and video to integrate into the visuals of the educational piece. For days at a time, I sat in a darkened room in a downtown Toronto production studio as we used visuals to illustrate the words. I hired a professional narrator to read the script, choosing a woman recommended by the studio. When she arrived at the studio, she discovered the FIC was the sponsor of the production and immediately refused to do the narration. I was shocked and convinced her to look over the script before refusing a juicy contract for a few hours' work. She perused the script; she saw that it was carefully worded to be non-controversial and pro-conservation. She then did a good job of narrating it.

The next step was field-testing it in a school, not an easy task as schools are reluctant to let just anyone have access to their pupils. Fortunately a school principal whose family went skiing at the same resort as my family let me show the video to a middle-school class. When the reaction was acceptable, the video was more widely distributed.

Reluctance on the part of members of the public to be identified with or associated with the fur industry was probably the key to the failure to build an alliance of animal use industries against the attack by the animal rights activists. We tried. At the peak of my FIC efforts, I chaired a committee of animal users. This group included medical researchers who were being attacked for their use of lasers on animal eyes, representatives from the dairy industry, from battery chicken outfits, from those who raised livestock and even from the zoo. Toby Styles, a Toronto zookeeper who had a moment of fame when an elephant ate his Tilley hat and he recovered it undigested sometime later, was perhaps the most well-known (and entertaining) participant. All agreed that animal users faced a major problem but eventually I could get no takers for an alliance involving the fur industry. No one wanted to risk their brand by identifying with fur.

When delegates from 50 countries gathered in Ottawa for a meeting of the parties to the Convention on International Trade in Endangered

Species (CITES)[24] the FIC set me up as a communicator available to any animal user group at the conference. If you represented farmers, big game hunters, medical researchers, Native people or any other animal-using group and found yourself under public attack at the meeting, I was there to help you. All you had to do was show up with your letterhead and your problem at my office and I would quickly craft you a news release that had a chance of attracting the attention of the national and international media.

I wrote a Canadian backgrounder for the media before the conference began. The backgrounder argued that the world would get more effective protection of endangered species by making those species commercially available than by restricting trade. This was counter-intuitive but true and an idea favored by many scientists but never got any traction with the public.[25]

The meeting took place in the old downtown Ottawa train station that had been converted to a conference center. I was surprised by the number and ferocity of the animal rights activists present. They sometimes disrupted the proceedings. On one occasion an enormous fish head was left on a desk used by one of the opponents of animal rights. After a couple of days, I began to take notice of the difference between the participants and the observers.

---

24 CITES is the acronym for the Convention on International Trade in Endangered Species of Wild Fauna and Flora, a multilateral treaty designed to protect endangered plants and animals by restricting export of materials from them. Today CITES has an overwhelming presence, affecting not just ivory traders, but guitar manufacturers who put some wood from endangered species of trees into their instruments, and anyone buying souvenirs containing ivory or turtle shell.

25 Most conservationists use an elephant example to illustrate this counter-intuitive truth. African farmers who have elephants tearing up their gardens or fields will shoot the elephant. If the ivory trade is banned, the dead elephant has no value and the farmer is simply out of pocket for the agricultural loss. On the other hand, if the farmer can have a trophy hunter called in and charge the hunter an exorbitant amount for a permit to kill the elephant, then the farmer can be compensated richly for his losses. This policy is supposed to encourage African farmers to conserve a population of elephants because they see the elephants as sources of income rather than as capricious vandals of farmland, as animals that only cause damage and hunger.

Sometimes it was amusing. When a buffet table was set out at lunchtime, the animal rights activists would look for the vegetable offerings and many of the delegates (especially those from Third World countries) would spear the meaty portions. One of participants pointed out to me that animal rights activists were representing small countries and actually had votes in the conference, having delegate status. He maintained that corrupt governments were bribed by the activists to let advocates represent them at CITES meetings and negotiations. I believed the story but I had no opportunity to confirm it. I knew from my freelancing days that if I did substantiate it, this was the kind of story the media would show no interest in printing. It didn't fit the prevailing narrative.

My job at the CITES meeting was to make myself available for crisis communications. Activist groups would arrive at the conference with attacks already prepared. The animal user groups, usually unprepared to deal with a public relations battle, would be caught flat-footed and without resources to respond to the attack. I became the only resource they had.

A steady stream of user groups showed up at the door of my communications room, bringing their problems and blank letterhead. I would discuss their issues and their planned responses. Sometimes I would advise them on how to phrase their response. I would craft a news release, type it on their letterhead, photocopy it and send it to the media room at the conference. The spokesman for the organization could use the news release to guide him in responding to media questions.

The tactic produced a number of minor successes and one major one. A visibly upset medical researcher arrived at my temporary office to tell me that animal activists were trying to stop international trade in chimpanzees. He was an AIDS researcher. Almost all research in this field was chimp-dependent. Stopping a steady flow of chimpanzees into research labs would effectively prevent further progress towards a cure for AIDS. The news release I wrote went around the world almost immediately and stopped the animal rights activists in their tracks.

My days with the fur industry and CITES ended when Kirk Smith moved to the Ontario government as communications director for the Ministry of Solicitor General. His new job description included being Director of Emergency Information for Ontario. Emergency preparedness being a low priority at the time, Smith began sending me in to play his role in exercises.

TransBord III[26] in 1989 was my first exercise. Thrown into the multi-party exercise as director of emergency information for Ontario, I was completely unprepared, ignorant of the protocols used in war gaming but dealing instinctively with whatever came my direction. I got sucked into giving a live interview to a Windsor radio station that had gotten wind of the exercise and somehow found the telephone number for the communications desk in the OPP war room. The description of events that I gave over the phone could have been used to start some kind of Orson Welles *War of the Worlds* panic along the Detroit River, but I guess the radio station, aware of that possibility, used the interview taking care not to cause alarm.

As TransBord III progressed I saw myself getting further behind and more bewildered. By the time the exercise ended with imaginary clouds of deadly phosgene rolling into Detroit, I had given up. The final news release I drafted was an announcement (tongue in cheek) that one of the bad guys had just been hanged in Effigy, an Ontario village just west of Windsor. In the confusion of that initial exercise, I regarded myself as a failure in crisis communications in a provincial director's role. What I didn't know at the time was that pretty well everyone else was muddled and trying to feel their way through the situation.

As I was leaving the war room, somewhat down in the dumps because of the three-day experience, one of the staffers stopped me. She asked what television station I was news announcer on. I suddenly realized I had fooled them. Despite feeling like a fraud and being confused beyond belief, other people thought I was on top of what was going on. That impression must have been relayed to the communications director at Solicitor General because I was soon sent to Ottawa for a tour of the national emergency communications center and to be trained in crisis communications by the Niagara Institute at a course given at the Chateau Laurier hotel.

---

26 TransBord III does not appear on the Internet, except for a notation that the documents from the exercise are in a Ronald Reagan-era collection in a library in California and that I played a role in the exercise. Other databases provide some news clippings on the exercise, primarily from Windsor, Ontario.

The course was basic media relations training teaching people how to take control of the message and how to handle television interviews with hostile interviewers. My working group chose me to represent them in the mock interview, my only appearance on television ever and I still have the videotape. I left the course feeling much more prepared to handle a crisis and to give clients guidance on how to communicate during a crisis and prepare communications plans for likely events.

I was Director of Emergency Information in Exercise Darlington 89. This was a full-scale rehearsal for a possible nuclear event during the commissioning of the new generating station on Lake Ontario east of Toronto. Unfortunately CANDU reactors are not very exciting. What might have been the absolute pinnacle of my work as a crisis communications consultant and crisis manager was somewhat underwhelming as a result.

I sat on a high platform in the war room, headed up the INFOGROUP, attended make-believe cabinet meetings, prepared statements that would be issued to the media and coordinated with the Ontario Hydro public relations person and various technical advisors. Dozens of people were involved. The war room in the old OPP headquarters near the Gardiner Expressway and Yonge was the real thing, a large, open room with hardwired telephones everywhere. The contact numbers for important people, including the premier, were posted on the walls. The numbers were covered up when the CBC television crew visited, so that the premier's phone number at his cottage would not accidentally appear on television.

The CBC did show up to do a story. These were exciting times in the nuclear industry with Darlington's first operational reactor commissioned just 10 years after the movie "The China Syndrome" terrorized the population and a few years after a Level 7 event in Chernobyl. There was widespread public fear of nuclear generating stations. We had to be prepared for over-reactions. So we gamed the possible developments. Nobody in the war room believed the anti-nuclear mantra that dominated the popular imagination after the problems at Three Mile Island in the US. The idea of a CANDU reactor burning a hole down to the earth's core was just Hollywood nonsense.

CANDU reactors have safety features that automatically shut down the reactor in the event of any major equipment malfunction and maintain cooling of the fuel in the event of a failure of the reactor cooling system. Any plume of radioactivity following a reactor incident is trapped in the containment building. One of the principal tasks of nuclear crisis communications was preventing panic. We had to convince people to stay home and not cause massive traffic jams that would only complicate matters.

One of the Hydro representatives wanted to make the event an educational experience—now that we had the public's attention, we could start feeding them information about the value of using nukes in electricity generation. There was considerable debate about how to handle publicity-seeking politicians. Some anticipated a politician would try holding a press conference on site, knowing there was absolutely no danger but appearing heroically bold to a nuclear-fearing member of the public.

There was one bit of excitement. A suggestion to the cabinet from the OPSGROUP (they were probably put up to it) of quietly evacuating an old folks home under cover of darkness was quickly scotched as a potential public relations and communications disaster. It could have started an uncontrolled mass evacuation of the Darlington area, something everyone in the war room wanted to avoid. Darlington 89 soon reminded me of a series of dull, bureaucratic meetings and overly technical discussions with Hydro staffers.

There were some perks. It was interesting sitting at a table on a raised platform beside someone playing the role of premier. If the OPP commissioner stood in front of me, I could go nose-to-nose with him while I was sitting down. It gave me insight into why kings sit on raised thrones; it's a power thing.

The exercise ended and I worked for a while on a communications plan for non-nuclear emergencies in Ontario. There already was one for nuclear emergencies, which were localized and well defined. Ontario's outstanding experience with a real non-nuclear emergency had been the train derailment in Mississauga in 1979 leading to the evacuation of nearly 200,000 people. Terrorism was always a possibility although regarded as remote. But as we joked, what were we going to do if a sizeable meteorite fell into Lake Ontario, sending a tsunami up to Richmond

Hill? I turned the first draft of the communications plan in to communications branch and forgot about it. Never heard any more about it. Never wanted to.

Turning my contract work into a permanent job in crisis communications might have been a possibility. But taking an Ontario job in emergency information would be like condemning myself to a life as a Maytag repairman of television commercial fame, forever sitting around waiting for something to happen

Darlington '91, two years later, was my last hurrah with nuclear crisis communications—as consultant to the INFOGROUP rather than a participant. Many communications branch staffers were involved, so I met with them in a boardroom at their office in Queen's Park to give them some idea of what to anticipate.

In those days, the first thing to expect after a nuclear event was a phone call. Calling trees had been prepared and when you got your phone call, you had a list of other people to call. My explanation was interrupted by a staffer who said, "Don't give me any people to call. Because as soon as I hang up my phone after a warning of a nuclear accident, I'll get in my car and start driving up Highway 400 as fast as I can." He was serious.

The people who planned Exercise Darlington '91 put a neat wrinkle in it. The scenario put a leak in containment. Problem: how are you supposed to keep people calm when they find out that airborne radiation is leaking and potentially blowing every which direction? It made for a more interesting exercise. But the overwhelming facts remain: nobody died at Three Mile Island (or at Fukushima for that matter) and that CANDU reactors are quintessentially Canadian—dull by design.

But I had acquired a good line on my resume: Acted as Director of Emergency Information preparing for the commissioning of the last North American nuclear generating station to go on line in the 20$^{th}$ century. I had developed knowledge and skills that I put to use for the rest of my communications consulting career.

Ron Truman

# 9.
# And h'it's in h'English!!
*More crisis communications 1992-2007*

My communications skills were the focal point of the final hour of a Federal-Provincial-Territorial Tourism Ministers' conference on SARS at Toronto's King Edward hotel in May 2003. The conference needed a communiqué to set the tone for media coverage. My job was to find the right words to tell the world what a baker's dozen of governments had agreed on. The first rule of crisis communications is to communicate in such a way that you appear to be in control and able to manage the situation— especially when the situation is out of control. It wasn't going to be easy. There was an overwhelming diversity of participants who had to agree to the message: a full-scale Federal-Provincial-Territorial Conference in Canada brings together representatives of 10 provinces, two territories and the federal government.

This conference dealt with the economic crisis brought on by SARS (Severe Acute Respiratory Syndrome), a viral epidemic that started in China seven months earlier and by early May had wreaked devastation on Canada's tourism industry. Fear was keeping potential visitors home, especially avoiding Ontario where the plague had arrived first in Canada, but affecting the tourism industry in every part of Canada. SARS was top of mind not only for the tourism industry, but was an item in almost every newscast.

Ontario tourism deputy-minister Jean Lam brought me to the conference. I was working for the province, not the Canadian Intergovernmental

Conference Secretariat (CICS), the federal bureaucracy that organizes those multi-party conflabs. CICS had a translator on hand, ready to produce a French version of whatever wording I managed to get agreement on. I had my own laptop and kept pumping out new versions of the communiqué based on the feedback brought to me by DM Lam, who negotiated with the other heads of delegation. Eventually, with revisions and tweaks of wording, we arrived at a final draft distributed to all parties. Quebec was going to be the key to getting unanimous endorsement of the communiqué and I was apprehensive when a delegate from that province arrived with my latest draft in hand. To my surprise, there were no notations on the text.

Speaking with a distinct French accent the Quebec representative said, "H'it's perfect. H'it says exactly what we want it to say." Then he added, as if he couldn't believe the words coming out of his mouth, "And h'it's in h'English!" [27]

I packed up my laptop, leaving the translator to work on the French version and went home. That was my last high-profile work related to crisis communications for the Government of Ontario.

My provincial role and responsibilities in the early 21$^{st}$ century were different from the ones I had in the late 1980s when I was involved as provincial director of emergency information in terrorism and nuclear exercises. Those had just been exercises and the crisis communications versions of war games. From 2001 to 2003 I had a minor role in real

---

27 NEWS RELEASE – TOURISM MINISTERS DISCUSS ACTION PLANS TO ATTRACT TRAVELLERS TO CANADA
TORONTO, May 10, 2003—Federal, provincial and territorial ministers responsible for tourism met today in Toronto to share ideas and discuss action plans to promote tourism across Canada.
At the meeting, co-chaired by Canada's Industry Minister Allan Rock and Ontario's Minister of Tourism and Recreation Brian Coburn, ministers agreed to extend marketing efforts surrounding Canadian destinations and attractions and to increase collaboration between provinces and territories. The ministers' goal is to assure the world that Canada is as ready and willing as ever to open its doors to tourists and reinforce its brand as one of the greatest tourist destinations in the world.
(The rest of the communique is just as dull and non-committal—a good example of the art of how not to say anything using many words in tricky situations.)

crises that had dramatic economic effects on the tourism industry—9/11 and SARS.

9/11 was a devastating blow to an Ontario tourism industry highly dependent on US visitors living within a day's drive of the Canadian border. Almost immediately, the province's tourism icon Niagara Falls was all but deserted; the casinos and slot machine venues that drew American visitors across the border to lesser destinations were practically empty. Americans began staying home. Less than two years later, the SARS outbreak in Toronto exacerbated Ontario's problems. The decline in tourism as a result of the reluctance of US citizens to travel abroad was intensified by the requirement of the Western Hemisphere Travel Initiative (WHTI) that US citizens get a passport to return to the USA, not just by air or water, but also when crossing the border in cars. Americans often do not get passports, so this effectively added another nail to the coffin for Ontario's tourism industry.

In September 2001, I was working as an in-house consultant for the Ministry of Tourism and Recreation, already putting in 10 – and 12-hour days. Tourism Minister Tim Hudak, an ambitious, energetic man in his mid-30s had set off on a summer tour in June with the goal of doing 100 events in 100 days. The demand for media advisories, speeches and news releases overwhelmed the communications branch (CB) almost immediately. (See Chapter 10)

The summer tour was something of an artificial crisis, brought on by one man's seemingly whimsical desires.[28] When I was called to see if I could keep up with the frantic pace, the CB gave me an office with a window when they found I was not only equal to the task but having a good time doing it.[29] The Internet helped make things manageable.

---

28  In the fullness of time, I have concluded that Minister Hudak was implementing a strategy to get into as many ridings as possible to make personal contact with party members who might support him in future leadership races.

29  Most of the speeches were delivered to small festivals and events or to present funding for arena improvements or cultural endeavors. Since I was a fast writer and a quick study, I often had time to spare and would amuse myself by doing things like working 26 Presley song titles into the minister's speech at the opening of the Collingwood Elvis Festival. I never complained about overwork. The Minister's Office staffers nicknamed me "Sport" because setbacks never deterred me.

By 2001, most of the organizations the minister met with and events he attended had established an Internet presence. Instead of providing him with speeches full of boilerplate paragraphs, I was able to go on the web and easily tailor each set of remarks to the audience of the day.

Then real crisis emerged. The Toronto International Film Festival (TIFF) was in full swing on September 11, 2001, the infamous 9/11. Hogtown was full of American celebrities and the minister was slated to address one of the TIFF gatherings that night. In the surreal shock of that day, CB modified the minister's remarks to make them more appropriate. Reality began setting in on September 12. Ontario tourism's Visitor Information Centers, which had been seeing a steady stream of American visitors looking for things to do, now were crammed with US residents seeking help to get home. Niagara Falls was deserted, with empty buses and boats. This was shaping up to be Ontario tourism's crisis of the century. (Until SARS came along.)

I was going to be involved, but only as a wordsmith. Nobody asked me for any advice or opinions on policy or suggestions about how to communicate with various audiences. I was told who was the target audience and the media being used (fax blasts, news releases, long speeches at conferences, statements in the Legislature) to get the message out. My task was to express things coherently and make them sound good if possible. (It was more than a year later, during the SARS panic, my role grew to include a few more advisory functions.)

The various small businesses that made up the tourism industry had to be kept informed. Many of them faced bankruptcy. They looked to government for help with their challenges. I wrote weekly bulletins that were faxed out to all the little enterprises on the tourism database. Some of the longest speeches I ever wrote were scripts for ministers' and deputy ministers' remarks to tourism industry gatherings.

I provided communications support—news releases and backgrounders—for various initiatives designed to give tourism a new start, a new direction. The ministry encouraged in-province tourism by promoting festivals and events. With US residents staying home, Ontario reached out to previously untapped markets from other provinces, including Quebec. I wasn't involved directly in that effort, but I did hear one of the marketing staff complaining after a trip to Montreal that the people in Quebec were not responding well and clearly "didn't like us anyway."

I was deeply involved in the bi-national initiatives designed to forestall further barriers to cross-border travel. Ontario attempted to build a consensus that the tourism industry was vital on both sides of the border in the Niagara Region, the Thousand Islands and the Detroit-Windsor area. I wrote long speeches and many news releases for bi-national conferences.

I have no evidence the conferences were successful in influencing the US federal government as it persisted in its plans to impose travel restrictions on its citizens by demanding passports for re-entry to the US. I saw the bi-national initiative as an attempt to play upstate New York and eastern Michigan against Washington DC's desire to tighten border crossing controls. It was a wasted effort, especially with the recalcitrance of the Ottawa Liberals, whom I regarded as basically anti-American, to cooperate in a continental strategy to keep terrorists out of North America.

Another thrust in dealing with the tourism crisis was an attempt to enhance Toronto's appeal to the artsy-fartsy segment of the population of North America. Fortunately, I was not involved with the dubious government sponsorship of a Princess of Wales Theatre production based on *Lord of the Rings*.[30] That was left to a small core of highly regarded and excessively privileged civil servants and their pet consultants operating independently and pretty much in isolation.

My preoccupation was the Toronto cultural renaissance—a government funding program for renovation and rebuilding of the Royal Ontario Museum, the Art Gallery of Ontario, the Opera House, National Ballet School, Royal Conservatory of Music, Ontario College of Art and Design. SuperBuild, a federal-provincial infrastructure renewal program had been rolled out pre-9/11. The Investment Development Office in the tourism ministry turned it into a tourism promotion program for Toronto. I used journalist Robert Fulford's books on the cultural history

---

30 I was working in tourism when the Lord of the Rings musical had a six-month run in 2006 and based on the press reviews, was not a success. Tourism-wise, it drew a total audience of about a third of a million. It received a number of awards and after a severe re-writing, opened later in London, England where it ran for a year.

of the city to create a narrative that politicians could use to promote more investment in downtown Toronto's cultural attractions.

During the declining months of the Conservative government, when Ernie Eves took over from Mike Harris, there was a revolving door for tourism ministers, reaching its nadir when Premier Eves fired tourism minister Cam Jackson. It was an impromptu dismissal just as Jackson was about to deliver a speech in Hamilton and had to leave the venue instead. The last tourism minister for the Eves government was Brian Coburn. In his brief stint at tourism, I found my role growing slightly from that of a wordsmith to being something of an advisor. When Minister Coburn had to answer questions from the US media on Ontario tourism, he took me to the teleconferencing facility in the parliament buildings to provide advice during the session. At a major tourism conference at the casino in Orillia, he had me attend to rewrite his remarks. Anticipating he would hear things during the day that he would have to address during his evening remarks, he wanted me there to do last minute revisions and additions.

That night, he faced a potentially hostile audience of tourism industry leaders, people who had reason to be unhappy with the provincial government's performance since 9/11 and SARS. His speech was well received. When he left the lectern to return to his seat, he made a detour to come by my table and express his appreciation for my wordsmithing that helped him to skate on thin ice.

Minister Coburn represented Ontario at the Federal-Provincial-Territorial conference on SARS. His confidence in my ability to find the right words in difficult situations was probably the reason I spent the day working on the communiqué that would be released to the press. In 2007, I did a little more work that was crisis communications-related when the Ministry of Tourism was making a last-ditch effort to stop the Western Hemisphere Travel Initiative (WHTI) from compelling US citizens to have a passport to get back into the country. It was doomed to failure. My role was as a wordsmith in the situation, writing speeches and news releases that would buck up the Ontario side and encourage US factions to support Ontario's position on cross-border travel.

After the Darlington Nuclear Generating Station exercises in the late 1980s and early 1990s I used some of my crisis communications skills in the provincial sector, but not extensively. I found more opportunity to use what I had learned in the municipal sector.

Disgusted with the NDP government, which I considered to be little more than a collection of misfits and morons, I pursued work in other areas than Queen's Park. When the first Mike Harris government took office in 1995, the municipal sector offered opportunity for crisis communications. I had some experience in the municipal sector. I carried an Association of Municipalities of Ontario (AMO) business card for five years and had run the media office at the AMO annual conference in 1990. Many municipalities were pushed into existential crisis as the Harris government announced its intention to amalgamate small municipalities into more efficient larger ones and backed away from the onerous regulations that made work for municipal government.

My break came unexpectedly, from a coalition of conservation authorities that found themselves under attack because of their unpopularity due to their high-handed interference with property owners and farmers. With the Harris government, they were without the unquestioning support of a provincial government that provided half their funding. They saw trouble coming and had hired a PR firm in Toronto and local lawyers to aid them in their lobbying efforts.

That wasn't going to bring them the support they needed for continued existence. When my phone rang and I was asked for a better solution, I suggested a public meeting with the public and local politicians to air the issue and build support for continued funding of the CAs. They bought the idea. I organized a large public meeting, wrote speeches supporting continued funding for CA executives and local notables, and ran the meeting. It was a great success. I also addressed several local municipal councils on the issue. Ultimately the CAs got the support of the local media and through municipal politicians' fear of alienating the press, kept their municipal funding. This was one of my best performances as a crisis communications manager. But it led nowhere for me in terms of more contracts to do municipal work.

Later in the 1990s I went into a brief partnership with a consultant who had worked with one of Toronto's leading crisis communications firms. He had learned a standard method (which he called a technology) of dealing with crises. From the communications perspective, it involved preparing clients to deal with "nightmare questions," developing effective talking points, and coaching clients to answer questions effectively. We had a couple of clients who contracted for our services and were not particularly satisfied with the results. The partnership fell apart—a result of the difficulties of making a partnership work and the interaction of the personalities involved.

The collapse of that partnership left a bad taste in my mouth and I no longer pursued anything to do with crisis communications in the private sector for the remainder of my working career.

# 10.
# Speech Writing

*You saved my ass 1983-2007*

Tim Hudak, an ambitious young tourism minister in the Ontario government, set out to do 100 events in 100 days in the summer of 2001. He actually did 101 events—an accomplishment his Wikipedia page lists first in the account of his stint in tourism. For the writers providing this tour with speeches and news releases, it was a task of Herculean proportions. Like the Augean stables to be cleaned by the fabled Greek god Hercules, before today's consignment of bullshit was disposed of, tomorrow's load was impending.

The tourism ministry's communications branch (CB) was overwhelmed almost immediately. A hundred speeches—each specifically tailored to the event, each brimming with content and messaging meaningful to the audience of the day—had to be prepared and approved in the course of three months. Each event required a media advisory and news release to be written, approved, translated, and sent to the wire service for electronic and snail mail distribution. It was going to be the summer from hell for CB.

It was only a matter of days before my phone rang. I was invited to come in, take an office in the CB, and write the bulk of the speeches and other communications products needed for this improbable summer tour.

Tim Hudak was in his early 30s, an unmarried, unencumbered bundle of energy, free to spend all his time advancing his political career. Already part of the Executive Council of the Province of Ontario, Minister of Culture, Tourism and Recreation in the Mike Harris government, he was well educated and intelligent. With a master's degree in economics and an uncanny ability to absorb, remember and use the information in his briefing books, he was an exceptional cabinet minister.

His 2001 summer tour, called "More to Discover," was pure fluff, involving a Winnebago covered with Ontario tourism messaging, a suitcase (to display the stickers, decals and badges of towns and festivals he visited), and brief speeches to whatever audience would gather to listen to a visiting politician. The festivals and events were usually exceptionally minor—fishing derbies, highland games, motorboat races, country fairs, moose festivals, apple fests, grape harvests, wine tastings, and local crafts shows.

Minister Hudak normally showed up at community events, public occasions that only people living nearby were likely to attend. Usually, he had a message from (and whenever possible, a check from) the government, tourism ministry-sponsored funding for advertising and promoting the event. Along with that funding announcement, there would be some boilerplate speechifying on how tourism created jobs, supported local economies all over the province, and celebrated culture.

Some writers might object to a steady diet of producing unserious material on trivial topics. But I get a kick out of writing, feel right at home in chaotic situations, and took it as a challenge to provide interesting speeches. By 2001, the Internet had matured and was a boon to a speechwriter. While search engines had not reached peak sophistication, you could gather plenty of information by going to the relatively primitive web pages produced by the festival or event.

The minister would be able to refer to coming events with accuracy. Often the web pages would provide photographs allowing me to add visual descriptions to his speech remarks. My goal was trying to provide a speech that was not just the standard bumf about tourism's benefits for the community—using the Internet I could incorporate visual and specific details that might catch the attention of the potential audience.

Basing my speech writing on the surmise that what most people hear when a politician starts speaking at a minor event is "Blah, blah, blah ... ," I tried to put something near the start of every set of remarks that might get people listening, possibly even thinking that this young denizen of Queen's Park knew what he was talking about.

Occasionally, I would have an opportunity to create a fun speech. The ministerial remarks for the Elvis Festival in Collingwood incorporated 26 titles of Presley hits. Once, when the minister was wearing his hat as Recreation minister announcing energy efficiency improvements for an arena near Point Pelee, I gave him some choice phrasing about the arena being the closest to the equator in Canada.

Tim Hudak remained tourism minister until April 2002, so I was a primary speechwriter for him for less than a year. I had very little personal contact with him. He dealt with communications through his advisors, did not customarily give briefings to speechwriters, seldom appeared outside of his office in the MO and never (as far as I know) visited the CB even for a walk-through.

Hudak became Ontario Leader of the Opposition in 2009 and promptly lost two provincial elections that his Progressive Conservative party was favored to win. He could have been premier of Ontario, but gave up those ambitions in 2014, resigning as leader. I believe the brief time in 2001 I dealt with his speeches at the Ministry of Tourism, Recreation and Culture was critical in his ascendancy in party politics. They also gave me some opinions about why he did not succeed.

His 100-event tour gave him an opportunity to build his political base in Ontario. He got to every part of the province at government expense, which means he got to meet and greet local PC supporters and party members. Many of his itineraries included non-official functions, which gave him time to build relationships with local conservatives who would be electing the next leader of the party. It seemed to me that he would be bright and thorough enough to keep notes on or be able to recall many of those encounters. The 100-event tour was his version of church basement and rubber-chicken banquet-circuit for building support. That tour raised his province-wide profile and may have been key to his rise in the party.

Working for the communications branch when he was minister gave me some insight into the reasons why he crashed and burned in his attempt to become premier.

The only advice I ever presumed to give him (via his advisors) was that starting a speech with a joke "to break the ice" was inappropriate in some cases. If, for example, you were at the Royal Ontario Museum with an important announcement for Toronto's elite, you didn't do yourself any favors by starting your remarks with a humorous anecdote about the guy you hired to paint your porch painting your Maserati instead. My advice was: you have clout; start by acknowledging your audience's importance and their influence. Make your announcement. Thank the audience for their attention and explicitly recognize that their continuing support is important.

I interpreted the joke obsession as a flaw in the minister's character. To my way of thinking, when you are speaking from a position of authority, opening with a joke with most audiences is an admission that you lack confidence and a clear indication that you may not have the alpha qualities that leadership requires. Tim Hudak never impressed me as an alpha. Perhaps our age difference of more than 20 years influenced my opinion, but I regarded him as a wanna-be, trying a bit too hard to pull it off.

The personal dynamics in his office were underwhelming. Here was a young, unmarried, powerful politician and not one of the young women I encountered in the MO was obviously head-over-heels in love with him.[31] His staff—male and female alike—was too often mildly contemptuous of him and the way he did things. They didn't bother to hide their indifference from a consultant. Hudak lacked charisma, to put it mildly, as far as I could see. So it did not surprise me to see failures ten years later when Hudak tried to win elections as potential premier. Not that being uncharismatic and/or a beta male is any barrier to becoming premier of Ontario, as proven by recent history.

---

31 Young women who work in the offices of the powerful often develop crushes that are obvious to people like speechwriters who have to deal with the female assistants as intermediaries between the text they are preparing and the cabinet minister delivering the speech. One young lady reminded me of an upland game hunting dog on point, actually quivering with excitement and anticipation as she waited for her boss to call her into the inner office, like a pointer going "birdy" waiting for the pheasants to flush. It's unusual to see a political office completely devoid of that kind of emotion, but I never saw signs of such infatuation or even mild hero-worship in Hudak's office.

But I will always be thankful for Tim Hudak—his ambitious summer tour was a big moneymaker for me and a test for my productivity and my ability to handle pressure when I was past my prime and nearing 60. And his demands let me put my foot solidly in the door as a tourism go-to speechwriter.

Although I wrote hundreds of speeches over 25 years for the Ontario government, it was never my intention to pursue that writing genre. I fell into it one day when I was in the tourism ministry organizing a tour for journalists visiting Ontario. When CB's writing coordinator unexpectedly needed some remarks for an event in 1983, he asked me to draft them. The resulting speech went through approvals, as the coordinator said, "like shit through a goose" and he began handing me speech writing assignments, almost all of them fluffy, tourism bumf rather than hard issues.

Then an attempted environmentalist panic in 1984 gave me my first big break. The latest fright wig scenario wasn't one of the big ones with universal appeal. By that I mean, for example: we were going to freeze under mile-thick ice or broil as temperatures soared, or that acid rain was going to bleach the human race right out of Gaia's hair, or that the ozone hole was going to open up so wide we would all fall through it or that corn monoculture was going to cause the erosion of every last bit of our arable soil, inevitably leading to mass starvation, or a nightmare on wheels, that we were going to reach something called "peak oil" prior to running out of gasoline and not be able to drive our cars. Any of those could incite public panic and demand a heavy-duty government response.

The 1984 scare was, believe it or not, that we were going to drink[32] the Great Lakes dry. It must have had limited appeal and been hard to swallow, because that angst had a shorter run than most of the other

---

32 I jest. Actually the real scare was that along with the greater domestic consumption by increasing populations, other things—diversions, increased irrigation and industrial use—were going to tap into the reservoir of fresh water left by the melting of the glaciers. That would leave the areas bordering the Great Lakes with permanently lower water levels that would affect consumers, shipping and industry. Of course, in recorded historic times, the lakes have always gone up and down—as this is written, several of the lakes are at or above their average historic levels after having been at spectacular lows in previous years. In 1984, the natural variation in lake levels must have had some appeal as a scare tactic. My memory of the 1980s is one of concern over high lake levels. In fact, Point Pelee in Lake Erie nearly washed away because of high water.

whack-a-mole alarums we have endured since the environmentalist religion took root in the 1970s. The Ontario Government didn't seem to take it too seriously, even though it had just produced a major study of the province's water resources and talk of worldwide water shortages and future global wars over access to potable water was and remains a popular evergreen topic with the chattering classes.

In June 1984, Toronto was the venue for a major international conference dubbed "Futures in Water" and environmental spokesmen and environment ministers arrived from all corners of North America—Ottawa, Washington DC and various state capitals.

I was puzzled about the tourism ministry being a lead agency for Ontario. The backstory I got at the time was the premier was originally supposed to be the provincial representative. He blanched when he received the invite and promptly passed it to the minister of tourism, who turned an even paler shade of white, called in his deputy minister and told him he was going. The deputy was severely outclassed on the panel—up against big guns, household names, famous environmentalists.

Even a popgun going against heavy artillery has to make some noise, and the buck stopped on my desk. No one really knew what to say, so I was given pretty much free rein to put words in his mouth. I researched and wrote a draft. After several revisions, the deputy had a text but no confidence. I attended the conference with him ready to make last-minute revisions to his speech if one of the previous panelists said something that needed a response. None was needed. He read his remarks and returned to his seat, relieved.

The next day I bumped into the deputy at the office. He was pleased, delighted. *The Toronto Star* reporter covering the conference had picked up on my concrete, visual and specific language. The *Star's* report on the second day of the conference was all about tourism and the deputy's warnings about Ontario Place surrounded by mudflats, marinas stranded high and dry, the thunder of Niagara reduced to a dull roar—words that I had put into his mouth in an attempt to save his ass. The deputy looked like an international hero rather than a provincial pipsqueak. Good speech writing made the day for the deputy.

I signed a huge contract with tourism and thought I was set for a while. But a new communications director in tourism didn't like my looks and didn't want me around. I never made a cent from that contract and didn't write another speech for tourism communications branches for the rest of the century. It was more than 15 years later that a prickly minister of tourism led to my callback to the tourism ministry. Cam Jackson of Burlington was firing speechwriters one after another and demanding better quality remarks. My phone rang.

Warned by acquaintances in the communications branch about the minister's complaints, I asked for a speech meeting with the minister before I wrote my first set of remarks. People had taken to dressing casually at Queen's Park, so I showed up in a suit and tie. I used a tape recorder to ensure that my speech could reflect his speaking patterns and vernacular. The feedback from his office was that he liked the speech and my professionalism.

That started a good working relationship lasting through his second stint as minister and until he was fired. The only hint of a problem was on one occasion in Ottawa, when Jackson set aside the speech I had written for him and launched into complaints about how expensive his speechwriters were. For years I kept that speech text and a copy of his verbatim remarks in a file folder that I labelled "Jackson Slags Me." I wrote the speech he was about to give in Hamilton before he got a phone call from Ernie Eves informing him he was no longer a minister—he was through in tourism. I stayed on.

My government speech writing career ended in 2007 right where it had started in 1984—in the tourism ministry. I was in tourism through 9/11, SARS and Ontario's effort to oppose the Western Hemisphere Travel Initiative (WHTI). All caused major economic crises for the Ontario tourism industry as they discouraged US visitors that the industry depended on. I wrote thousands upon thousands of words, short speeches to business owners, statements to the legislature, complete texts of hour-long addresses to conferences. To me, those crises had an upside, creating demand that favored those who could work under pressure.

Tourism communications branches were easy picking as far as I was concerned. Tourism is a minor ministry forever being bounced around in cabinet shuffles, getting lumped together with Industry and Trade or Culture and/or Recreation. That led to churn in the communications branch. Every time some ministry like Industry and Trade or Culture was split off, the cream of the crop of communicators seemed to go with the new ministry. Every reorganization left the tourism CB with more of the communicators nobody wanted, either because they were lazy and incompetent or because they caused problems. That created headaches for branch directors and work for consultants like me.

Speech writing, for those who have the knack, can be one of the best ways to make money in freelance writing. Once you are established, you can often recycle material from previous speeches and make lots of use of boilerplate material the minister repeats to every audience. Sometimes you can knock off a speech in a couple of hours, cutting and pasting from old speeches and invoicing for hundreds of dollars. On other speeches, weeks of research and rewriting lead to invoices for thousands of dollars.

You need a thick hide. The writer who treats his words as sacred and his handling of the concepts as impeccable is going to find speech writing difficult. One such writer, winner of a national newspaper award in a journalism career, actually confronted a cabinet minister's advisor who had revised his speech. He pointed out bluntly how much more he as a writer knew than the man who was going to take responsibility for the words. Not a good career move.

You make more money going with the flow. A communications director in the Ministry of Energy once handed me extensive revisions on an important keynote speech. We discussed them for a half-hour and he concluded by saying, "That's why I enjoy having you around. You're just as enthusiastic about revising something as you were about writing it in the first place." He was right. I charged by the hour and was getting not only more opportunity to play with words (one of my favorite pastimes), I was also getting more money.

You also have to deal with some strange quirks. One tourism minister disliked delivering anything that was even remotely like bad news. At an event, he would scan his speech text before his turn at the lectern and if he didn't like the content, he'd put the speech aside and tell his audience, "Normally I read what I'm given, but because I'm among such good friends, I'm just going to speak off the cuff. Copies of the prepared text are available at the back of the room for you to pick up if you're interested."

That annoyed tourism ministry staff, who were determined the industry needed to improve its act to be more competitive in the world. The business owners needed to be told the bad news that the minister was so reluctant to give them. Often, staff would not hand the minister his remarks until the very last second, in the hope that he would not have time to preview them and dodge delivering the messages.

Towards the end of his tenure as minister, demands arrived from his office for speeches with *no bad news at all* in them. Finally, one day his communications advisor arrived at my cubicle with a speech draft in hand. "We thought we told you—NO BAD NEWS," she said. The next moment the air was filled with sheets of paper as she threw the speech in my general direction. "Bad speechwriter!" she shrieked.

Before 9/11 turned tourism writing gloomy and serious, working on projects for the various ministries of tourism was relatively light-hearted labor. Much of the verbiage was promotional and encouraging. There was no overwhelming concern that every word written would be parsed by interest groups taking conflicting positions on the issues.

I got into speech writing about more contentious matters between 1985 and 1993 working for the Ministry of Natural Resources (MNR) and the Ministry of Energy (MoE).

A natural fit with MNR because of my hunting background, experience writing on wildlife management for *The Globe and Mail* and lack of strong opinions on most of MNR's contentious issues, I wrote speeches for the MNR starting when Alan Pope was minister, continuing through the term of Mike Harris and into the time of Vince Kerrio.

When hunters were adapting to selective harvesting in moose and deer hunting, it was good to have a writer who was capable of understanding the difference between party hunting and party killing of moose.[33] My

---

33 Some communicators hired by MNR did not have a clue either about biology or hunting. One of the amusing incidents that wildlife biologists related to me involved a young woman in the communications branch who was drafting an information piece on how hunters were to comply with selective harvest regulations. She was having difficulty with the requirement to identify the sex of a harvested animal by putting the identification tag (like a ski tag—a wire with sticky paper) in the appropriate location (directly through the genitals) on the carcass. She was on deadline and the moose biologist was in a meeting when she burst in and interrupted the proceedings with an urgent question. "What's a vulva?" she asked. Hilarity ensued.

ability to communicate with both wildlife biologists and hunters put me in a good position to produce the speeches and backgrounders needed.

In Pope's ministry I wrote only for the deputy minister, but tackled ministerial speeches under Harris and Kerrio. Both were enjoyable to work with, as they took the time to brief their speechwriters. My speech writing at MNR came to an abrupt end when the left wing of the ruling Liberal party became ascendant—beginning an anti-hunting trend and an absurd focus on endangered species[34] that continues to this day. I mark the turning point as the day the Minister of the Environment made an announcement on a controversial issue that was in Kerrio's mandate, effectively usurping his power. Demand for me as an MNR speechwriter dried up as I was identified with the hook-and-bullet crowd and therefore politically out of step, *persona non grata*.

Energy speech writing provided better opportunities. Ontario's energy situation in the late 1980s was precarious. The economy was in overdrive, expanding so rapidly that large companies began worrying the province was going to run into electricity supply shortages. Increased automation of manufacturing processes meant that the slightest variation in electricity supply (causing a brownout or voltage regulation) could be devastating—interrupting an automated assembly line with the result that all the semi-completed product on the line at the time was junk, causing great losses to the manufacturers.

At the same time, the environmentalist religion was broadening its focus from wildlife issues (anti-sealing and anti-trapping) to energy issues (anti-nuclear). This made it politically tricky to build desperately needed new nuclear reactors to meet growing demand for electricity.

The Association of Major Power Consumers of Ontario (AMPCO) sponsored a conference dubbed "Running on Empty" to raise public awareness of the need for increased electricity supply. I was asked to prepare the minister's speech for the conference. While preparing it I learned a lot about the anti-nuclear and anti-supply attitudes of the ministry staff. One draft of my speech was returned with a sarcastic comment

---

34  When resources are limited, why pour them into species that are on their way out? Better use those resources to improve habitat and management for species that have a future. Many species getting special treatment as endangered are simply at the northern fringe of their range in Ontario and are thriving in other parts of North America.

on how pro-nuclear it was, which led me to better educate myself on the demand management side of the electricity debate. During the weeks before the conference, rumors circulated that Ontario Hydro was going to "flip the switch" and leave the province in darkness for a few days, influencing the debate on the need for new supply. That idea infuriated the pro-demand management advisors in the ministry and some of them started muttering about the kind of dire punishment Ontario Hydro executives deserved if they pulled that kind of trick.

Later in the 1980s, just before Darlington Nuclear Generating station was commissioned, the MoE held a series of major public consultations dubbed Energy Choices Conferences. I wrote the keynote speeches for those events and attended the one in Toronto to watch the media give lavish attention to the anti-nuclear voices and promote dubious ideas like NegaWatts—the glib notion that it is both effective and far cheaper to reduce demand than increase supply. One of the communications staff warned me that the public component of the meeting would largely be "dirty, long-haired hippies sitting around on the floor and breast-feeding their babies in public." The staffer was far from wrong.

After the 1990 election, in which the pro-nuclear stance of the Liberals helped to cause their surprise loss to the NDP, the Ministry of Energy turned into a clown show run by the NDP government. Rumors circulated in the communications branch that one of Bob Rae's energy ministers did not distinguish between hydrogen bombs and nuclear generating stations, actually calling a delegation from Atomic Energy of Canada Limited (AECL) evil men and demanding they stop making weapons of mass destruction.

I was never asked to write a major energy speech in the early years of the Rae government, for which I was truly thankful. When the NDP government decided to tackle the Ontario Hydro issue, the communications branch director asked me to write the Power Corporation Act Amendments speech and all the background material for the legislation. It was a long job, full of contentious detail and basically boring for someone who didn't really give a damn about Ontario Hydro or its shenanigans as long as the lights went on when I flipped the switch.

When the legislation was introduced, I was appalled. The minister of energy was Will Ferguson, a former boxer and previously an executive in a waste management company called Dusty's Disposal. He had worked his way up in the NDP government. He gave the speech I wrote, which was designed to sound moderate, reasonable and pacific. He delivered it to the provincial parliament aggressively, a welterweight minister literally punching the air at what he thought were the main points.

Again, I was not asked to write speeches at MoE for a long period. Then they needed me for the ministerial remarks to the Municipal Electric Association (MEA) annual conference. The minister had exactly seven minutes to speak at lunchtime. He was to follow the MEA president and precede Maurice Strong, whom Premier Bob Rae had installed as President of Ontario Hydro. The Ministry of Energy had been merged with the Ministry of the Environment and the new minister was Bud Wildman; this was his first speech as head of the new combined ministry.

The result was total embarrassment. Wildman went feral. Departing from his seven-minute script, he spoke endlessly and incoherently, misquoting Shakespeare and referring to a succession of Bob Rae governments to be elected in future, when everybody knew by that time that the Dippers were toast in Ontario. That afternoon, I sat in the writing coordinator's office at Energy, listening as he fielded call after call complaining about the execrable performance of his minister at the MEA.

The Ministry of Energy disappeared for a while, subsumed by the Ministry of the Environment. I did no speech writing for the first Mike Harris government elected in 1995, so that Energy/Environment speech was the last of my speech writing until the century's end. Then, in the new millennium, Cam Jackson's personality and Tim Hudak's burning ambition gave me a new start in my speech-writing career.

# 11.
# Combatting Preservationist Balderdash

*Saving all kinds of things in the wilderness 1983-1995*

They were dire warnings. In the early 1980s, abandoned hearths and chimneys stood on a number of prominent points in Algonquin Provincial Park. It was heartbreaking. Where once there was a family cottage carved out of the wilderness, only the stonework remained. Every other portion of what was once a delightful personal retreat was gone. It was a deliberate visual provocation. Like gibbets—rotting bodies of executed prisoners suspended in iron cages—the fireplaces served notice to the park's remaining cottage leaseholders that they were destined to be purged from the park in a purification process.

Earlier in the century, the provincial government had invited cottagers to establish summer residences in the park. The cottagers would provide a measure of security for the isolated park and its visitors. But a new age of environmentalism and protectionism had dawned. People had to go. Park authorities brooked no nonsense from humans inhabiting territory designated as parkland.

Algonquin's summer residents knew well what happened in New Brunswick a few years earlier. Acadians living on land coveted by Parks Canada were tear-gassed. They watched as bulldozers levelled their homes. They rioted to no avail. The Acadian crime leading to this second expulsion: they did not promptly vacate land they had owned for generations.

The land was now ordained to return to wilderness park status. Parks authorities did not fool around when it came to dealing with little people.

Unfortunately for the Ontario provincial government and the environmentalist-wilderness groups they were kowtowing to, many Algonquin leases were held by members of the Toronto and Ottawa elites. Playing Bigfoot with them—stepping in and enforcing new rules that little people would have to obey—wasn't going to be a cakewalk. Cottagers promptly built an effective, multi-faceted resistance. Their opposition efforts involved a consulting job for me. It provided me a role in a success guaranteed to last to 2017. That was nearly 30 years—the next thing to permanence in today's world.

In the late 1970s and early 1980s, Algonquin was part of my freelance beat for *The Globe and Mail*. Along with the usual fishing, canoeing and camping features, I wrote about the formal review of the park master plan. I was sympathetic to the precarious situation of the cottagers and the critical dependence of local communities on the natural resources in the park. In magazine articles, including my regular column in *Outdoor Canada* magazine, I didn't hide my cynicism about plans to return the park to an untouched wilderness.

My relations with the wilderness and parks groups lobbying for purification and re-virgination of the Algonquin wilderness had been problematic from the beginning. For one of my first *Globe and Mail* stories on the park, I interviewed the president of the Algonquin Wildlands League (AWL). Instead of performing as a stenographer for his poetic-emotional descriptions of the park's wilderness and esoteric value, I asked him some uncomfortable questions. It turned out that he had seen Algonquin Park only from a Ministry of Natural Resources truck touring along the park logging roads. I immediately suspected he was a phony, preaching a wilderness party line to impress his fellow academics.

Later, when I worked in the communications branch of the Ministry of Natural Resources (MNR), staffers would talk about the urbane-ness and lack of field experience of the leadership of various groups advocating saving old growth forests and wild rivers. People who actually knew what was going on spotted phonies, poseurs and publicity-seekers everywhere among the advocates of protectionism and purification.

Ron Truman | 119

The original decision to remove leaseholders from Algonquin Park was taken in the mid-1950s. When the issue of cottagers in parks heated up in the 1980s as more leases began to expire and children's' camps and logging operations stayed, I wasn't entirely surprised to get a phone call from the Algonquin Park Residents Association. In a meeting with their executive, I was astounded when I was offered a contract as their lead consultant. I agreed, somewhat reluctantly, as long as they would use a team of Doug Roseborough and me. There was no way I felt I could do an adequate job working alone.

Doug, who had recently retired as director of MNR's wildlife branch, had begun his career in the 1950s setting up the interpretive program in Algonquin Park. He was an expert on Algonquin and its history. He brought gravitas to our presentations and was exceptionally effective at getting under the skin of MNR parks employees who were not in agreement with him. He tormented them with stories of waste, inefficiency, dubious park user surveys, and MNR staff's lack of authority to make decisions. He derided them publicly as nothing more than rule-followers who had to look up every decision in a book of rules provided by Queens Park.

My role in the consulting process included lining up support for the cottagers. I approached outside organizations and media outlets, presenting the cottagers' point of view. I encouraged loggers and other people who were not ideological environmentalists to attend public meetings and speak in favor of multiple use of the park. With the media, even small town reporters, I usually could not hope to get a pro-cottager story. Softening reporters up, convincing them that there was another legitimate point of view as opposed to the black-and-white ideology of the Algonquin Wildlands League, was about the best that I could hope for.

Some outside organizations supported the leaseholders readily. To my surprise, one I had some difficulty with was the Ontario Federation of Anglers and Hunters (OFAH). Jack O'Dette, a former president still powerful in the organization, had come from an era in which naturalists and hunters cooperated. He believed there should be parks in which no hunting would be allowed. The OFAH executive director was impressed that I was able to bring the former president around to supporting multiple use in Algonquin.

I also cultivated cottagers, encouraging them to speak on their own behalf. In that, I had invaluable cooperation from Dan Gibson, a man I had gotten to know while iceboating on the Bay of Quinte. Dan had a cottage in the park and a formidable reputation among the naturalists and environmentalists. He was a high-profile Toronto photographer, filmmaker and sound recordist (the Solitudes series) who would eventually become a member of the Order of Canada for his environmental contributions.

At the crunch public meeting in the Waverly Hotel in downtown Toronto, I introduced the representative of the AWL to Dan Gibson. It was a simple appeal to celebrity. I had briefed Dan on what I hoped he would do. The AWL representative was awed by Gibson's reputation and willing to listen to Dan's argument that cottagers do more good than harm in the park. When the AWL rep agreed with Gibson that multiple use was the ideal solution for the park's future, I buttonholed the reporter from the *Toronto Star* and brought him over to make sure he got the story.

The next day, the *Star*'s article on the Toronto public meeting quoted the AWL executive as endorsing multiple use in Algonquin. Alfred Holden wrote that the league had done an about-face. That was valuable because the *Star* was (and is) virtually the house organ for the provincial Liberal party. The Liberals were in government at the time.

When the public consultation was all over, the provincial government announced the extension of all cottage leases to 2017. That 21$^{st}$ century date seemed like forever back in the 80s, but as this memoir is written, the deadline is mere months away. The province had simply kicked the can down the road. I hope my efforts as a consultant for the cottagers helped to get their stay of execution. I have never been sure why Queen's Park backed off, wondering if it had been political pressure from the elite or a credible threat by some high-profile lawyer-leaseholder to drag the province into court. I hope I helped.

The Algonquin leaseholder's gig is my fondest memory of the years I spent consulting on wildlife and conservation issues. It was my only real success; all the rest turned out to be efforts on behalf of losing causes. I was always swimming against the current, despite the fact that I believed I was fighting for the righteous.

The environmentalist movement was reaching its full fervor in the 1980s. Extremist advocates of the cause, mostly urbanites, were going to save all kinds of things in the Ontario hinterlands. That included the old-growth forests (Temagami), wildlife in general, the wilderness itself, and an extensive list of plants, birds and animals that might be considered endangered species. Destroying is the other side of the coin when it comes to the tactics of ideological movements. There were lots of things targeted for destruction. The environmentalist movement was going to eradicate, if possible, the seal hunt, the trapping industry, logging in parks and elsewhere if possible, introduced plant species in parks, and, of course, leaseholds in parks.

In the late 1970s, Wildlife Branch director Doug Roseborough was convinced that emotional and animal rights-flavored ideas about wildlife were making his job more difficult. Wrong-headed efforts to help or protect animals were actually doing long-term harm. There wasn't much he could do about the Hollywood entertainment industry with its Bambi movies and the endless cartoons presenting talking animals with human emotions.

Education, however, is a provincial responsibility. Roseborough saw a flawed education system as providing and supporting disinformation about wildlife and its management. He wanted to tackle the root cause of the problem by starting to change the attitudes and information that students were exposed to in the classroom. He wanted to provide school kids with more accurate, less emotional material, eventually inoculating the public against the concept that animals were human.[35]

Hiring me to promote better attitudes to wildlife management, he first sent me to Federation House in Toronto as a consultant. My task was to convince teachers to explore changing the way wildlife management was

---

35  Roseborough often could not find a wildlife biologist to talk effectively to the public. Wildlife biologists made a life choice to deal with animals not people. When they came in from the wilds and took a job in the bureaucracy, they were, from that time on, working with *homo sapiens*, a species they regarded with ambivalence and often wanted to avoid. I felt sorry for many of them. For example, when working for a federal wildlife organization, I watched a grizzly bear specialist being abused by a clerical worker who was preparing a document for him. When the clerk-typist left the room, I challenged the biologist, pointing out that he was famous for fearlessly standing his ground against charging grizzly bears yet he was completely intimidated by an unpleasant, uncooperative woman. He looked at me mournfully, explaining, "I always know what a grizzly bear is going to do next."

being presented in schools. Roseborough wanted me to start with endangerment. There was constant silliness about flourishing common species (Canada geese, for example) being endangered. Species on the northern fringe of their range in Ontario were scarce but supposedly endangered and their status was added to public lists making it look like mass extinctions were imminent. Schools were full of emotional appeals to the younger set with slogans like "Extinction is Forever" and art lessons that produced anti-fur and anti-hunting posters.

Roseborough faced pressure from the public and from provincial politicians to use more of his limited wildlife management resources on management of endangered species. He saw this as a waste of money. Why use your scarce resources to try to help species that were doomed, on their way out, when it would only delay their demise? Better spend the money enhancing habitat for wildlife that might thrive with improved living conditions.

My first and only meeting with the teachers' representative took place in a little boardroom at the headquarters of Ontario's teachers' federations. I launched into my pitch. The federations' curriculum representative was surprised. She may have been expecting someone from wildlife branch would be bringing material and ideas to help get the message out that we should love and protect our little birdies and furry animals. Perhaps I would be bringing money to help produce teaching materials for the effort.

What I had to say about endangered species did not please her. She went from being discomfited to being annoyed. After a short time stirring in her chair, she cut off the interview and did everything except admonish me not to let the door hit me on my way out. My first consulting assignment produced my first professional bum's rush. It wouldn't be the last failure in the years I was involved in this endeavor.

Roseborough and I began working together in a loose partnership. He was well into his retirement before he gave up on his efforts to educate the public on the right ways (not the animal rights way) to manage wildlife. When he left MNR about the time I left *The Globe and Mail,* we considered ourselves a consulting team for the rest of the decade. My role was usually to develop ways to reach the public. Using his credentials as retired Director of the Wildlife Branch to get published, I would ghost write for him. I penned letters to the editor over his name and wrote an op-ed piece published in *The Globe and Mail*.

Roseborough opened the door for me at the Fur Institute of Canada, Canadian Wildlife Federation and Canadian Wildlife Service. That led to consulting work for me at the humane trapping research facility in Alberta. I dealt with Greenpeace and other anti-trapping groups at Ontario Trappers' Association annual meetings. I provided talking points and backgrounders for the nation-wide editorial board tour by Alan Herscovici, the author of a book on animal rights. I ran a communications facility for animal user groups at the Ottawa meeting of the parties of the Convention on International Trade in Endangered Species (CITES conference).[36]

Roseborough's changes in moose management in Ontario led to my being hired to be writer/editor of *The Moose in Ontario*. This was a 90-page booklet for a moose hunter education program he hoped to introduce. I spent several winter weeks at the Leslie Frost Centre in Dorset working with co-editor Mike Buss to turn material submitted by moose biologists across northern Ontario into a readable and coherent version of an educational manual. To make the publication more useful for non-hunters, we separated out the chapters on moose hunting and put them in a second volume. The first volume was intended to be sold in Algonquin Provincial Park, where moose are frequently seen along the Highway 60 corridor. Visitors frequently have questions about moose.[37] Drawings by a professional wildlife illustrator from the Royal Ontario Museum made the final version appealing; review by all Ontario moose

---

36 Many of these are dealt with in this book's chapter on crisis communications.

37 On a visit to the park in 1992, I was pleased to find the book display at the West Gate included the first volume of the moose book, being sold exactly where I wanted it to be peddled. On a visit in 2010, finding the book was not available at the East Gate, I stopped in at the park's interpretive center and found that the main library did not have a copy of it and that the person in charge of the library materials had never heard of it. Yet the staff at the park said that most of the visitor inquiries about wildlife involved moose. It was probably the logo of the Ontario Federation of Anglers and Hunters on the booklet that led to its disappearance from Algonquin Park outlets. The Frost Center where I wrote the book, once a venue for training of foresters and later a camp where children could learn skills useful for hunting and fishing, was turned into an environmental camp and then closed.

biologists ensured it was accurate. The biologists involved were pleased with the results. They designated me as co-author of one of the chapters, giving me the only scientific credential to my name. The book has since gone out of print. Roseborough's hopes for a moose hunter education course never reached fruition.

My stint of wildlife consulting ended where it began, with an attempt to get realistic material on wildlife management into the schools. The Fur Institute of Canada (FIC), using its bountiful funding from the federal Department of External Affairs, hired me to produce a video on the trapping industry. The FIC provided all the visual material in terms of still pictures and video clips. It was up to me to write a script and to work with AKO Productions Ltd. in Toronto to create a 15-minute video that could be shown in schools, an alternative to the anti-seal hunt and anti-trapping propaganda films that were being used.

This was my introduction to video production in the pre-digital era, when Betamax video player-recorders required a seemingly endless number of hours to patch together a few paltry minutes of video worth watching. It was a time-intensive and labor-intensive project that discouraged me from emphasizing video production as part of my bag of tricks.

When the video was completed and dubbed to VHS tapes, I was asked to field test the project. The biggest challenge was getting into a school to show the video. In southern Ontario the doors were closed to me once school administrators found out the FIC was involved. Eventually, a school principal that I knew from skiing in Vermont allowed me into his school to try the video on middle-school classes. I submitted a report indicating that the children had a ho-hum reaction to the video and were more likely to have strong responses to videos that played on their emotions rather than our video, which appealed to logic and reasonableness.

The Ontario Federation of Anglers and Hunters (OFAH) was another organization that wanted into the educational system. They wanted to counter the anti-hunting propaganda being preached. They had developed a slide show and presentation. They wanted federation members to go into schools, show the slides while reading the accompanying script and answer questions—providing an opportunity for urban middle-school students to meet and ask questions of people who hunted.

The OFAH executive found that they could get into the schools if individual teachers invited hunters they knew to talk to their classes; what they needed were OFAH members who would volunteer to make the presentation. Using a grant from the Toronto Sportsmen's Show, OFAH hired me to go to zone meetings in every part of the province to demonstrate how easy it was to do the presentation and encourage members to make use of it.

Most of the OFAH zone meetings in Ontario were fairly small, attended by a relative handful of dedicated federation members. In Kenora, I gave my presentation at dinnertime to a full ballroom in the large hotel that sits on the shoreline of Lake of the Woods. I sat at the head table chatting with the mayor before my turn came to speak. Everybody who was anybody in Kenora was at that zone meeting, one of the major social events of the season. It was refreshing to be in a milieu where people shared my beliefs about what was truly protection of the environment and what was emotional nonsense. By the late 1980s, the only place I found an atmosphere pretty well free of ideological animal rights activism and environmentalist fanaticism in Ontario was in the far northwest of Ontario, where the Canadian Shield met the prairies.

In retrospect, as I write this memoir looking back over my years of consulting on wildlife projects I realize they provided a great deal of fun and excitement—from playing a part in an international conference in Ottawa to being a speaker at events in remote parts of the province, meeting all kinds of people with different takes on life. But my efforts did not make much of a difference in the shape of events.

I took on wildlife consulting projects until the mid-1990s, when I decided that fighting a losing war wasn't entertaining any longer. I had flown all my missions and moved on to other fields. The environmentalist-animal rights religion was steadily gaining ground, pushed by the media. I was swimming against the current, winning a few battles but utterly failing to stop what I considered to be the corruption of public attitudes towards wildlife management.

I eventually came to a McLuhan-esque rationalization for my inability to make significant progress with changing public opinion. One of my outstanding memories from my university days was that of watching

Marshall McLuhan, who coined the phrase "the medium is the message," being booed for minutes at a lecture, almost driving him from the stage.

McLuhan was arguing that the slaughter and outrages in Cyprus (the Turk-Greek Cypriot imbroglio) had been going on for centuries. They had only become a public issue when new media like television appealed to people's feelings and got them emotionally involved. I decided McLuhan was right. I was getting nowhere trying to oppose emotionalism with logic and facts. The pen may be mightier than the sword but the video camera is trump.

All the logical words I wrote on wildlife management and on animal use for things like medical research and food were falling on deaf ears. Facts were simply beside the point compared to how someone feels. The media were compliant and sometimes complicit. Two examples.

Doug Roseborough claimed that Peter Worthington of *The Toronto Sun* was his cousin (how distant he never said). He took it personally that he saw Worthington as an animal rights activist who supported the outrageous animal rights behavior of the Toronto Humane Society[38]. Worthington refused to print some of the material Roseborough put his name to in an official capacity as director of the provincial wildlife branch. According to Roseborough, Worthington made excuses by lying about not having received some letters from him.

At the ECO-ED[39] conference in Toronto in 1992, I was one of two people who challenged one of David Suzuki's producers. The television producer had just made a presentation that I considered to be full of distortions. The other challenger was Diane Francis, editor of the *Financial Post*, someone I thought might have some clout. We badgered the producer for a considerable length of time without making any impression.

---

38 The Toronto Humane Society was a hotbed of animal rights activism in the 1980s. It is one of the few organizations to ever condemn me publicly. I was a low-profile journalist and consultant. A hunting organization was another to attack me. After an article I wrote about the moose tag lottery displeased Timmins-area hunters, I was hung in effigy in South Porcupine.

39 The World Congress for Education and Communication on Environment and Development (ECO-ED), held in Toronto in October 1992 drew more than 3000 delegates from 75 countries, 500 presenters and 275 speakers. I attended, sent by the Ontario Ministry of Energy.

I had the distinct impression his attitude was: facts and details don't matter; as long as you *feel* you are right. Maybe in television—and in the real world—that's what counts.

# 12.
# Thin Skins for Cree Women

*Native issues 1986-2005*

In October 1986, the village of Winisk on the shore of Hudson Bay was gone. Fourteen weeks earlier, a late spring ice jam led to a flash flood that swept the entire community (all but two buildings) from the face of the earth. It was a catastrophe of biblical proportions. Two residents drowned; others waited for days to be rescued, floating around in canoes. The community was being rebuilt as the village of Peawanuck, 30 kilometers upriver. Our de Havilland Twin Otter was one of the first fixed-wing aircraft to land at the village's just-completed airport.

*Like the snow of yesteryear that I am holding in my mitten, everything else in the photo (except me) is gone. The Village of Winisk was swept out to sea by an ice jam. The airport, which survived the flood, was dismantled and removed in a clean-up of the old radar stations in the north.*

Our immediate challenge was getting into town; the road between the airport and the community was not yet drivable. Solved by helicopter. Passengers and crew of the Twin Otter piled aboard a work chopper and sat on the floor for the quick trip to town. In the village we encountered a frenzy of activity with helicopters, lumber, windows, shingles and insulation, power tools and gas-powered generators—a frenetic race to complete the new village before winter set in. After a brief look around, staying out of the way of the construction activity, we sought out the band council, meeting in a partly completed community center. A handful of band members, on break from building tasks, sat around a television set receiving TVO educational programs broadcasted from a satellite. The children's program had to be boring for them, but the satellite television was a novelty.

The chief sat at a makeshift desk near the north wall of the building. We lined up in front of him and introduced ourselves. Then, with as much formality as is possible on a construction site, one of the Ministry of Natural Resources (MNR) staffers took out a substantial bundle of checks held together with elastic bands. Gravely, he presented it to the chief announcing this was part of the compensation for the villagers' losses in the springtime deluge. This was serious business, designed to help bring closure to what was possibly the greatest tragedy ever to befall this small Native band. We anticipated a serious response, something with gravitas and deep emotion.

The chief took the bundle, then, while still looking at us, casually flipped the checks over his shoulder. They landed on a shelf behind him with a resounding thump. More than 400 thousand dollars in checks. Aghast, the staffer who had made the presentation waited a few moments in shocked silence, then asked, "Aren't you going to put them in the bank?" The chief replied, deadpan, "We could do that. What is it, early October? We'll have a bank here soon—a snowbank." [40]

---

[40] The chief, I found out many years later, was dissatisfied with the amount of money his band had received. The members got everything they asked for, but had not claimed all the items they should have. He was annoyed at the band members, not at the provincial government.

*We visited Peawanuck before roads were built as the new community replaced Winisk, a village washed out to sea in the spring of 1986. After hitching a ride by helicopter in from the airport, we explored the village in all-terrain vehicles.*

Our delegation was stuck for words, although some of us chuckled quietly. The subject changed to the progress being made in building the new village and landing facility. We did a little more perfunctory touring of the town site. Then, not wanting to be in the way, we choppered back to airport, and boarded the Twin Otter to return to Polar Bear Provincial Park Headquarters, also located at the mouth of the Winisk River, but on the slightly higher south bank. Someone shouted out an appeal to fly close to ground level on our way back[41]. The pilots, both of whom were

---

41 Pilots prefer the smoother air at higher altitudes but biologists and tourists being flown to Hudson Bay Lowlands destinations commonly nag their pilots to fly low enough for the passengers to enjoy the rare view of the flora and fauna of some of the world's most southerly true tundra and permafrost.

CL-215 water bomber pilots in fire season, were delighted to comply with a request for more exciting aviation antics.

There were few trees to provide a guide to how low we were flying. Nothing grows much more than knee-high in that tundra. But to me it felt like we were almost skimming the surface of the water. It was a roller-coaster ride down the river. Some passengers hung on to the seat in front of them, taking a white-knuckle grip as the Twin Otter made its way down the meandering river to the abandoned Mid Canada Line radar station — Royal Canadian Air Force (RCAF) base that had become Winisk's airport.

This was the second day of a three-day tour, stopping in at all the Cree villages along the James Bay-Hudson Bay coastline between Moosonee and Manitoba. I had visited Winisk airport in a previous antediluvian year, had time to explore it in daylight and found it to be a time capsule. RCAF fire engines, service vehicles and antique half-tracks dating from the mid-1950s rusted slowly near a crumbling air control tower. A deteriorating hanger with doors that could still be closed provided shelter for planes staying overnight. It had a little hotel and was one of the rare spots to do an overnight stay along the coast of Hudson Bay.

Two years later, the hotel was gone but most of the other RCAF buildings, abandoned 20 years earlier still stood. When we landed in Winisk on a late afternoon in early October 1986, after a long flight over some of the world's most southerly tundra and permafrost, my first thought was for food. George McCormack, the Ontario Ministry of Natural Resources assistant deputy minister known as *King of the North* had food and fuel caches strategically located in his huge domain. While other people on the aircraft did the housekeeping necessary for the Twin Otter's safe storage and refueling, I plundered the food cache's large freezer for frozen pork chops, steaks and ham, a veritable feast for hungry men.

I was in for some major disappointments. Taking my carnivorous prize to one of the low-profile buildings surrounded by oil tanks, radio towers and obsolescent radar dishes that had become temporary headquarters for Polar Bear Provincial Park, I discovered there was a lot to be done before frying pans could begin to sizzle. The park had one caretaker, Mike Hunter, a former chief of the Winisk band, who had been living alone in a building that could sleep more than a dozen. Living solo, he had indulged his disdain for doing dishes and the entire dining area was littered with remnants of many previous meals. It would be an hour of cleanup before we could cook.

During that hour, one of the members of our party, an avid hunter, went out in pursuit of geese. He was wildly successful, to the delight of many—and to my complete dismay. All my delicious farmed, corn-fed and smoked meat was put aside. We sat down to a meal of snow and blue goose, a meal I considered to be barely edible. Starved, I managed to choke down enough dark, stringy goose breast to hold off starvation until breakfast.

Our location in a provincial park had some extraordinary rules. We were all armed to the teeth, literally loaded for bear. When you are on Ontario's Arctic tundra, you want to be carrying something big enough to stop (or at least slow down) half a ton of fearless predator. The park regulations required you to be suitably equipped with firearms. I packed a 12-gauge shotgun with rifled slugs for ammunition, figuring that several half-ounce balls of hot lead, applied at slightly under the speed of sound, might be enough to deter a bear. I never had to use the gun but I was happy to comply with the regulation.

There was another diktat, one I ignored. There were severe restrictions on alcohol. We were north of the 50th parallel in Ontario, deep into dry country where many reserves had banished booze. I had the foresight to include a couple bottles of rye whiskey in my luggage. For a good reason. My previous experiences in the Hudson Bay watershed taught me that residents of the area, when they saw someone toting a camera bag and a notebook, tended to avoid him like an STD. My strategy for starting a conversation became sitting down at a table with two chairs. On the tabletop I would display my spiral notebook and two glasses accompanied by large bottle of whiskey—a forty-pounder of Canadian Club. Suddenly I became as attractive as a nubile young blonde in a topless bathing suit. People simply wanted to be near me and chat me up. The most reticent of sources could become blabbermouths with the judicious application of whiskey—whether they told the truth or were feeding me a line was another question.

That evening, after the disappointing goose dinner, I sat with Winisk's former chief. While we drank, I listened to one of the most amazing stories I was ever to hear in my journalism career: his life story—that ended up with him living alone in a seldom-visited park.

Mike contracted tuberculosis (TB) as a child in a residential school on James Bay and was evacuated to a convalescent hospital for children in Toronto. Come ice-out, his father was dismayed that he wasn't back in Winisk. That triggered one of the epic journeys of Ontario history. His father, taking his whole family along, paddled back up the Winisk River to its headwaters, portaged long distances to the source of the Attiwapiskat River, which he followed downstream to the James Bay community of the same name. Then, launching his fragile craft into the dangerous, open waters of James Bay he made his way to Moosonee's railhead and connections to Toronto.

The rest of the family stayed behind, but after a long train ride Mike's father had a few days to spend with his son in the Queen Mary Hospital convalescent hospital in Weston before he had to backtrack to get home in time to set up his trap line for the winter. The visit had taken a full ice-out season. A fabulous story, an epic journey.

Mike learned English in the hospital. Later in his childhood his mother established a relationship with one of the airmen at the Royal Canadian Air Force Base-Mid-Canada Line radar station across the river from the village of Winisk. He learned to function smoothly in both cultures and eventually became chief of his village. But, he confided in me, he felt that he didn't fully belong to either culture and that people in both regarded him with suspicion. When I met him, he claimed to be quite content living by himself in park headquarters on the abandoned radar station.

I have often wondered how much of that story was verifiable, but I've had no way to check, so this is the first time I have written it. Once I had drafted it for this memoir, I picked up my phone and called the number listed for M Hunter in Peawanuck. He answered. Now 80 years old and living with all the modern conveniences just upriver from where I met him in 1986, Mike confirmed the details.

Our flight moved on to Fort Severn, the most northwesterly community in Ontario. It was relatively new as a native settlement, built about 10 years previously at the mouth of the Severn River for a band that had been living further inland and decided to move to an ancient coastal site, the original location of one of the first Hudson's Bay Company fur trading posts in the late 1600s.

Many newer houses were built on stilts, holding them above the ground. I wondered in passing how cold the floors would be in winter with the wind blowing under the building. But I had bigger fish to fry, another problem to solve. I had run out of booze. I had downed the last drop the previous night. I needed to talk to people and with just a few hours in town, I had lost my quick-start icebreaker.

So I decided to use behavioral tactics to get someone to talk to me. While the rest of my group was doing the "hail fellow well met" greeting at town center, I ignored the socialization and, as sullenly as possible, headed for the community center. I got a cup of coffee, sat at a table and took all my camera bodies and lenses out of the camera bag. Head down and totally silent, I busied myself cleaning and polishing the equipment, ignoring any activity around me and appearing as uninterested as possible, looking only at my camera gear and the floor right in front of me.

Eventually a pair of blue jeans came into my line of vision. A voice said, "What are you doing here?" I looked up, smiled, and said, "Have a seat. I'll be more than happy to answer all your questions. Then I have a few to ask you." The speaker, one of the leaders of the band, was taken aback. He was too polite to refuse. We had a good chat, although not as personal or revealing as a conversation lubricated with liquor might be.

What *was* I doing there? My primary task was to interview women who were doing Native crafts using hides donated by big game hunters in southern Ontario. Caribou and moose hide, readily available in the Hudson Bay Lowlands, was thick and tough, hard to work. The Cree craftswomen much preferred the thin skins of the white tailed deer, an animal whose range reached its northerly limit several hundred miles south of Hudson Bay.

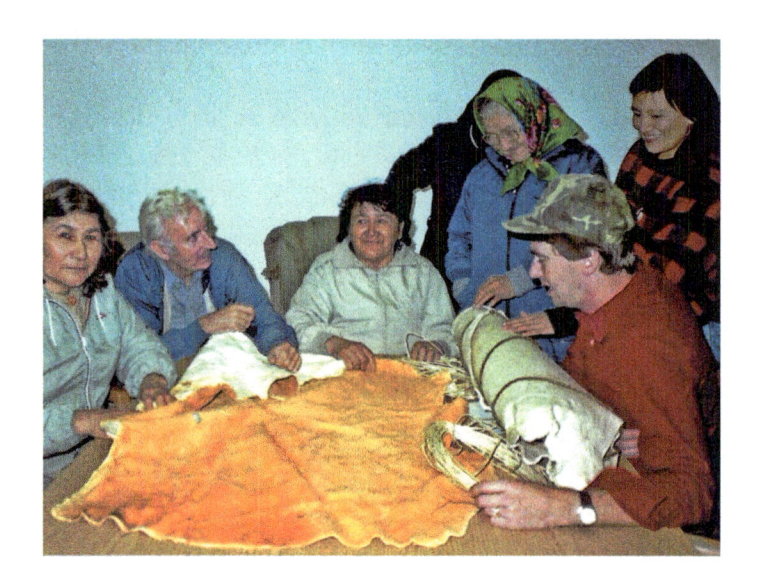

*Cree craftswomen in Fort Albany discuss the advantages of using deer hide from southern Ontario as opposed to locally available moose hide. Representatives of the Ontario Ministry of Natural Resources Moose and Deer Hide program that shipped tanned deer hides to the Hudson Bay lowlands are also in the picture.*

*The Koostachins of Fort Severn, Ontario's northernmost community, pose with some of the tools, raw materials and finished products of craft production in the Hudson Bay lowlands.*

Southern hunters have little use for the hides of the deer and moose and often leave them in the forest as food for scavengers. MNR set up collection points for the hides every late fall, rewarding hunters with an orange cap for donating a hide. Later MNR distributed the tanned hides to craftsmen and women in remote Native communities. Moose hides were used for moccasins and ceremonial drums. The more readily workable deer hides became a variety of products, many of them decorative.

My task was communications: produce stories that would encourage hunters to participate in the program. Inform the broader public about a provincial program designed to support the economy and preserve the culture of Native groups in remote communities. My first stop was at the Cree Cultural Interpretive Centre in Moose Factory, a village accessible by water taxi from Moosonee. It's a facility that exists today with a website featuring "animal carvings from wood and stone, dream catchers, tamarack birds, and moose hide gloves and moccasins." From there, we held meetings with craftswomen in every coastal community up James Bay. The Toronto accountant who handled the finances of the program was on the excursion and had an opportunity to pursue his own agenda in the meetings.

*The crew on the Moose and Deer Hide program tour load themselves into a freighter canoe that is the main transportation between Moosonee and Moose Factory, where the Cree Cultural Centre is located.*

Not being artsy in nature or a collector of souvenirs, I saw and photographed many craft items and came home empty-handed. But I twigged to the cultural nature of the program. Someone at Queen's Park was worrying about the disappearing way of life of the James and Hudson Bay communities. Some of the Cree craftswomen had the same concerns. They presented their craft-promoting efforts as an attempt to get younger women to participate in traditional cultural activities. Bull sessions with other people on the trip made it clear to me that the provincial government was doing everything it could to promote Native trap lines, so that people could live "the Old Way" without all the drudgery that the Old Way entailed.

The traditional way of life along the coast was that in winter the Cree were scattered in the interior, running trap lines and hunting. Come spring and ice-out, they would move downriver to the coast and sell their furs to the Hudson's Bay Company. They would hunt the geese that nested on the tundra. As the days got shorter, it was time to head back to the hinterland, to spend the winter in isolated camps. By 1986, the Old Way was a pretty much a thing of the past. Younger generations living year-round in permanent villages on the coast seem to have tuned out on the Old Way completely.

I deliberately posed a trick question to a young woman who was working in a band office. She told me she had been educated in southern Ontario, sent to high school in a medium-sized city. Pretending to be confused, I asked, "In the Old Way, did the people go up the river in the fall or in the spring?" Her answer, after a few seconds of thought, was, "I don't know. I'll have to ask my grandmother about that."

In Fort Severn, I had one of the more interesting interviews with a married couple engaged in crafts. She made beautiful beaded mittens and moccasins and even had a pair of gloves made from polar bear hide, which unfortunately did not fit the colossal meathooks that I have for hands. Her husband had a problem. The polar bear he had killed earlier in the year, as part of the band's annual quota of the animals, was devalued. If you looked closely at the hide, you could see a huge letter and number that someone had put on the bear's fur with Lady Clairol hair dye. Now he'd have to sell it for less than he usually got and would like to be compensated. I smiled but didn't mention that I had been involved in the tagging program that led to the blemished fur. I had accidentally discovered a connection with someone in the lowlands of Hudson Bay.

The tour ended in Fort Severn and we were to fly back to Timmins cross-country and non-stop. Someone mentioned that a former band chief was living out somewhere to the west, between Fort Severn and the Manitoba border. He didn't want to come back to town that season and preferred to live the Old Way. We decided to go looking for him. We never found his camp on the seemingly endless tundra but we did find a flock of willow ptarmigan, spotting them from the air when they took flight. Their seasonal plumage, still mainly chestnut brown, stood out against the snow-covered ground. At the urging of one of the passengers, who wanted to add a ptarmigan to the list of birds he had shot, the pilots landed the Twin Otter on an elevated beach ridge.

I had landed on the tundra before, but only in slow-moving Single Otters equipped with huge, underinflated tires. I wasn't even aware that Twin Otters with ordinary tires could be used for tundra landings. But after a couple of passes over the potential landing strip to ensure there were no projecting stones or petrified trees on the ancient beach, we landed without incident. While the hunter went out to bag his ptarmigan, I climbed out to take pictures of a Twin Otter sitting on the tundra.

*A de Havilland twin otter sits on an elevated beach ridge west of Fort Severn. This was my last tundra landing and the only one in a twin otter with regular tires.*

Then I saw the ptarmigan flush low and the hunter about to shoot. I knew I was right in line with where the birds were going to be when he pulled the trigger. Unwilling to drop to the ground and risk damaging my cameras, I turned my back to the action, trusting my heavy hooded anorak would stop any shot coming my direction. Sure enough, I was in the direct line of fire and the pellets hit, but not hard enough to penetrate the material.

This was my fourth time being in the line of fire and the third time being hit. Fortunately the only time someone was shooting at me deliberately was the time I was missed. The only time I was injured was as a teenager, when a shotgun accidentally discharged and pellets bouncing off a hard surface hit my leg and I had to dig some Number 9 shot out of my skin.

As the Twin Otter took off in a cloud of snow and ptarmigan feathers to return to home base in Timmins, I had the feeling that a chapter in my life was concluding. My days of roaming northern Ontario seemed to be coming to an end. They had been some of the most exciting in my life. There were times when I had bush planes or float planes at my disposal. I had worked on enforcement with conservation officers, tried to walk down moose in a traditional hunt, had voyageur-like canoe trips in the Arctic watershed, participated in polar bear tagging operations and sturgeon research. There were times when I carried enough firepower to stop a large predator, and I was always packing a burdensome load of camera equipment.

I was losing interest in doing the exciting things I had once desperately craved. Since I turned 40, I had already turned down one exciting-sounding assignment, an offer to tag caribou on the tundra. Rumors about the tagging procedure had the biologists using rockets to launch nets from the runners of helicopters and that there was a risk that a mis-launched net could cause problems with rotors. I had to admit to myself that I had become middle-aged and more cautious—I could find quite enough excitement in sitting behind a desk trying to manage communications when events were out of control. But a decade of adventure with *The Globe and Mail* and *Landmarks* had provided me with a lifetime's worth of vivid memories and unusual anecdotes.

I wasn't totally deskbound—yet. Five years after I returned from my last northern adventure for the Moose and Deer Hide program, a telephone call from the Ontario Native Affairs Secretariat (ONAS) gave me another kick at the can, another opportunity to wander the near-north in Algonquin Provincial Park and report on goings-on there.

In the early 1990s, the New Democratic Party government soon walked into a firestorm of bad publicity, not only in the local press but also in the Toronto media, by allowing Natives to hunt in Algonquin Provincial Park. Highway 60 was an ideal venue for road-hunting moose. The problem was compounded by lack of communication. The provincial government, responsible for setting park policy, seemed to have gone silent. By the spring of 1991, interest groups in and around the park were seething.

Native affairs had become high profile in the 1980s. The Oka crisis dominated the national news in the summer of 1990, a full-blown violent incident that involved the unsolved murder of a policeman and required the Canadian military to keep the lid on. Native issues repelled me like gun control issues—things that would eat up a lot of time and generate controversy without accomplishing much for my career or making me much money. I actually avoided writing about Natives or land claims.

My assignment came with the vaguest of instructions. I was to go into the park, talk to everyone and anyone who would talk to me about the land claim, the hunting and fishing issue and the response of the provincial government, then submit a report to communications at ONAS.

In late spring of 1991, entered the park through the East Gate in Whitney and made my way westward, eventually ending up in a donut shop in Huntsville where I talked to an official who preferred the relative anonymity of the coffee shop to having me interview him formally in his office.

*En route*, I began tracking down everyone I knew—a field biologist while actually in the field doing research, with a mirror on a stick long enough to hold above a bird`s nest to check the progress of the fledglings, the acquaintance who ran the Portage Store on Canoe lake, another who once was a park ranger and had become a lawyer in a nearby town. I sought out cottagers who had temporarily stopped worrying about imminent dismissal from the park because of environmentalist-preservationist pressure and were now worrying about being forced out by another set of challenges. I spoke to lodge and restaurant owners in nearby communities, and the owner of a canoe manufacturing and rental operation. I did random, man-in-the-street, interviews, standing on the dock at popular canoe launches. Extending that streeter program to guests at luxury lodges, I turned it into an excuse to spend a night at Deerhurst Inn. I made every effort to contact people who were involved with the politics of the park and the MNR employees who were responsible for the management of the renowned facility.

Every interview was open-ended and unstructured, starting with the promise that I would incorporate their comments (or the gist of them) into my report. At times, I felt like a lightning rod. Many people were angry, as much because they had been kept in the dark as anything else. Some people mentioned that they had been trying to get responses from Queen's Park and were being stonewalled and that the local MNR authorities seemed to be as much benighted as anyone else. I was the first person connected to any provincial agency who had asked their opinion.

On my way back home, I stopped at the Golden Lake reservation and talked to members of the band council, once again in a non-directed, open-ended fashion.

When the interviewing was done, I wrote the report, not with recommendations but as a summary of the various opinions expressed. I did try to emphasize the idea that the park has an iconic status, particularly in eastern Ontario. Anything that happens in the park quickly becomes a larger issue, punching far above its weight.

Not that I ever expected what I wrote to be heeded. I thought my pages would quickly hit the circular file. I believed I had been sent in to the park to allow people to let off some steam and give the locals a large, slow-moving messenger to shoot at. Later in the year, when the Golden Lake band and the provincial government announced they had negotiated an agreement that would prevent hunting during the time when lots of tourists were in the park, I decided I had been little more than cover for ongoing secret negotiations.

Decades later, I asked the former communications director at ONAS if that was the case. He said no, that the executive director of ONAS wanted an opinion on what was going on in the park from someone other than an MNR type and I was chosen to do the survey. When I retired, I shredded my copy of the report along with other materials that might be considered confidential.

Other than the Moose and Deer Hide tour and the one ONAS consulting project, I wrote very little about Natives. I recall doing one feature for *The Globe and Mail* on a Native who built birch bark canoes. As a communications consultant hired to promote tourism in Ontario, I familiarized myself with attractions like the Woodland Cultural Centre in Brampton and Native-oriented tours promoted mostly in Germany. What I wrote was pure tourism bumf designed to attract visitors to Ontario.

Although I wrote a monthly opinion column for the OFAH magazine and another for *Outdoor Canada* magazine, I usually avoided comment on Native issues. When self-government became an issue in the early 1990s, I dealt with it in passing, once putting a paragraph in a magazine column stating it would be no big deal if the powers of municipal self-government devolved to Native bands. This brought forth an immediate reaction from the NDP cabinet minister in charge of Native affairs. He denounced my opinion. I was surprised. I always figured cabinet ministers had better things to do with their time than engage in controversy with columnists in magazines with circulations of under 100,000. I could see no point in wasting effort in battles with fanatics and I had no particular interest in the issue, so I didn't deal with it again. When the OFAH magazine changed hands in 1992, I discontinued my outdoor writing activities, so I never had anyone asking me to look into the issue.

A water crisis in Kashechewan in 2005 changed my mind briefly. The problem got national publicity and I happened to know that the James Bay coastal village was taking its drinking water out of the river downstream of where effluent from its sewage treatment plant was being dumped into the river. CBC and the national newspapers were having a field day. The federal government seemed to be prevaricating about evacuating people and the provincial government complicating things.

The media, which have an obsession for looking for root causes or underlying reasons for things like criminality or terrorism, had an ideal opportunity to discover the real root cause for the *e coli* outbreak in the village. So I contacted the *Canadian Press* reporter covering the story and started feeding him information and the names of some contacts on water issues. Eventually he called me, wanting to quote me as an authority on water treatment issues. I refused, not only because I had no expertise in water treatment, but because my limited experience dealing with the north and with Native issues made me cynical and unwilling to engage in any public controversy relating to them.

As far as I know, one of the real reasons for the village's water problems—drinking their own diluted sewage—didn't make a big splash. Facts are next to irrelevant when dealing with some kinds of problems.

# SECTION IV
## Technology and Energy

*Buoyed up by an erbium-doped amplifier*

I acted as Director of Emergency Information for Emergency Planning Ontario when Darlington Generating Station, the last North American nuclear facility to be brought on line in the 20th century, was commissioned. I was Director of Project Development, getting the permits that allowed construction of the first utility-sized solar farm (temporarily "the world's largest") in Sarnia, Ontario early in the 21st century. Those are the outstanding milestones in my career in energy and technology.

Technology was never really my bag. But electricity is too important to be left to the private sector in Canada. Politicians take charge and meddle furiously, usually screwing up royally. The politics of electricity in Ontario drew me into the field—as a speechwriter, as an advocate for demand management and conservation, as a crisis communicator, and as someone who could write sensibly about alternative generation compared to the idealistic babble produced by ideologically driven save-the-world environmentalist writers.

Working for Northern Telecom (later Nortel) provided me a basic education in contemporary technology. My penchant for novelty attracted me to the emergent digital world in the early 1980s. While a lot of technical stuff went over my head, I got enough grounding by writing marketing literature for digital switches and technical literature on topics like erbium-doped amplifiers that I could usually manage to swim rather than sink.

# 13.
# Digital Revolution and Building Energy Management

*Writing about technology 1983-1995*

The company's vice-president, shaking with suppressed emotion, demanded, "You're from Northern Telecom, right?" I nodded, adding that I was a consultant, not an employee. He picked up the phone from his desk, shoving it towards me. The phone required two hands; it was one of the sleek new Meridian phones big enough to have both a dial pad and a string of soft (programmable) keys linking it to a digital Private Branch Exchange (PBX) which would forward calls, put them on hold, send them to voicemail, conference in other people and do numerous other esoteric or previously unheard-of things.

I prepared to duck or dodge, thinking he was going to throw the phone at me, but he simply held it out, pleading, "Get rid of this. Take it away. Give me my old phone back. I haven't done a decent day's work since they installed it. Half my calls get screwed up or lost. It's the biggest time-waster that's ever been forced on me."

Unable to help him, I sympathized and later kept my promise to mention to my boss back at Northern Telecom (NT) headquarters that some people were having problems adapting to the new technology.

It was the mid-1980s and digital technology was mind-blowingly new. Digital switching was suddenly allowing the transmission of data, text, images and sound over telephone lines. Today, if you interrupted someone watching a movie on their smartphone to inform them that "in the digital world, sound, text and images are all the same," you might get a response like, "I never thought of it that way, but it's true." In the mid-1980's most people would give you a blank look or wonder out loud about your sanity. The revolution in technology that would usher in the 21st century world was difficult to comprehend and disruptive to everyday life.

*A Northern Telecom Displayphone. One of my first writing jobs at NT was doing case studies on Displayphone. I would visit a company and write a short feature story on how the new technology was being put to use.*

I was there just as it started affecting people, the business community first. I was writing about digital technology when the leading edge commercialized device was a Displayphone, a dumb ASCII terminal hooked up to a phone line. Transmission was slow (300 bps). Speed was measured in baud rates—a unit that was left over from telegraph days—not gigabytes per second. I would travel to various locations writing up applications for NT marketing that were trying to sell Displayphones.

Only a year or so later, when sophisticated digital PBXs came into widespread use, researching the marketing applications became more interesting. I visited hotels in Toronto, distilleries in Eastern Ontario, law firms in Halifax and schools of dentistry. I wrote about the use of PBXs in digitizing dental X-rays, managing hotel guest registration and saving time for executives who could make their own long distance calls rather than wait for the company switchboard operator to place them.

It was exciting to deal with novel ideas that would become everyday commonalities. When Caller Name Display was introduced, for example, it was used in an upscale hotel at the Toronto airport to allow hotel staff to greet by name guests using telephones in the hotel. Big deal! Today, we can glance at the display screen on almost any phone we pick up to know who is calling. In the 1980s, it was new and exciting, almost magical; it impressed hotel guests who were greeted by name.

I attended telecommunications trade shows in Toronto and Montreal, which gave interesting glimpses of the future. One in Montreal had an amazing demonstration of video-teleconferencing for businesses—something that is now an everyday household reality called Skyping. Back in the 80s, it required the use of eight telephone lines to transmit voice accompanied by jittery pictures of the speakers.

The thrill of working at the leading edge of telephony wore off as the technology became both more commonplace and more sophisticated. I found NT wanted me to write literature that was highly technical and destined for an industrial audience rather than a commercial or residential one. My typical article would have a headline like "Boosting digital signals with erbium-doped amplifiers," and be published in the switching and transmission newsletter. I became less enthusiastic about working in the field. The good money was welcome. But money was never enough to keep me coming back.

I worked sporadically for NT and its successor Nortel. When the company ran into difficulties, as it often did in its death spiral, the need for freelancers to do the work of laid-off employees would arise. I would show up and find some well-paying assignments.

I did my last writing for Nortel at the time the lobby of its Brampton headquarters had huge banners announcing, "The Future is Wireless." The mid-1990s would have been an ideal time to look for a permanent niche in telecommunications writing. The future was indeed wireless and you could make a fortune promoting it. But I was still more interested in excitement and novelty than in spending my time writing explanations of why a new dialing system (10-digit) was needed for North American telephony and technical briefs on why four-and-five digit in-house dialing systems could be a bad idea if not implemented properly.

*At telecom conferences, telcos use their imagination to attract attention to themselves. This photo by Bell posed me with a guitar, not that I ever played one. It was a prop to make the photo more interesting, perhaps in the hope that I would hang on to it. Taken about 1992.*

As usual, the future was hard to predict. E-commerce on a business-to-business (B2B) level was a hot topic for my writing, identified by NT marketing staff as a potential area for growth. No one seemed to imagine that 30 years down the road, bricks-and-mortar stores would be closing and sales tax collectors would be tearing out their hair because retailing had migrated online.

Nor did anyone anticipate the dismal future of long-distance telephony, the cash cow for many telcos and a gigantic cost for many companies. One of the most ridiculous statements I put in marketing material was that digital technology held out the promise that the cost of long distance telephony would eventually fall to 10 cents a minute. Today, of course, it's basically free, with unlimited amounts of long distance included in many monthly residential bills.

Some people pooh-poohed the promising ideas NT and Nortel were promoting. Just as I was leaving the high-tech telephony field, a book entitled *Silicon Snake Oil* made a huge splash, arguing that computerization was going to change next to nothing at all. With my experience with NT, I knew the author had his head where the sun don't shine, a fact he later had to admit. But the reception of his book and the widespread publicity surrounding it were an indication of how much resentment and confusion the new technology was creating.

In retrospect, working for NT was like writing science fiction that would come true almost immediately. NT encouraged me to be an Internet early adopter, using a modem for filing stories when computer-to-computer communications was done through electronic bulletin boards and modem-to-modem telephony.

My early days writing at NT gave me the basic education I needed for writing about energy, another field in which computerization was having a pervasive impact. From the mid-1980s to the mid-1990s, energy-related topics were often near the top of my agenda. My experience at NT proved handy later at the Ministry of Energy, leading to my appointment as editor-writer of *Ontario Energy Network*, a quarterly publication promoting building energy management to the MUSH (Municipalities, Universities, Schools and Hospitals) sector.

My first project at the Ministry of Energy (MoE) was writing a 1986 booklet on generating electricity from wind power in Ontario. MoE communications needed something to send people who were demanding information on how to make their own electricity from wind power. This was an aggravating group largely made up of back-to-the land advocates, environmental fanatics and cranks nursing a grudge against Ontario Hydro.

The ministry had a few specialists who kept an eye on what was happening with wind power. They followed the latest wind technology, which included Darien wind turbines that looked like giant eggbeaters. In any serious discussion of reliable contributions of power to the provincial grid, wind power was regarded as hopeless nonsense. The province wasn't about to invest in wind. There was no MoE literature to help Ontario residents set up their own home generating stations using wind turbines.

After interviewing the ministry's specialists, writing 90 pages and submitting it for technical review, I turned in the manuscript for approval. My comment was "The frontispiece of this pamphlet needs a warning message: "Don't read this! In Ontario, the wind doesn't blow, it sucks."[42] For years after that I heard no more about wind-generated electricity.

I started a personal photo collection on wind power. From Galveston Island in Texas to Polar Bear Provincial Park on Hudson Bay, I took pictures of broken or disused wind generators, evidence of the impracticality of wind-generated electricity. Years later, I chuckled every time I saw the towering industrial wind turbine that dominated the landscape at Ashbridge's Bay in the left end of Toronto. It seemed to be always standing stock-still. I nicknamed it a "windmill *statue*," a moniker I later applied to all of its kith and kin springing up across the province.[43]

My cynicism about non-conventional energy was getting deeper while demand for writing propaganda in favor of it was growing. I continued producing bumf on renewables, literature to satisfy what was evidently an emergent demand for information about environmentally friendly electricity. Public opinion polling in the late 1980s put environment at the top of the list of people's concerns.

I rewrote a wood burning publication left over from the 1970s energy crisis. MoE experts were cynical about fireplaces for heating houses. One said the most efficient fireplace was a free-standing one built outside your house. Watch through the window as it burned. Otherwise you were losing more heat than you gained. My draft of the revised pamphlet reflected this cynicism. Before the booklet was reprinted, an NGO advocating wood burning was hired to put positive spin on the publication. The result was a cheery and positive wood burning booklet that contained some mild warnings of the dangers of open fires, soot buildup in chimneys and pyrolysis.

---

42 My copy of the pamphlet, an official one with Energy Minister Vince Kerrio's name on the cover, has been donated to the Ontario Provincial Archives and can be found in the Ron Truman fonds (collection).

43 Windmills are preponderantly nocturnal in Ontario. That's when the wind blows— as any keel boater who has drifted all day on Lake Ontario knows, he can be filled with resentment when he is trying to get to sleep at night as he listens to gusty winds set the halyards to rattling against the mast. The electricity that windmills produce at night is usually un-needed as Ontario's nukes, which produce power for up to 99 per cent of the time, can easily meet night-time demand without any help from windmills, which tend to unbalance the grid at night and put money in the pockets of windmill owners.

When MoE wanted to reach out to children, someone dreamed up a comic booklet useful for schools and hired me to write the text. It was hilarious in parts. Among the people I was told to interview was a woman who believed that after showering, you should wipe as much water as possible off your body with your hands before using a towel. That way you were saving energy by not requiring as much energy for the towel in the electric dryer. The booklet was a resounding success—among energy bureaucrats anyway. The publication was translated into French, marketed with huge posters and picked up by the federal Department of Energy for national distribution.

*One of my favorite photos from my collection of defunct windmill statues. These were in Galveston TX in 1995. My photo series includes broken and non-functioning windmills from Polar Bear Provincial Park to Hawaii. I found that old windmills were often just left to deteriorate, becoming even more of an eyesore in the fullness of time.*

Ron Truman | 153

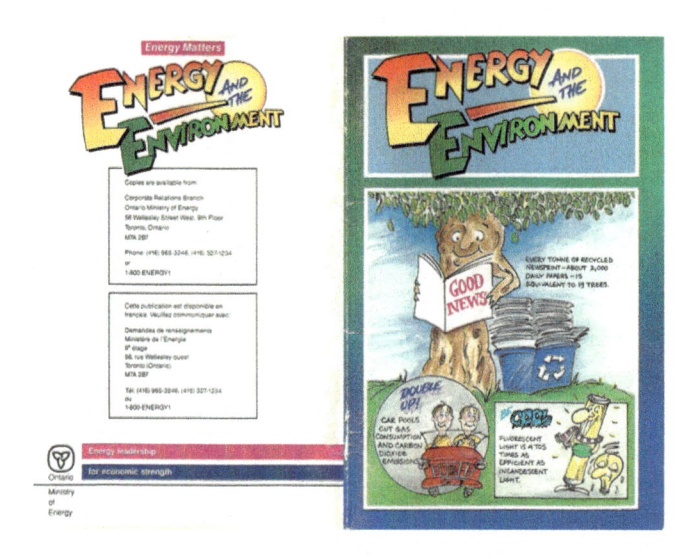

*I wrote the text for only one comic book. Energy and the Environment was distributed widely by the Ontario Ministry of Energy. Bureaucrats loved it. It was reprinted and distributed even more widely the federal Department of Energy. I have no idea of how it was received in its target market of elementary school students, but I was pleased to see large posters promoting it in the lobby at the Ministry of Energy.*

At the same time I was writing delusional material for the kind of people whose basic belief seemed to be that we should live in the dark in grass huts with dirt floors, I got a grounding in the realities of Ontario's evolving electricity policy. I wrote many keynote speeches for a series of energy ministers.

In the 1980s the province seemed to be running short of power. Ontario was in a long economic boom with steadily increasing demand for electricity. Advocates for increasing supply (i.e. building and commissioning new nuclear generating stations) organized a conference called "Running on Empty."

I wrote the minister's speech, getting introduced to the debate about energy at the upper levels of the government. One incident of note: in the weeks before the conference, rumors circulated at the MoE that Ontario Hydro executives were contemplating "flipping the switch."

This could force the province to suffer through the political ramifications of a few days of blackout. (This foreshadowed the massive blackout that happened by accident in the summer of 2003 and had a dramatic impact on that fall's election). This idea caused conniptions among senior bureaucrats at the Ministry of Energy.

Provincial politicians recognized the urgent demand for increased electricity supply in the late 1980s. Their answer to the fierce opposition to nuclear energy by the anti-nuclear crowd was a series of public conferences in the late 1980s. I was asked to write the keynote speeches for the "Energy Choices Conferences." Opposition to additional nuclear energy reached the highest levels of the ministry. One senior electricity advisor called an early draft of my Energy Choices keynote speech "one of the most blatant pieces of pro-nuclear propaganda he had ever read." [44]

Some Ministry of Energy staff regarded the opponents of nuclear energy as a bunch of hippies. They could be expected to show up unshaven (faces, armpits and legs), wearing dirty clothes, nursing babies in public and whining endlessly. I attended the Toronto conference. It was my first encounter with the herd of independent alternative energy thinkers and anti-nuclear babblers. It was almost comic how they conformed to that clichéd description.

The Energy Choices conferences had faint hope of influencing public opinion. The opponents of nukes had long since made up their minds. The media found nuclear scare stories good for selling papers, especially after events at the Three Mile Island and Chernobyl nuclear generating stations. The anti-nuke activists were good quotes and entertaining theater. Newspaper and television reporters, most of them left-leaning in politics, tended to be anti-nuclear or sympathetic to anti-nuclear points of view.

The result of public and media hostility to nukes resulted in demand management taking precedence over supply management. Policy wonks were keenly aware that controlling even the rate of growth in Ontario's demand for electricity was going to be exceptionally difficult. Ontario

---

44 The bluntness of that statement reflects the fact that senior advisors who dealt with me as a speechwriter knew that I had a thick skin. When something I wrote was unacceptable, I could be told in no uncertain terms. Instead of being offended, I took their comments as a challenge to find an alternative way to express things. They liked my cheerful willingness to rewrite until I had it right. I did it, not just for additional billing hours, but because I enjoy rewriting as much as writing.

would not be able to increase supply adequately because of political barriers.

Electricity political advisors started looking to demand management and conservation to help delay the ultimate browning out of the province.

Based on a theory referred to as Negawatts—that it was far cheaper to save a watt than to generate it—provincial energy policy encouraged, among other things, reduced used of energy in large buildings. Building operators would de-lamp until visitors had to keep one hand on the wall as they walked down gloom-filled hallways. Employees tried to organize desk locations so that work could be done with light coming through the windows. The heat was turned down to the shivering point. Proximity and motion switches saved energy by heating and lighting rooms only when there were people occupying them.

Municipal governments are major energy users. Electricity costs, along with other energy costs, are big budget items that can be managed. What the province really wanted was not to save money for local governments but to get a handle on province-wide growth in electricity demand.[45] It was a provincial priority, not a municipal one. My communications skills were needed in the provincial effort to convince its hundreds of municipalities to use free money to do energy efficiency improvements—to accept bribes to save money

A quarterly newsletter called *Ontario Energy Network* published out of the Association of Municipalities of Ontario (AMO) was my platform. It covered what had to be the dullest issue I ever worked on: building energy management in municipalities. Now there's something truly deserving of the boredom-inducing descriptor "worthwhile Canadian initiative." *Network's* purpose was to support the Municipal Energy Conservation Program (MECP) and publicize its accomplishments—as few and far between as they were. I tackled the newsletter with gusto. It offered me a regular income for nearly seven years. The program also provided me with a generous expense account accompanied with a

---

[45] No one at the MoE was naïve enough to think that you could actually reduce electricity use by municipalities. What the policy wonks wanted to do was reduce the rate of growth of electricity demand, which seemed to be completely out of control province-wide until the Rae recession began in 1990 and industrial consumption tanked.

"magic" Amex card that I could use as I pleased. I never saw the bills or was asked to account for purchases.

Working for the newsletter provided me with a fully equipped office in AMO headquarters in downtown Toronto. It allowed me to attend conferences, including the Electric Vehicles Conference in Toronto, the World Energy Conference[46] (WEC) in Montreal and AMO annual conventions. I could travel the province at will, in search of stories on small and medium-sized municipalities that were making progress in energy management.

MECP was struggling. No matter what the energy advisor did, including a province-wide dog and pony show with an energy efficiency expert, mid-sized municipalities showed little interest. As one of the MoE officials in charge of promoting the program said, shaking his head at the incredulity of the situation, "We can't bribe (municipalities), actually giving them the two dollars they need to invest so they can save a dollar every year for the next 20 years."

At AMO, MECP began falling apart. The program's energy efficiency technical expert departed. The policy advisor fled to greener pastures in the west. The replacement advisor didn't seem to have a clue about the task, planning to take the money that was supposed to be used for bribing municipalities to invest in energy retrofits for city halls and use the funds to buy T-bills, hoping the ministry would be happy to get back more money than they gave the program in the first place. Wiser heads prevailed and the major effort put forward by the program that year was a funny-money casino night at the AMO annual conference. All that

---

[46] At the 1989 Montreal World Energy Congress (WEC), I was curious about why France had been able to continue to build a network of nuclear generating stations despite the election of François Mitterrand's anti-nuclear socialist-communist government. In a one-on-one interview with the director general of Électricité de France, I asked the English-speaking official how he made progress after the election of a leftist government whose election promises included the stopping of building of nukes. His answer was humorous. He said he was building a nuclear generating station at the time of the election. He stopped, fulfilling the new government's promise. It was a matter of downing tools and walking away, leaving the uncompleted station to decay. Then he said, "I moved to a new location and built a new generating station. And I built yet another nuclear generating station every year for the next 10 years. France does not have a problem with electricity supply."

casino event accomplished was attracting politicians to come to a room where some MECP information was available.

Eventually a new AMO executive director informed MoE that all links with the energy program were being severed. The simple and blunt message was: GET OUT. The energy policy advisor stayed with AMO as a personal assistant to the executive director. I suspected the newsletter would continue. Municipal energy management was a high priority at MoE.[47] After all, the province had more than 600 municipalities. They used a lot of energy. It was a huge break for my career when my contact at MoE asked me to find a new municipal partner for MECP—a daunting task.

Setting out to visit both municipalities and provincial municipal organizations, I looked for answers to MECP's failure and searched for possible partners for a revived program. I concluded that elected politicians preferred to invest time in projects that led to ribbon cuttings. New insulation, dimmer hallways, building automation systems, low-emissivity ceilings and water-saving urinals didn't fit the bill. It's hard to cut a ribbon on an innovation in deprivation. I even sought out elected municipal politicians reputed to be smarter than the average bear. My efforts to educate them on the importance of energy to both the economy and environment of the province were met with blank looks or indifference.

The administrators of smaller municipalities had enough irons in the fire; they didn't need to add projects that would not get them accolades from their elected bosses. If a municipality was big enough to be run on a businesslike basis, it was probably already taking advantage of MECP. The provincial government, on the other hand, recognized the importance of

---

47  When I visited Thunder Bay, the minister of energy had me met and picked up at the airport. The minister gave me a personal half-day introductory tour of efficiency efforts in the city. I was impressed with how important my little newsletter was considered to be in achieving Ontario's energy goals. That tour of Thunder Bay was one of my longest times with a minister, who usually associate only with their own advisors.

energy to the economy [48] and looked to the municipal sector as part of their efforts to get a handle on problems with out-of-control growth in demand for electricity.

My experience with the Association of Ontario Municipalities is an illustration of the failure of elected officials in the province to appreciate the role that electricity supply plays in the provincial economy and future.

I saw the municipal energy management problem as fairly basic. Local politicians can get their picture in the paper cutting the ribbon to open new arenas or swimming pools. But there's no ribbon-cutting ceremony when a low-emissivity ceiling is installed. You can't even see the energy-saving gizmo; it's way, way up there. With no major cost crisis and no ideological drive (environmentalism focused on energy) to spur the energy conservation program on, it failed to gain favor with municipal politicians.

Municipalities also resisted because energy conservation in buildings was becoming high-tech, with computer-based building energy management systems getting more important. It was harder to explain to people, a steep learning curve. Resistance to computerization, something that is almost non-existent today, ran strong in the late 80s and early 90s.[49]

I covered the southern portion of the province from Sarnia to Cornwall in my search. The response was underwhelming. The lack of enthusiasm sometimes surprised and dismayed me. I dragged my supervisor to St. Jacob's for a meeting with the executive of the municipal association of chief administrative officers (CAOs). After interviewing some CAOs who were professional engineers and seemed to twig to the importance of the energy-and-cost saving program, I thought the CAOs

---

48 At the provincially sponsored Energy Choices Conference in 1988 Senator Michael Kirby warned that people in Ontario expect the lights to go on when they flick the wall switch. If the lights ever fail to come on because we don't have enough electricity "they will seek out whoever is responsible and punish them severely."

49 Municipalities tended to resist innovative technology. My favourite example involves fax machines. I had a meeting in a city east of Toronto and had faxed some advance documents to my contact. When I arrived, he did not have the faxed material. There was a problem. The municipality had a modern, glassy building with soaring atria and high-speed elevators but only one fax machine. They turned the fax off overnight so people would not be able to communicate with them when they were not there. Talk about not getting the idea.

association might be the way to go. A partnership with CAOs would give us an in with the top official in every sizeable municipality. It was a complete waste of a dog-and-pony show. Most of the executive did not seem to even be paying attention to our presentation. I was disgusted.

Eventually the search took me to the North York offices of the Ontario Recreation Facilities Association (ORFA), an association of arena managers, the kind of people often disparaged as rink rats and Zamboni drivers.

ORFA had become the most professional of organizations. Why? Because there *is* something that concentrates the mind more wonderfully than the prospect of hanging. That is the possibility of having to fix a big hole in your work—at center ice while a dozen National Hockey League players, two linesmen and a referee chomp at the bit and half the country watches on television waiting for the Stanley Cup Playoffs to resume. Many of us can remember seeing an arena manager or icemaker with a fire extinguisher patching a hole in the ice to allow the game to continue. A good measure of ORFA's success is that many of us can't remember the last time we saw it because it was so long ago.

Arena managers face some of the most intractable problems in building energy management. The ice must stay frozen solid and the players cool while the spectators expect to stay comfortably warm. Lights are focused on the ice surface, adding heat, especially when the candlepower is ramped up to permit color telecasting of games. Add to this the fact that outside air (often warm in spring and fall) must be introduced into a huge building and you have a set of conflicting energy demands that is mind-boggling.

ORFA had built itself from the ground up to train its members—from the operators of tiny municipal arenas to icemakers in National Hockey League venues—to make and maintain good ice. An association of practitioners, they developed no-nonsense certification and training programs. ORFA ran a full-scale summer training program at the University of Guelph each summer, published an informative magazine supported by advertising, maintained a library of up-to-date information and held regular local meetings in every part of the province. This was a dream come true for someone peddling municipal energy management.

ORFA members also knew the importance of energy management as a cost-controlling measure. Many of them ran municipal arenas and had restricted budgets. About the only expense they were allowed to manage was the cost of energy consumption. The slightest increase in the price of electricity had dramatic effects on their entire budget.

Unfortunately, ORFA, unlike most Ontario municipal organizations, had never attempted to put a liplock on the provincial government teat. The organization was not only hugely successful, it was self-sufficient. Some of the executive were not sure they wanted to take grants from the provincial government. Eventually, with the support of the organization's executive director John Milton, ORFA agreed to take the king's shilling and become a partner in energy management.

The next step was to reach out to utilities, including Ontario Hydro and local municipal electrics, municipal politicians and other interest groups to build momentum once MECP had a primary partner in ORFA. The vehicle for support-building chosen by Ministry of Energy program directors was a charrette, a pre-Internet vehicle for creating a consensus over a short period of time.

The basic idea of the charrette is to define a problem and invite about 100 people to a one-day brainstorming session to find possible solutions, then establish an action agenda. It appealed to energy policy wonks because charretting had been successful in getting the Deep Lake Water Cooling project off the ground in Toronto. That electricity-saving project was just a pie-in-the-sky idea until a charrette created an action plan that eventually led to an efficient, lower-cost cooling system for downtown Toronto buildings.

The charrette leader had to be a writer, and a fast one. The 100 people in attendance, broken into sub-groups, would analyze a component of the problem and submit their reports to a leader, who would, in the course of a lunch break, summarize those reports and later present them to a plenary session for discussion and establishment of action items. The real trick was the final report, which had to appear only a few days later, when the discussions were fresh in the participants' minds.

I was selected to organize and run the charrette. I knew from the get-go what the final report would say. For my purposes the whole day of talking and sub-groups and reports was for getting flavor for my final report and people to attribute quotes to. We chose a city hall in a municipality north of Toronto to hold the charrette and had excellent participation. After the day of conferencing, I took all the material and shaped it into an action agenda, a list of small steps that could be taken to move in the direction of our overall goal, that of reducing municipal demand for electricity.

Every attendee got a copy of the report, so he or she had something concrete and specific to suggest at his or her place of work. Then we devoted an issue of *Network* to the charrette. Then we waited for something to happen. I didn't expect a groundswell of new enthusiasts. We didn't get one.

ORFA members who attended the charrette endorsed the idea of selecting one person in a municipality to champion the cause of energy management. Usually, because ORFA members managed the most energy-intensive buildings, that would be one of theirs. The organization developed a recognition program for its members and a first-rate training course in energy management that they integrated with their ice-making program held every summer in Guelph. This became the best-ever initiative in energy management in my field. I stayed on as *Network* editor until the mid-1990s when the provincial grants that paid my fees were no longer forthcoming.

In retrospect, although technical subjects weren't always thrilling, I was assisting at the early stages of the digital revolution and playing a part in effective implementation of reasonable energy-saving measures. Technology was one of the fields in which I had history on my side. It wasn't a guaranteed loser the way my efforts to defend hunting, the fur industry or freedom had been.

# 14.
# Rent-seeking in the Sun

*Permits for the world's biggest solar farm and other energy scams*

I had been out of the energy field for 10 years when I got an unexpected job offer. From a "green" corporation in the private sector, no less—a type of business I had never worked for.

A California-based company was planning the world's biggest solar farm in the intense sunshine of southwestern Ontario—10 acres of photovoltaic panels generating 40 megawatts (MW) of clean, carbon-free and nuclear-free electricity. It was a multimillion-dollar project that reeked of environmental enthrallment. The project was greener than grass, as Christ-like as composting, saintlier than Suzuki… What was I doing as their Director of Project Development? Reputed to be a cynical, pro-nuclear realist about energy, I was no crunchy granola environmentalist idealist.

I gave little thought to solar photovoltaics before I joined the corporation.[50] Since then I wondered how badly I fit in. The corporation's organizational culture was unlike anything I had encountered in the past.

---

50 Much of my information on solar photovoltaics (as opposed to passive solar) came from doing a news story on the Darwin-Adelaide solar car race in 1999, focussing on a Canadian entry from Queen's University that placed second. At that time, I believed that solar photovoltaic cells never produced as much energy as it took to manufacture them—evaluated over their full life cycle, they were a net energy loss even in the sunburnt country of Australia.

Wildly different. There were times when I thought I had been teleported into a simulation of the popular situation comedy *The Big Bang Theory*, a television show teeming with nerds, girlymen and narcissistic females.

The company had a real-life version of the sitcom's engineer, Howard Wolowitz. He was a self-promoting beta-male who radiated low self-esteem, constantly sought the spotlight, brazenly hit on women, bragged about his sexual successes and brashly rambled from mistake to misstep to *faux pas*. We also had a socially inept prodigy, a man so introverted he had to be dragged to meet cabinet ministers and was almost completely tongue-tied once he was face-to-face. The company had a genuine genius who dreamed big. He was planning to build enormous solar farms not only in North America, but also all over Europe—wherever progressive or socialist governments were irresponsible and inane enough to subsidize them. I sometimes wondered if he, like Sheldon on *Big Bang*, fantasized about winning a Nobel Prize. We even had an equivalent to the sitcom's astronomer Raj—a senior executive from the Indian sub-continent—a man who had successfully completed energy developments all over the world.

A few of the people involved in the corporation had experience that might be relevant to the task. Others had none. Some had legitimate engineering degrees from the most impressive of US schools. Others, passing as knowledgeable professionals, had "studies" degrees[51] from universities that would graduate a potted plant, or even the pot itself.

The human resources people, the legal staff and the technical staff appeared to be legitimate. I had my doubts about the communications types, as personable as they were. Communications staffers often have erratic and peculiar pasts. A number of the women were very, very good looking; some of them could be relied on to keep day-to-day business on track. The company got away with much of the inexperience because the solar farm was a genuine first. It was destined to be one of the world's first utility-size solar farms.

---

51 To me, any degree in a science-related field that contains the word "studies" is suspect. A degree in anatomy is one thing. A degree in anatomy studies might indicate nothing more challenging or educational than four years of examining Playboy and Penthouse centrefolds with a magnifying glass.

The 40 MW solar farm got built as an 80 MW project, twice as large as originally proposed. Short term impact: it was, briefly, the "World's Largest Solar Farm,"[52] letting Ontario politicians temporarily spout off about "global environmental leadership." Long term impacts: the electricity bill that Ontario ratepayers will be footing until around 2030 (at an outrageous 42 cents a kwh) will be twice as big as originally projected; any hopes for substantial long-term job creation were ephemeral; and almost 100 acres of Canada's most fertile soil (Class A farmland) had been removed from food production. A bad bargain for transitory bragging rights.

*Construction began on the Sarnia solar farm in 2008. I am shown standing beside the first solar panel to be installed. The farm eventually became the largest in the world. Another company later purchased OptiSolar and all the original panels were torn out, sold in the Peterborough area and replaced with a different type of photovoltaic panel and base.*

And I—an environmentalist cynic—also came to a bad end, which raises the question: Why did I get the phone call, out of the blue, from the corporation asking me to help out with communications—dealing with the public, the media and local governments?

---

52 It actually became the world's largest in September 2010, when Enbridge bought it and expanded it to 80 MW.

Ron Truman | 165

Three reasons come to mind. One, I had a background going back more than 20 years in electricity, renewable energy, demand management and energy conservation. Two, unlike many gullible, starry-eyed and utopian communicators in the business of promoting alternative energy, I was grounded in the realities of Ontario energy policy. Three, Ontario was departing from its normal approach of relying on nuclear, coal-fired and hydraulic electricity generation stations for its electricity supply. There was an emerging, unprecedented emphasis on green energy that was going to culminate in the Green Energy and Green Economy Act, 2009 (GEA). Communicators with experience dealing with energy supply issues were needed.

There is an important back-story to the 21$^{st}$ century reorientation of Ontario electricity policy under the Liberal Party of Ontario. From 1990 to 2003, the years the Liberals were out of power, very little was heard about green or alternative generation of electricity. The New Democratic Party, in power in the early 1990s, concentrated on demand management, not supply increases.[53] When the Progressive Conservative party took over from 1995-2003, green energy supply was not a priority.

In fact, green energy wasn't even known by that name. Alternative generation was called Non-Utility Generation (NUG).[54] It was small potatoes. One MoE advisor said NUGs were a sop to "bored dentists with money to burn looking for excitement by investing in micro hydro installations."

Ontario Hydro had done a thorough job of developing the province's hydraulic (water) resources, but there were some peripheral sources that remained untapped and old dams that had fallen out of use. There were isolated incidences of facilities with high demand for both heat and electricity investing in natural gas-powered engines that they would use for cogeneration, meeting their electricity requirements off-grid. Some northern mills would burn waste material to generate electricity. A few

---

53 The NDP was anti-nuclear and made an issue of environmental damage done by energy use. The question of creating large amounts of new electricity supply was moot during their time in power, as the recession that accompanied their term of office ensured that existing electricity supply would meet demand.

54 Non-utility generation is probably a better name as nuclear and hydraulic generators produce no carbon dioxide and are thus "green."

landfill sites generated electricity by burning the flammable gases generated by the moldering garbage.

A more concerted NUG funding effort was provided by the Ontario Energy Corporation (OEC). OEC was a public teat created with money the province had somehow managed not to lose when it sold a 25 per cent interest in the oil company Suncor. OEC put major efforts into getting Native bands to develop hydraulic resources on reserve lands.

Why the sudden change after 2003, when the Liberals regained power? My explanation is that the Liberals had been traumatized by their totally unexpected defeat in 1990. One of the wedge issues in the 1990 election was the completion of Darlington Generating Station. The anti-nuclear crowd, led by Greenpeace, not known for shyness or reluctance to do public theater, was prominent among the protestors. Demonstrators harassed the Liberal premier in the September 1990 election, showing up at almost every event to attempt to embarrass him. I believe the Ontario Liberal Party has been gun-shy about nukes ever since. They have taken to heart political advice to "hug the tree-huggers."[55]

Fast forward to the 21$^{st}$ century. Once the Liberals won a majority after 13 long years in the wilderness, history began threatening to regurgitate. The Liberals made election promises in 2003 that included one dangerous greenie-pacifying plank—to close the province's coal-fired generating stations by 2007. They had committed themselves to an impossible timeline.[56] When it became obvious that there was no hope of closing the coal-powered stations on time, the Liberals feared they were going to be hammered from the left in the 2007 election. They have failed to keep their energy promises.

---

55 The major published analysis of the 1990 Ontario election, *Not Without Cause*, by Georgette Gagnon and Dan Rath, devotes more than 50 pages to a chapter on the protestors who pursued the Liberal premier "like an angry mob of bill collectors."

56 The promise was unrealistic, as detached from the reality of energy supply as the idea that renewable energy could become the only source of energy for the province. The idealists wished, as hard as they possibly, possibly could, for a world powered by tiny generators cleverly concealed in tinkling brooks, photovoltaic panels activated by healing sunshine, gentle breezes setting picturesque windmills awhirl, and the CO2-free spontaneous combustion of unicorn farts. Anything but nukes or coal.

The Renewable Energy Standard Offer Program (RESOP) legislation was rolled out just in time. In the words of the 2006 news release announcing it, RESOP[57] was "a bold new step that will *allow hundreds of small, local, renewable energy producers* (my italics) to get into the energy market."[58] At the heart of the program was a fixed price to the generator for power supplied. The fixed price was generous. In some cases, RESOP would pay up to 82 cents a kwh for electricity the local utility would sell for eight cents.

RESOP addressed a real and pressing need—and a political necessity. I saw it as designed to help keep raucous anti-nuclear and anti-coal activists happily preoccupied with building and running miniscule electricity-generating installations. They would be anticipating 20 years of cashing generous checks for intermittent power production. They would be busy patting themselves on the back for walking the talk of being green. Most important, they wouldn't have the time or incentive to interfere with the re-election of the governing Liberals at Queen's Park in 2007.

As the 2007 election approached, the Ontario Power Authority (OPA) was about to announce the first projects to be funded by RESOP. My phone rang. The company that called was anything but one of the "small, local, renewable energy producers" mentioned in the initial news release. It was a Canadian subsidiary of a large, vertically integrated California corporation named OptiSolar.

One of the first things the OptiSolar representative explained to me was how a loophole in the legislation allowed international corporations to participate in a renewable energy program ostensibly designed for community organizations and diminutive collectives. RESOP limited the size of each solar installation to 10MW. The corporation was doing an end run by building contiguous 10MW solar farms. Put a number of 10 MW solar farms side-by-side and end-to-end, you had enough solar farm in one location to make construction feasible—economy of scale.

---

57 Sometimes referred to as SOP (Standard Offer Program).

58 The stated purpose of SOP was "to ease the strain on Ontario's electricity system, reduce air pollution, promote reliability, protect the environment and create new, high-skill jobs." The presence at the news conference of "world-renowned scientist" Dr. David Suzuki—media darling of Ontario leftists—suggests another agenda.

OptiSolar planned to manufacture photovoltaic panels in California and install them in Ontario, collecting $0.42 for every kilowatt hour of electricity they generated over 20 years. The first solar farm was going to be 40 MW. The 20-year bill for Ontario ratepayers would be almost $20 million for the approximately 45 million kwh of electricity it could be expected to generate. That same amount of electricity, if bought from the provincial grid by a householder at $0.08 @ kwh would cost in the vicinity of $3.5 million. A good deal for the corporation; a ridiculous deal for the province and for Ontario ratepayers.[59]

Although I found it distasteful to be exploiting a loophole, even a gap in a naïve green energy initiative of the Liberal government, I agreed to get involved. Four years of under-employment, a result of Queen's Park being inundated post-2003 with consultants who had worked for the recently defeated Liberal government in Ottawa left me anxious for work.[60]

At first, I was an independent communications consultant working for OptiSolar. I assisted in the public announcement of the plans to build the world's largest solar farm in Ontario, part of OptiSolar's plans to "jump out of the bushes" with a surprise revelation of ambitious plans. That was followed up with town hall meetings informing the local communities of OptiSolar's plans for its first three solar farms.

After a recruiting visit to the company's headquarters in California, I shut down my own business to sign a contract with OptiSolar. All seemed propitious. OptiSolar developed and manufactured its own thin-film solar panels[61] at its home base in California. They bought a humungous

---

59 If 1000 MW of solar farms were built and put into operation, the Ontario taxpayers would face an energy bill of approximately half a billion dollars over 20 years to pay for the electricity they would generate.

60 Anyone who has read Lewis Namier's *The Structure of Politics at the Accession of George III* recognizes this phenomenon is not one exhibited exclusively by Ontario's liberals. Time out of mind, the foundation of all politics has been patrimony, patronage and favouritism. Political DNA.

61 Demand for silicon was at an all-time high in 2007 and the cost of solar-grade silicon was soaring. A thin-film approach to manufacturing panels would allow the manufacture of more panels using less silicon, thus saving money for the solar company and improving the return on investment.

abandoned US air force facility in Sacramento to scale up for mass production of panels. The company was securing a large land base for installations both in Ontario and in the US Sunbelt states.[62] The corporation had money coming out its ears. Venture capitalists were pouring money into the operation.

For the first time in my communications career,[63] I became an employee rather than a self-employed contractor. I became Director of Project Development for the Canadian subsidiary. Part of my job was to develop strategy for keeping the community informed and pacified, produce newsletters, news releases and website updates.

I was to deal with the municipalities and get the major permits needed for construction of a number of solar farms. I spent much of the summer of 2007 working on a comprehensive public document on the potential environmental impact of the Sarnia solar farm. I would attend council meetings and committee meetings dealing with permits.

Zoning could be challenging, as southwestern Ontario included some of the province's best farmland. Sarnia would be the site of the first solar installation because the municipality had re-zoned a substantial acreage in its southeast corner from agricultural to industrial land.[64] Because the city had taken the first step by rezoning, getting the permits would be much easier. Land in other municipalities where the corporation planned to build would present greater zoning and permitting challenges.

I also was asked to keep an eye on the provincial government and its evolving attitude towards solar energy. At first the Ministry of Energy seemed to ignore us—our Queen's Park news conference announcing our project was approved only hours in advance. A few months later, in the heat of an election, the idea of having the "world's largest" solar

---

62 Solar energy requires extensive acreage to generate enough electricity to serve the needs of even a few hundred houses.

63 In 1989 I had signed a contract with the provincial government. I became a writing coordinator at the Ministry of Energy. It was a matter of weeks before I discovered that I much preferred to be a self-employed contract writer and resigned the position.

64 The re-zoning was a component of an attempt to attract a large automotive company to start manufacturing on the site. That would have created thousands of jobs in the Sarnia area. A solar farm would create a few hundred jobs during construction and a handful of long-term jobs maintaining the farm.

farm in Sarnia seemed to have greater appeal. OptiSolar's plans were prominently played up on the premier's webpage in the fall of 2007. Solar energy, despite its expense and limited productivity in terms of meeting Ontario's electricity demand, had the unqualified blessing of the provincial government.

Things didn't work out so well when the voters in Sarnia-Lambton went to the polls. The provincial riding was not only future home to a solar farm producing 40MW but also the location of a coal generating station producing nearly 2GW of electricity and a significant number of local jobs. It was slated to close.[65] The Liberal incumbent in Sarnia-Lambton—a provincial cabinet minister—lost the election. It was a substantial loss. She got 6,000 fewer votes than she had received in the previous election.

I organized a meeting with the Progressive Conservative member of the provincial parliament who won the election, filling him in on our plans. He listened politely, but I had no further contact with him. I continued to monitor relations with the provincial government. Eventually my responsibilities included being the point of contact between OptiSolar and the archaeological surveys that had to be approved by the Ministry of Culture, the contact for relations with municipal-provincial conservation authorities and the organizations that would organize the replanting of vegetation with plants native to the short-grass prairie that had once predominated in the Sarnia area.

I knew from the get-go that public relations and project development weren't going to be easy. There would be mistakes and unforced errors. We were groping our way through something that had never been done before in Canada. But I was astounded by some of the missteps.

One of the first involved pipelines. When I saw the Sarnia solar farm site for the first time, I noticed a wide swath of land clearly marked as an easement for buried pipelines—part of the transportation system for raw materials and finished product to and from petrochemical industries visible to the west of the site. I was puzzled, figuring nobody could

---

65 The Lambton Generating Station produced approximately 50 times as much electricity as the 40 MW solar farm. Far more jobs as well—solar farms are not labour-intensive operations compared to coal-fired plants.

possibly overlook the fact that you could not install any kind of structure over buried pipelines. Farmers were growing wheat and soybeans on the easement. Easily removed annual crops covering the land could be dug up and discarded if an urgent repair was needed to a pipeline. Digging up hundreds of solar panels on concrete bases along with their accompanying wiring was a different matter.

I didn't mention the pipeline issue at OptiSolar until the first draft plans for erecting solar panels arrived. I noticed that the pipeline easements had been slated as areas for construction. I pointed out you can't build there. The existence of the easements stunned some of the senior executives, who soon found out that I was correct. Of the hundred acres of land they had expected to build on, a significant number of acres were not useable. An expensive oversight and one for which there seems to have been no recourse. Look on Google Earth at the site of the solar farm today and you will see a wide swath of unused land running east to west near the top of the farm.

Flooding had been overlooked. The Sarnia area is prairie, flat as a pancake, ideal for fields of solar panel installations. It also makes flood plains expansive as a sudden surfeit of water will spread far and wide. Water and electricity are usually kept apart—it is, for example, not advisable when breakfasting in the bath to let your electric toaster teeter on the edge of the tub. Yet solar panels were slated to be installed over an area that had not been properly evaluated for flood risk. It was a potentially shocking oversight.

The lack of basic geographical knowledge, ignorance of what a pipeline sign denoted, and absence of common sense on the part of company executives was obvious in other ways. When exploring for new sites near Windsor they were puzzled by the number of abandoned mine heads they found. They were surprised to learn from me the briny history of the area—famously home of Windsor Salt. They were astounded that the Ontario government maintained a library and database in London to provide guidance and regulation on how land once used for salt mining could be used in the future.

People issues were even more challenging than geographical issues for OptiSolar. The public had a variety of reactions to the solar farm proposals. Municipal politicians and staff seemed to come onside easily.

In Sarnia there was some discontent on the part of city planners about turning over 100 acres of land to a use that was not going to create jobs like a traditional manufacturing industry would. Media support varied from intrigued to supportive. The general public, thoroughly brainwashed by green propaganda at that time, seemed to be generally favorable, even enthusiastic.

It was the denizens of dump lands—people who had been living near a recently closed major municipal landfill site—who did much to make life difficult for OptiSolar. You would think these local Sarnia residents, who had put up with years of garbage truck traffic, dirt, and noise living next door to a landfill would be delighted. The new use for 100 acres of land just west of the artificial hills of the closed dump would be relatively benign. The solar farm would be low in vehicular traffic, quiet, and passive in nature. It would actually ease existing seasonal annoyances of drifting soil and snow.

Town hall meetings in all three communities—Sarnia, Tilbury and Petrolia—gave neighbors and the public a chance to react.

In Tilbury, the solar farm was in an industrial area separated by Highway 401 from the residential part of town. There seemed to be little opposition. In Petrolia, a town with a long energy history, objections were minimal at the meeting. When we had our feet wet and were more satisfied with our presentation, we held the town hall meeting in Sarnia. That was the first opportunity for the people who lived within a mile or so of the old dump to express their opinions. They took that opportunity at a well-attended meeting in the auditorium of a local arena.

Cross-referencing the names and addresses on the sign-in sheet with the objectors during the question-and-answer session at the meeting, I learned where the most vociferous opponents lived. Almost all near the old landfill site. In subsequent meetings, it became obvious that living near the dump had encouraged the neighbors to become organized.

Initially the neighbors demanded that OptiSolar guarantee their property values. They didn't want to see the value of their homes negatively affected by the presence of a solar farm. When no guarantee was given, relations with the neighbors took a turn for the worse. A substantial group of neighbors showed up at the Sarnia council meeting that approved the major permits for the farm.

They later chipped in about $25 each to cover the cost of an appeal to Ontario Municipal Board.[66] The OMB had the power to review the Sarnia permit and revoke it, stopping the construction of the solar farm. Even though a large group helped pay the fee for the appeal, only one person could sign it. They chose one of the neighbors who had been married to a lawyer.

We implemented pacification measures. It was nominally my job to handle relations with the neighbors, visiting them to assess their situations and view of the solar farm. I tried to establish what kind of screen planting would satisfy their desire not to see the solar farm.

Screen plantings were basically all they were offered by OptiSolar. The plantings were both costly and valuable. This was expensive custom landscaping that would improve the value of any property. The process went along without major surprises until I discovered that one of the people living in the southeast corner of the proposed solar farm had been using a pond near her property. That pond was going to be fenced into the solar farm, preventing any further use of it by her grandchildren.

I reported that she coveted that adjacent property. I forgot about it until the day I was told to make an appointment to visit her. My instructions were to give her no reason for the visit—just secure a time when OptiSolar could visit. I went along to the meeting, where the OptiSolar executive presented her with fully prepared legal documents deeding over the pond and surrounding land. It was a complete surprise (to me anyway). I wondered (after suppressing my conflicting desires to flip my biscuit or roll on the floor laughing at the optics of the situation) if the OptiSolar executive was playing King of the Dumplands, presenting a surprise boon to one of the peasants who lived nearby.

The homeowner looked at the documents. Without missing a beat she demanded several thousand dollars for landscaping the gift property. OptiSolar executives seemed surprised when other neighbors did not appreciate one of homeowners being singled out for special benefits and began demanding more for themselves. Things got even worse when it

---

66 The Ontario Municipal Board (OMB) is an independent, quasi-judicial, administrative tribunal responsible for handling appeals of land-use planning disputes and municipal matters. It had the power to stop construction. Any withdrawal of the appeal would end the hopes of the neighbours for a hearing in front of the board.

turned out that the homeowner who got the extra property was the signatory of the OMB appeal. She was the only participant who had the right to withdraw the appeal. She did exactly that. Her withdrawal of the OMB appeal allowed construction to begin on the solar farm.[67]

In subsequent weeks, more consequences came in as the neighbors became increasingly restive. One of the more interesting results was a challenge to a technical study supposedly proving that the solar farm was (unlike windmills) completely benign. OptiSolar's reflections study minimized the impact that reflected light from the solar panels would have on vehicles travelling nearby roads or shining reflected light into nearby homes. Instead of having the study done by qualified people, one of OptiSolar's executives did the math, physics and optics. He would not allow internal company challenges to its accuracy. When OptiSolar set up dummy panels, one of the neighborhood residents tested the validity of the study by driving past the panels when the sun was at a low angle in the morning. He painted marks on the road indicating the locations at which light reflected from the panels would affect drivers on the road. The study's conclusions, along with the company's credibility, were cast into doubt.

Neighbor relations had been set back. Any progress I had made was wiped out. I was blamed for it, but it wasn't failure in neighbor relations that led to the end of my career in photovoltaics. As much as anything it was relations with the province. There was a crisis triggered by a brief moment of OPA sanity in Ontario's headlong rush to bankruptcy, de-industrialization and have-not province status with reckless spending on renewable energy.

There was a renewable energy gold rush going on in the spring of 2008, with numerous large corporations frantically seeking contracts to build solar farms that would sell electricity for 20 years at an outrageous price of $0.42 @ kwh.

In early 2008, there were clear indications the OPA was having misgivings about the potential aggregate cost of solar electricity. They began delaying the approval of contracts that should have gone through swiftly.

---

[67] It has always seemed to me to be an odd coincidence that the landowner who got the pond was the only one who could withdraw the OMB appeal.

Ron Truman | 175

That was a clear indication to me the OPA was coming to its senses and putting a stop to the greed-fueled fervor.

Since a meeting at the Ministry of Energy in December 2007, I had been cautioning my corporation that the provincial government was getting antsy about the titanic financial commitment they were making to solar energy. In that meeting I believed I could see from the bureaucrats' body language[68] they were suddenly realizing that the province was going to face a colossal bill for a smidgen of electricity and a paltry number of long-term jobs.[69]

In 2008, OptiSolar was talking about getting contracts for a gigawatt (GW = 1000 MW) of solar installations. Ontario's electricity planners projected bringing only a few dozen megawatts of solar online by 2025. In fact the OPA projected only 1000 MW of electricity from all renewable sources. We were proposing to provide that amount on our own. While I was not directly involved in seeking OPA contracts for OptiSolar,[70] I was appalled by the frantic race for more and more and more contracts.

RON TRUMAN
Director
Project Development

OPTISOLAR FARMS CANADA
*Growing Clean Energy*

416 926 1616
rtruman@optisolar.com
www.optisolarfarms.ca

In mid-May, the OPA made an announcement clamping down on the standard offer program. Existing projects could continue, but there were

---

68 I knew several of the bureaucrats at the meeting from my decade of consulting at the ministry. By 2007, they were in more senior positions.

69 From following the media clippings originating in Europe, I was getting the first hints that Germany and Spain were having second thoughts, if not regrets, for their headlong rush into wind and solar.

70 The search for contracts only involved me when I was asked to scout an area for its suitability for solar farms. Other people in the company identified transformers with unused capacity that made them suitable for solar energy contracts and submitted the applications.

new restrictions on use of transformer capacity—no company could have more than 10MW on any one transformer. Furthermore, no company could have more than 50MW under development. It was intended to take the wind out of the blades and cast an umbra over the photovoltaic panels of the renewable energy industry. OptiSolar, with its desire for a gigawatt (GW) of solar, wanted to develop 20 times the amount of solar generation that Ontario stated it wanted. Furor ensued.

I discovered the name of the person who had been advising the premier on energy matters. I found out he was a free agent, having left the Ontario Premiers Office. I arranged a consultation meeting for OptiSolar but was told I could not be present at the meeting. Emotions were running high at OptiSolar in the aftermath of the devastating OPA announcement. Losing my cool,[71] I got into heated arguments with other OptiSolar executives.[72] From then on, it was all downhill.

My dissenting views on OptiSolar's moral obligation to create Ontario jobs also undermined my popularity. I believed that when OptiSolar took Ontario money, there was some onus on them to spend that money in Ontario, creating long-term manufacturing jobs and encouraging research. The short-term employment created by construction just wasn't enough.

My first foray into a personal "Buy in Ontario" initiative was supporting a team of engineers in an evaluation of a company manufacturing inverters in Burlington. OptiSolar would require a large number of inverters to convert the direct current produced on its solar farms into alternating current that could be fed into the grid. The Burlington company was a prime Ontario candidate for the job. Their inverters were being used by the US military, a fact that I considered to be concrete

---

71 This is one of the rare occasions I lost my usual calm at work. My health was a factor; I had been diagnosed with severe heart failure a few months earlier. I was sick enough that the Peter Munk clinic was about to recommend that I be implanted with a cardiac defibrillator.

72 The interview with the former OPO staffer would be my first opportunity to get some insight into policy development at the provincial level. This was something I was used to doing as a consultant and speechwriter. I wasn't accustomed to being told who I could and could not talk to. I guess I suffered from poorly developed followership skills and was annoyed to be excluded from a meeting I had initiated.

evidence of their high quality. The contract to build inverters was given to a company outside Ontario.

Questions regarding the manufacture of solar panels in Ontario were routinely deflected. As far as I am aware, OptiSolar planned to do all its photovoltaic manufacturing in California. I discovered that a significant number of Ontario politicians visited the California headquarters of the company, presumably attempting to change their minds. Surprisingly, one of the Ontario visitors was former Progressive Conservative premier Ernie Eves. No one—former premiers, current cabinet ministers or Liberal aides—made any noticeable progress on the issue in my time with OptiSolar.

Ontario had been foolish enough to sign a contract that didn't specify a *quid pro quo* on manufacturing in the province. Later in the renewable energy fiasco, Ontario tried to impose where-to-manufacture restrictions on its rent-seeking corporations. The province ran into World Trade Organization restrictions that hampered efforts to create jobs in the province. When I was around, the attitude seemed to be that suckers don't deserve an even break. They were stupid enough to sign the contract; let them pay.

By June 2008, I was in deep trouble with some OptiSolar executives in the Canadian subsidiary. I found allies in the California headquarters who sided with me. As a result, I was able to face an unusual situation—including being accused of things I was incapable of doing—with my usual placidity. I was confident that in the end, I would come out on the winning side.

Unfortunately, the financial crisis of 2008-2009 finished the company. OptiSolar was sold to a larger solar company and in the transition, my services were no longer required. That's not something you can fight easily. I already had a major battle on my hands—trying to recover from severe heart failure—so I retired and left the field.

I made some half-hearted attempts to battle the headlong rush by the province into the green energy abyss and a dismal post-industrial future. Health problems interfered.

One of the last things I did for OptiSolar was mildly encouraging. I attended a council meeting in a township hall north of Cobourg. The meeting's purpose was to get municipal approval for a solar farm along

Lake Ontario's shoreline. The room filled up with people. Normally council meetings don't draw a big crowd in small townships. I was puzzled until I recognized two of the people as former cabinet ministers in the federal Liberal Chrétien government. Putting two and two together, I concluded many of the participants were affiliated with them. There's 20 years of easy money from the outrageous profits the solar farm would generate if the council approved permits to build the farm.

The story ends with some heartening news. The Hamilton Township permits were approved, but the facility has never been built. Apparently the solar company could not get conservation authority permission to cut a stand of trees that would cast shadows on part of the farm. That will save Ontario's ratepayers a lot of money. In other news, the former Liberal cabinet minister who chaired the meeting on behalf of the solar group has been convicted of fraud on an unrelated matter.

# SECTION V
# Cardiovascular Adventures

*The Miracles of Medicine*

In 1978, when I first began writing *Globe and Mail* features on cardiovascular medicine, surviving any heart attack or stroke was a matter of chance. The odds were often in favor of dying or facing a future with severe disability. Rehabilitation programs were at an early stage of development. Cardiac patients were seldom encouraged to exercise. Many stroke survivors spent the rest of their lives hidden away in back rooms.

In the mid-1980s, I got a call from the Ontario branch of the Heart and Stroke Foundation. Directors were transforming the Heart Foundation to incorporate the closely related problem of stroke. They needed someone who had the ability to write on the subject as recovery odds were improving.

Initially, I wrote material for their new literature on stroke. Later I produced press kits for the February fund-raising campaign, interviewing cardiologists, neurologists and patients to produce stories that would appeal to the general public. I wrote radio ads, a review of *The Heart Healthy Cookbook*, ghost-wrote an article for the journal of the College of Family Physicians of Canada, and produced many articles on research in progress and advised the foundation on dealing with animal rights activists who opposed medical research.

I'd like to believe my communications efforts made some contributions to the impressive progress in cardiovascular medicine. Today, a significant number of heart attacks and strokes can be stopped in their tracks. Heart-restarting defibrillators are prominently displayed in many buildings. Interventional radiologists can reach directly into the brain of someone suffering a stroke and remove the blood clot causing the blockage. Rehabilitation programs for cardiac and stroke patients routinely take aggressive measures to return survivors to normal life. Death and disability rates have dropped remarkably.

At a personal level, it was education for me. I finally learned I shouldn't smoke, so I quit for good. I discovered that much cardiovascular disease was heritable. One of the best preventive measures was choosing your parents carefully. I concluded that because there seemed to be very little cardiovascular disease in my family, I didn't have much to worry about.

I couldn't have been more wrong. My 60s were a long battle with cardiovascular catastrophes. At the age of 62, I developed severe heart failure. My heart was barely able to circulate my blood. At 69, I had two embolic strokes in three days. The second stroke left me in a locked-in state, unable to speak, barely able to breathe, and completely paralyzed on the right hand side of my body. It was more than a near-death experience; it actually left me dead for nearly half a minute.

Today, if you met me in person you would find it had to believe I have had catastrophic heart failure and a massive stroke. My heart, which once pumped out only about 12 to 15 per cent of the blood in it on each contraction, now ejects 50 percent of its blood from its left ventricle. I walk and speak normally, have no vision deficits, exercise regularly, ride my bike to the gym where I lift weights. I can tell you about some residual problems from my cardiovascular mishaps, but unless you are a medical professional examining me, you are unlikely to notice them.

This section tells the story of my cardiovascular misadventures. I believe what I learned from the people I interviewed when I wrote on the subject influenced my dealing with the crises and my recovery from each.

# 15.
# Recovery from Cardiomyopathy and Heart Failure

*Getting tired was my first clue*

I don't remember ever writing the word "cardiomyopathy" in the decade I wrote about cardiovascular disease[73] for *The Globe and Mail* and the Heart and Stroke Foundation. Thirty years later, I was diagnosed with it.

Dilated cardiomyopathy (DCM), in which heart muscle becomes weak, thin, and unable to efficiently pump blood around the body, is among the most serious of cardiovascular afflictions. DCM is a relatively rare cardiovascular disease but a leading cause of heart transplants.

I never even worried about cardiac disease in any form before I was diagnosed with DCM and severe heart failure. In the late 1980s, when my contract with the foundation came to an end, I made a conscious decision not to concern myself at all about cardiovascular problems. I decided that the best thing to do to avoid an early death from heart problems or stroke was to choose your ancestors very carefully.

After a decade in which I interviewed dozens of survivors of cardiovascular disease and many cardiologists and stroke specialists, genetic themes played large in my mind. I encountered a mother of two children who both required heart transplants. I heard stories from cardiac patients

---

73 I never wrote exclusively on the topic. With the newspaper it was occasional feature stories. I had a steadier diet of cardiovascular writing when with the foundation, but it was only one component of my workload.

who discovered that familial toddlers who died mysteriously had actually suffered heart problems similar to the ones they were dealing with. Scariest of all were tales of cardiac infarctions down the generations with grandfather, father and son all dying suddenly in middle age. It all seemed to be inherited.

I had one grandfather who died of a sudden heart attack in his 50s and an uncle with a pacemaker, but that seemed to be the extent of the problem. My immediate family seemed relatively free of cardiovascular disease. There didn't seem to be a lot you could do about it if you had a propensity for early-life heart attack or stroke. It's never hard for me to believe something is primarily genetic. So I simply decided not to worry.

Perhaps that's part of the reason I didn't recognize the indications of heart failure that I experienced in the last half of 2007. My only symptom was fatigue, an overwhelming exhaustion that I couldn't attribute to anything, certainly not my heart. I was never in pain, never felt that my heart was beating with unusual rhythms or skipping beats. But I was at the end of my rope from tiring out almost instantly when doing anything physical. I had no energy and was sleeping too much.

*On a sailing cruise relaxing at a lunch near Picton Harbor.*

In September, on a sailing cruise in the Thousand Islands, the first thing I checked when we moored at an island was the location of the outhouses. I was dismayed if the facilities turned out to be on the other side of a hill. I wouldn't know if I could make it over the hill on my way to the washroom. I had plenty of strength, but no endurance. I could do ordinary sailing tasks, was still the muscle, the winch gorilla. I could pull the anchors and set the sails. Then I would go below for a nap.

I thought I had just let myself get out of shape and didn't see my GP about it. I had been overworked in the summer of 2007, regularly commuting four hours each way between Sarnia and Belleville. The weekday routine I had been following up to the end of March—working 10 hours or more at a desk followed by an hour-long session at a luxury gymnasium—had gone by the wayside. I figured I had simply let myself get out of shape when I was no longer spending four or five hours a week using the cross-trainers and lifting weights.

My GP was in Toronto. I wasn't feeling sick enough to make an appointment and a special trip to downtown Toronto to see him. But after the sailing trip in September, I got progressively more worried about my lack of energy and increasing fatigue. I wondered if I had contracted something like the "yuppie flu" and just had to wait until it ran its course.

Despite my writing experience in the medical field, until the end of December, I didn't have a clue I was having heart problems. I had written the obvious symptoms of heart problems many times—shooting pains down the left arm, tightness in the chest, pressure, indigestion. I had none of those.

I self-diagnosed cardiac difficulties on December 30, 2007. I was on vacation in Tampa and suddenly feeling like I couldn't breathe if I tried to lie flat on the bed. I had a distinct sensation of drowning. Clearly, whatever was wrong with me had precipitously become catastrophically wrong. That actually frightened me but I had no idea of possible causes until I put both hands on top of my head in an effort to breathe easier. I put my hands on top of my head about as often as I cross my legs, which is almost never.

As soon as my hands were above my hair and my fingers interlocking, I remembered a long-ago interview with a cardiologist who told me that cardiac patients often put their hands on their heads to relieve the pressure on their hearts. A light went on. Suddenly I understood. My six months fighting fatigue had not been yuppie flu.

"It's my heart!" I said to my wife and immediately lost my cool. I decided I was on the verge of collapse—and that time was of the essence. In the hotel lobby, I got directions to the nearest hospital and drove myself there. I ran red lights on the way, stopping briefly to look for traffic, then barreling through rather than waiting for a green. (Lights take forever to change in Florida.)

My blood pressure was sky-high when I was admitted, a phenomenon I attributed to stress and panic.

I spent a little more than 36 hours in the Tampa Heart Institute. Given a diuretic to make me "piss like a race horse" and put on oxygen, I soon felt better. The doctors gave me various tests, including my first MRI. I don't remember getting an echocardiogram which would have given me some idea of the disastrous condition of my heart. It seemed to me the physicians were ruling out other possible causes of my fatigue and water retention. On discharge, a cardiologist informed me that the left side of my heart was not up to par. He advised me to see a doctor as soon as I got home.

Even after being hospitalized in Florida, I had no inkling I was suffering from something long-term and serious. I felt considerably more energetic after getting rid of the fluid that had accumulated in my lungs. My obnoxious, headstrong personality kicked in. After refusing my insurance company's offer of a medical escort on the return flight to Toronto, I was allowed to walk out of the hospital (no wheelchair to the door). I flew home accompanied only by my wife.

An incident in the hospital also led me to take my situation more lightly than I should have. A young man in his 20s who was in the same hospital room was visited by his cardiologist as he was discharged. I overheard him being told his episode had been a temporary viral attack on his heart. The symptoms had vanished; he was free to go. I suspect my subconscious was processing that event as parallel to my own experience. My extreme symptoms had evaporated. I had lived with the usual symptoms for months, so I wasn't going to worry.

I arrived in Toronto late on the night of January 1, 2008, blissfully unaware of the severity of my problem. I spent half an hour chopping ice and clearing snow from my car before driving more than a hundred miles home. My wife was beside herself because I had turned down all offers of help. She was afraid to go outside the hotel lobby where she was waiting because she might be a witness to my dropping dead. She was convinced I was seriously ill. I was persuaded only that it was time to see my GP to get to the bottom of things.

The startled look on Dr. Calvin Lei's face when he put his stethoscope to my chest a few days later was the first incident that led me to think that something truly out of the ordinary was happening. A day later, the MD who was stress-testing me on a treadmill stopped the test almost immediately. My heart was behaving poorly. Continuing the test might have led to serious problems. That was scary.

My referral to a cardiologist came almost immediately. Dr. Anup Gupta arranged my first echocardiogram and effectively explained to me that my heart was performing poorly, not squeezing out enough blood with each contraction. He scheduled an angiogram. Again, no alarm. Nothing seemed hurried. There was no rushing me to the hospital in an ambulance. My appointment was a week or more away. By the time of my angiogram I was in severe heart failure with Grade IV dilated cardiomyopathy, one of the least encouraging of diagnoses.

It was a phenomenon I had never even heard of. I had to go to the Internet for information. When I looked it up, I discovered that dilated cardiomyopathy was a leading cause of heart transplants. Non-surgical treatment had improved to the point that it was no longer true that victims had only a 50 per cent chance of being alive after five years. This was deadly serious business, a rare heart condition.

I began taking miniscule doses of beta blockers immediately. I had to cancel a planned business trip to California, but I continued work. I felt better than I had in the autumn, much better than I had in the last week in December. The staff in the Dr. Gupta's office, where I continued to be a patient until June, treated my condition as more debilitating than I did. Arriving one day in the spring, I asked for the key to the washroom. The receptionist asked if I needed help getting down the hall. I replied that I had just walked a mile from the train station to the office.

It was mid-April 2008 when I got a referral to the Peter Munk Cardiac Clinic at Toronto General and had my first appointment with Dr. Heather Ross. The clinic, according to an article in the *Toronto Star*, had a patient roster of the 1500 sickest cardiac cases in Ontario. Dr. Ross is head of heart transplant at TGH. She pulled no punches in our first appointment, telling me I could expect some improvement and could learn to live with heart failure. I could anticipate living with some degree of heart failure for the rest of my life.

Dr. Ross doesn't have an effective poker face. In our frequent appointments in the next two months, I wondered if she was thinking that each visit might be the last time she saw me alive before my heart stopped and no one got to me with a defibrillator in time.

I felt sicker in the late spring, more easily fatigued than ever. With the return of good weather, I began taking walks. At first I could go no more than a quarter of a mile, walking from lamp post to lamp post and breathlessly holding on to each one a for a few minutes before I could continue.

Later, the safety officer at the solar farm in Sarnia told me she didn't think I was going to survive. An experienced emergency room nurse, she said she could see in my eyes that I was pretty far gone. Strangers noticed as well. One day, a car pulled up beside me on the street as I plodded down the sidewalk. The woman in the passenger seat asked me if I would like a ride home as I was in obvious difficulty. I refused, thanking her as nicely as I could for the offer.

June was a breakthrough month. All of a sudden, after being able to walk only a few blocks, I was able to hoof it all the way down to the yacht basin on the bay, a round trip of nearly two miles. I attributed it to the effect of the beta blockers and ACE inhibitors. I had started out on a pediatric dose of beta blockers, 2.5 mg pills taken twice daily, with instructions to stop driving for an hour after taking a pill. Apparently some people do not adapt easily to beta blockers. Dr. Ross doubled my dosage regularly, as I got used to them without problems. But clinical test results from regular echocardiograms and MUGA scans did not reflect how well I felt.

At the end of June, I was surprised to receive a letter from TGH announcing an appointment with a surgeon. He explained that I needed an implantable cardiac defibrillator (ICD),[74] a small device surgically inserted near the left collarbone with two wires that led to the heart. The

---

74 There are cardioverter defibrillators, providing heart pacing functions as well as defibrillation. As far as I remember, I was slated only for a cardiac defibrillator.

ICD would sense when my heart had stopped. It would deliver a jolt that would feel like the kick of a horse. My heart, hopefully, would restart beating regularly. Implanting it would require an overnight in the hospital. This would be followed with weeks of immobilization of my left arm so that I would not pull the electrodes out of place in my heart. The first date open for the surgery was six or eight weeks away but the permission forms were ready for me to sign.

Although my cardiomyopathy was classified as idiopathic—cause unknown—the surgeon said he was 99 per cent sure that it was a result of a virus attacking my heart. I liked hearing that. To me it meant that my devastating problem was the result of an accidental encounter with some vile polio-related virus. It was not a genetic thing that I might have passed on to my children or—heaven forbid—something that I might have brought on myself by failing to take slightly elevated blood pressure seriously. (The jury is still out on that one. Not every medical professional will subscribe to my preferred diagnosis.)

The fact that I was non-ischemic (not dealing with high levels of plaque in my arteries), had no previous history of heart problems and had been a non-drinker for years ruled out some of the other possible causes of cardiomyopathy. They also made me a suitable candidate for an ICD or even a heart transplant, should I need one and should they ever have a heart available for a man in his 60s.

In an act that I would later describe as signing my own death certificate, I put my scrawl on the permission forms. I had just been told that I was likely to die in the near future, but that a jolt from the ICD would revive me to give me an opportunity to die again—and again, and again. Then I was sent to have a MUGA scan, one of the most accurate tests of heart function. After the technician injects radioactive particles into your bloodstream, the machinery does an accurate count of the number of radioactive particles in the left ventricle and records the percentage pumped out of on each contraction of the heart.

The result is the Left Ventricle Ejection Fraction (LVEF). A normal, healthy heart will eject more than 50 percent of the blood in its left ventricle on each contraction. I know my LVEF had been below 20 per cent for a period of time. I believed it had gone as low as 12-15 per cent. While it had improved since January, it must have still been in the 20-29 per cent range in June. Hence the referral for an ICD.

On that July day, my feeling that I had turned a corner was confirmed by the MUGA scan results. The surgeon told me that my LVEF was at 38 per cent—outside the range that indicated a need for an ICD. Instead of getting confirmation of an appointment for the implantation of the ICD, I got to fill in an application to participate in a study of ICDs. I went home with mixed feelings, delighted with the test results but concerned that my heart had been so bad for so long that I had been considered for an ICD.

That night, at dinner in a crowded restaurant, I had a chance encounter with Belleville cardiologist Dr. Peter Hollett. His daughter had dragged him to our table because the little girl wanted to talk to my wife, who had been her kindergarten teacher. Elaine introduced us men and let us make small talk while teacher and former student caught up on the child's progress in life.

The ICD was on my mind, and Elaine had introduced Dr. Hollett as a cardiologist, so I told him I was debating whether or not to sign up as a potential candidate for the study. After hearing his thoughts, I decided to apply for the study (but was never chosen.) I had my bottle of beta blockers on the table, ready to take my evening dose as soon as I had something to eat. Before he left to walk his daughter back to their table, he said, "That's a heart transplant in a bottle." Those words were prophetic.

Over the summer, medication seemed to work magic on my heart. I could walk greater distances and got fatigued less frequently. At the end of September, in my next regular appointment with Dr. Ross, she said I was getting the "best possible results" from my drug regimen. I was cleared to start a rehabilitation program at Toronto Western Hospital.

The year-long cardiac rehabilitation program began with a classroom session on nutrition and exercise and moved on to weekly sessions in a hospital gymnasium. Sessions began right after lunch. Participants sat in a hallway while the rehab staff took their blood pressure and heart rates, then moved into the gym where they changed into exercise gear, walked on treadmills, pedaled stationary bicycles, used elliptical cross trainers and arm exercise machines. The staff circulated, taking heart rates with devices that they clipped on fingers, helping ensure that patients did not overwork their hearts. A defibrillation cart stood at the ready in the room.

Many of the participants were obviously seriously ill, some barely able to walk on treadmills. The age range was wide—many were elderly, some were surprisingly young. Staff included a cardiac nurse, physiotherapists, exercise therapists and a nutritionist. Records were kept on each patient and treadmill stress tests at regular intervals assessed progress.

The year in rehabilitation was a pleasure. The staff was friendly, supportive and attentive. I was delighted to exercise on machines in the hospital gym. I had owned heart rate monitors for at least a decade, starting with the early models and progressing to new, GPS-equipped ones as the technology evolved. I had always felt I was lazy on aerobic machines and used the monitors to ensure that I was running my heart at a suitable rate, a little higher than the recommended rate for my age. In rehabilitation, I used the monitor to ensure that I did not exceed the limits set for me by the clinic. In my walking program at home, I used a GPS-equipped monitor to track my distances and speed as well as my heart rate.

Metrics became a vital component of my recovery exercise program. I would download the GPS-equipped monitor's results to my home computer, attempt to analyze my progress and watch for irregular heart patterns. Somewhat disappointed that the beta blockers made it difficult for me to get my heart rate up to the 123 beats per minute that I wanted, I tried to compensate by going longer distances and spending more time exercising. One winter in Florida, I tried to cycle 10 miles every day, accumulating 1500 miles according to my GPS by the time I returned to Canada in the spring.

Motivation came from my burning desire to get better; I enlisted music to reinforce it. Thirty to 45 minutes is a long time to spend on an elliptical cross-trainer and I had an iPod loaded with enough music to fill the time. Each session on the machine, the last song I played was Meatloaf's nine-minute anthem ``Bat out of Hell.'' The final chorus to the energetic, somewhat cacophonic rock song, repeated a number of times—"the last thing I saw was my heart, still beating, breaking out of my body and flying away, like a bat out of hell,"—was inspiring. Once I felt I was on the path to recovery, I declared total war against cardiomyopathy. I did not intend to live with my illness; I was going to recover. In the words of Meatloaf's cardiovascular battle hymn, I planned to "hit the highway like a battering ram on a silver black phantom bike."

My bike was nothing more than a standard 15-speed hybrid that I regularly pedaled five miles to the local YMCA where I worked out at least five times a week once Dr. Ross gave me permission to resume. She wrote a letter to the staff at the YMCA branch, telling them what I was allowed to do. Other than taking my prescription medications, exercise was the only other component of my rehabilitation efforts. My perception was that I was getting better. But at the Peter Munk Cardiac Clinic, perhaps to avoid raising my hopes and perhaps because what was happening was so unexpected, the feedback I got at appointments seemed vague to me. It was encouraging, but not specific.

The bluntness that I had appreciated when I was very ill seemed to give way to indirectness and evasiveness as I got better. At one appointment, Dr. Ross's associate seemed startled by my progress, inquiring incredulously "Just how much exercise are you getting?" I asked for a copy of the results of that day's echocardiogram, which would give me an estimate of my LVEF. I got a simple refusal. For some reason, I wasn't going to see the report. I suspected that the results that morning were so good that they weren't credible and were being treated as some kind of outlier. I took no for an answer. As a matter of personal policy, I never questioned or objected to anything that happened in the clinic,[75] so I never asked why I could not see my results.

I knew I looked better, was projecting a healthier image. I was no longer the exhausted pedestrian who looked so pathetic that strangers offered him a ride home or the executive who looked to the industrial safety nurse like he had one foot in the grave. One day as I checked in at the clinic, the receptionist asked, "Who are you here to see, doctor?" She was somewhat surprised when I explained I was not a visiting doctor but a patient. I just didn't look like a seriously ill senior citizen who belonged in the ambulatory cardiac clinic waiting room.

I had little to report in most of my clinic appointments, no pains, no odd sensations in my heart, no irregular rhythms. Having nothing to talk

---

75 My contrarian views got exposed only once, in a difference of opinion with a nutritionist. The rest of the time, I simply kept my mouth shut and did as I was told.

about led me to mention a minor annoyance—I was having some sleeping problems. I had already been through sleep apnea testing, spending a night in the hospital, wired up and slumbering like a log for six hours. Asked if I was exercising late in the day, I said no. The next question surprised me. "Would you see a psychiatrist about those sleep difficulties?"

I knew that interrupted sleep could be a symptom of depression and the clinic kept a close eye on its patients—seriously ill heart patients can be inclined to slip into the depths of hopelessness. I said yes immediately, not because I thought I might be depressed but because I was being offered an opportunity to have my rationality evaluated by a medical professional who could settle, once and for all, the question of my sanity. Given my approach to my career and some of the unconventional things I had done, I had endured more than my share of unsolicited amateur opinions on that subject.

I saw Dr. Brian Baker, a pleasant professional originally from South Africa who takes referrals from the Peter Munk Cardiac Clinic. I had five sessions alone with him, then one with my wife participating before wrapping things up with a final session. I answered all his questions honestly and thoroughly. In our final session, I didn't have much to say, but sought his opinion. He said I had a difficult personality. He could prescribe drugs that would make life easier for me, but he knew I was unlikely to take that route. Fortunately I had a wife who was the best thing going for me. All of which were the absolute truth as far as I was concerned. Then he said the words I wanted to hear from a psychiatrist—a person who could certify me and put me away—after a lifetime of listening to amateurs make snide remarks. He said, "You are sane."

He also confirmed I wasn't depressed and didn't regard my cardiac condition as overwhelming. By the time I was seeing Dr. Baker, I knew my performance was satisfying and believed I was getting significantly better. $VO_2$ max stress testing was giving me concrete and specific results that confirmed I was getting back to cardio-pulmonary normalcy. Unlike the customary treadmill-based stress tests, the $VO_2$ max tests were done on a stationary bicycle, computer-controlled to get harder to pedal every 60 seconds. As well as having electrode patches stuck over much of your body, you wear a neoprene mask that guides your breath into electronic equipment measuring how much oxygen you inhale and how much carbon dioxide you exhale, an effective guide to the performance efficiency of your heart and lungs.

I liked the way the $VO_2$ max results printout sheet compared my performance on the bicycle to the results a healthy man my age might get in the same circumstances. I was always shown my results, a sheet of paper that said I was performing, for example, at 93 percent of the efficiency of a healthy 65-year-old or, later, 100 per cent as well as a healthy 68-year-old. That meant something to me; it was data I could get my teeth into. It gave me a goal to pursue for the next test.

I didn't like some things about the $VO_2$ max. One was that the test kept lowering the bar as you got older. I would have preferred all results comparing me to a 60-year-old man. I would never get to 100 per cent but I would have a better idea of whether I had stood still, improved or declined between tests. So I started setting goals based on how long I could last on the machine before I stopped because of leg fatigue or was stopped because my blood pressure or heart rate went too high.

The other thing that bugged me was that the system factored weight into the final results. If you were heavier than your BMI said you were supposed to be, your final result would be lower. I always figured it should go the other way—rather than being penalized for being heavy, you should be rewarded because your heart and lungs can do more work.

I began training for the stress tests, a process I referred to as "gaming the results." I would exercise regularly between $VO_2$ max tests; in the weeks immediately prior to my appointment, I would focus on increasing the intensity of my exercise, pushing myself harder. Resting a day or two before the test, I would put my best effort into the 17-20 minutes I hoped to be on the bike. Knowing that the computer would make the bike harder to pedal every 60 seconds and that the sudden increase in resistance could slow me down below the 60 rpm you are expected to maintain, I would try to speed up my pedaling to 75 rpm in the 15 seconds before the resistance went up. That way I wasn't playing catch-up—I just got slowed down a bit as the bike got harder to pedal.

By April 2013, it paid off. I got 100 per cent of predicted on oxygen consumption per minute divided by my weight. Persistence rewarded an overweight man whose heart had scarcely been pumping six years earlier. My cardio-pulmonary performance finally was equivalent to that of an average, healthy, slender man my age.

Late that morning, in a consultation with Dr. Ross, I got the news I had long hoped to hear. I had recovered. Everything was in the normal range. We were both delighted and chatted about how this was an unexpected outcome and that few of her patients ever receive such good news. Before I left the clinic, she put a bug in my ear that my recovery made her suspicious that the cause of my heart failure may have been failure to control my blood pressure. I got slightly revised prescriptions, but I remained on the maximum doses of beta blockers.

I asked no questions about restrictions on exercise. I figured that if I had recovered, those no longer applied—asking about them would just be inviting trouble and limitations on the things I could do. The problem was that I had been restricted to lifting nothing heavier than 30 pounds for years. I like pumping iron and always much preferred to do five or six repetitions with as much weight as I could lift than doing endless repetitions with lighter weights. So that spring and summer, I went back to cycling, began lifting heavy weights and made plans to train even harder for the stress test I expected to take in April 2014.

*Retirement. In Florida during the winter, I played croquet almost every day and rode my bike up to 1500 miles each season in an effort to rehabilitate myself from heart failure. I am shown here in croquet whites, about to ride to the courts.*

In the fall, I invested in an Elliptigo, a fancy and expensive combination of bicycle and elliptical trainer.[76] You ride it standing up and it's more strenuous than a bicycle. I figured it would avoid the discomfort of sitting on a bike seat and allow me get my heart rate up higher than an ordinary bicycle would. If I rode all winter on Florida bike trails, I would be ahead of the game and able to perform at perhaps 110 per cent of predicted when I was tested. Getting used to the Elliptigo seemed a bit like learning to boardsail—challenging at first, but relatively easy once you got the hang of it. I was just beginning to feel comfortable on the strange machine when my world collapsed.

---

76  See http://www.elliptigo.com/ for more information

# 16.
# Stopping a Stroke in Progress

*My life and the squeaky toy*

New cardiovascular problems struck me like the vengeance of the gods less than nine months after being told I had beaten heart failure. I had two strokes while on winter vacation in Venice FL.

Dr. Charles Gordon told me I died on New Year's Day, 2014. My eyes rolled back in my head. I stopped breathing and lost consciousness. I stopped squeaking the rubber toy in my left hand.

An interventional radiologist, Dr. Gordon was sitting beside me at waist level at the time. He had just pushed more than two feet of catheter to a blood clot in my brain stem, where an embolism was growing larger by the second. Getting the catheter to the clot had been tricky. The artery near the problem area was so convoluted that the sheath guiding the catheter had to be removed and held over a boiling kettle, heating it up with live steam to make it more flexible.

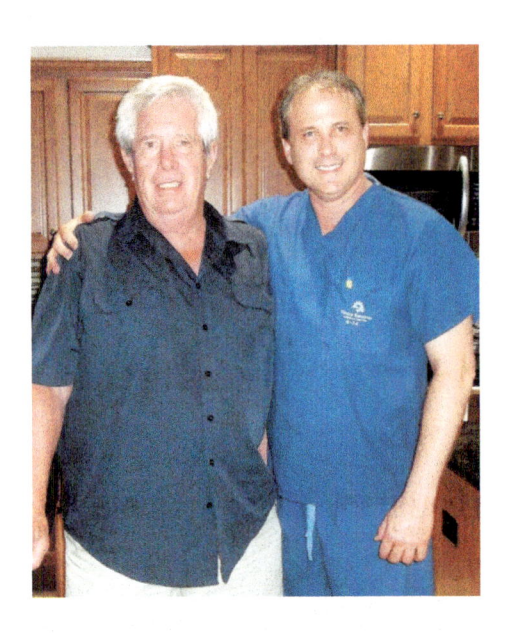

*Dr. Charles Gordon, the interventional radiologist who saved my life when I was paralyzed, aphasic and barely able to breathe, told me that I had actually died in the cardiac studio. He and his team had almost given up on me when I announced my return from the dead by squeaking a toy in my left hand. With the clot removed from my brainstem (almost directly between my ears), I was able to breathe, move and speak immediately. – photo by Howard Van Nostrand*

He inserted a stent opening up a flow of blood in my brain stem. As the blood started streaming around the clot, the embolism began to enlarge like a pearl in an oyster, adding layers. More and more of my brainstem—the part of the brain that controls breathing, heart rate and other existential functions—was increasingly deprived of a flow of oxygen-rich blood and progressively shut down.

I stopped breathing. My heart slowed down, precursory to stopping forever. My left hand went limp; I stopped pumping the squeaky toy I was holding. I was gone. Dr. Gordon changed the wire from a device used to insert the stent to a penumbra device, a tiny vacuum cleaner. He sucked the blood clot from my brain [77] and used clot-busting tissue plasminogen

---

77  There is an animation of how the Penumbra system works on a blood clot at https://www.youtube.com/watch?v=ajcgsAr6K2A

198 | Polar Bears and Other Scares

activator (tPA) — to remove more of the embolism that remained. It was a mechanical intervention followed up with a pharmacological one. In domestic terms it was analogous to dealing with a blocked kitchen sink by vacuuming away the solid and gooey stuff jammed in the drain and following that up with a shot of Drano or Liquid Plumber to dissolve the remnants. The results were dramatic.

Less than half a minute after I stopped breathing, the toy in my left hand squeaked. I was back. My only instruction from Dr. Gordon had been to keep squeaking the toy; don't stop. It was the first thing that came to mind when I revived. So I squeezed it. This is how a Lazarus announced his return from the beyond, not with a shout but a squeak. In the minutes that followed, blood reached parts of my brain that had been oxygen-deprived for hours. I could move my right side again. My arm and leg—completely paralyzed since the major stroke began—responded to my attempts to move them.

I was still flat on my back on the cardiac operating table when I regained my ability to speak. I had been fully cognizant, able to form words and thoughts in my mind. Grunting was the only thing that came out when I tried to voice them. I was aphasic, locked in, fully aware of everything going on around me but helpless and incommunicado. My wife saw me briefly in the hospital room and cardiac studio before the procedure began. I tried to communicate with her using my left hand, the only thing that would move for me. When I found I had my voice back, the first thing I did was speak to Dr. Gordon. My first words were "Thank you." It was, everyone agreed, a truly incredible outcome. The medical team thought they had lost me and were overjoyed with the squeak that announced I was alive.

The hour of drama in the cardiac studio was the culmination of two days of an evolving cardiovascular accident (CVA) that had built up to a crescendo of paralysis and aphasia. I remember much of what happened in the 60 hours from 5:30 p.m. on December 29—when I had a minor stroke—until January 1, when I was on the operating table in a cardiac studio feeling the warm glow in my head I had been told to expect. That's when I passed out. My memory of the critical half-minute is rather prosaic—I seemed to drift off to sleep, then wake up with a start, feeling that there was something important I was supposed to be doing. I wasn't doing it. That was squeaking the toy. So I squeaked it.

Unlike my experience with heart failure, which had sneaked up on me almost without symptoms for months, this cardiovascular accident announced its presence suddenly and with some pain. It began on a croquet court. Playing aggressively as usual, I tried to put a ball through the first wicket and all the way down the field to the second one. But it bounced off the first hoop. It was a hot Sunday afternoon. While waiting my next turn to hit the yellow ball, I went to a nearby sun shelter and picked up a bottle of water. Prickly heat spread across the right side of my face. The thought crossed my mind that I should splash the cool water on my face. But I treated the symptom as an annoying and puzzling hot flash of some kind—a reaction to the heat of the day—and kept on playing. Or tried to.

As I turned to address the ball, I stumbled like a drunk. Finding it difficult to steady myself for a shot, when I swung the three-pound croquet mallet in what was intended to be a gentle, precise stroke that would reposition the ball in front of the wicket, I swung too hard. I had no control. I missed the ball completely, taking a divot out of the turf. The other players saw I had problems, sat me on a bench, got me an aspirin and called an ambulance.

I knew my difficulties were real and serious. I wasn't even tempted to get in my car and drive myself to the hospital. I cooperated quietly when I was loaded on a stretcher and put in an ambulance.

Less than an hour after the initial sensation of prickly heat on my face, I was in the hospital emergency room talking with a neurologist. She was assessing whether I was having a minor brain attack, a Transient Ischemic Attack (TIA) that would resolve itself on its own or a stroke, a Cerebrovascular Accident (CVA) that might be treated with immediate application of clot-busting medication. She described me as having unsteady gait and slurred speech.

I didn't qualify for clot-busting, a risky procedure that is used with caution. At nightfall, I found myself in the Intensive Care Unit (ICU). My wife called at 7 p.m. She was at home for Christmas and due to fly out of Toronto in the early morning of December 31. While she was away, she called me in Florida every day. When my cell phone rang on December

29, I was in ICU and still struggling to speak clearly. At first, the only words Elaine could understand were "hospital," "Venice" and "stroke."

Eventually, she understood enough to get my message that the stroke seemed minor. There was no panic and she didn't need to get an earlier flight back to Florida. I was not in pain and I was getting good care, including MRIs. She should finish her wintry break from our Florida vacation as planned. I would be fine and when she called again on December 30 I would talk to her on my cell phone unless I was getting a medical test of some kind.

She immediately called a friend in Venice, who came to see me in the hospital. Dennis Day had difficulty understanding me and could see the left side of my face and mouth were somewhat paralyzed. He described me as dopey and tired.

When I woke up the next morning, I was surprised to find myself tied to the bed, with my ankles in Velcro-closed cuffs that prevented me from getting up—presumably a precaution taken for patients with dementia. I was anything but demented. Removing the cuffs and asking for a phone in my ICU room, I called my insurance company, told them that I was in the hospital and was going to have extensive testing, including an MRI. I had tests that day and much of the next, being rolled around on a stretcher.

Elaine arrived on New Year's Eve as scheduled. Dennis picked her up at the airport. She found me somewhat mobile, apparently making steady progress in recovering from a cerebrovascular accident (CVA) of moderate severity. I had been moved out of ICU. We visited until late afternoon. I suggested she should go to our Venice accommodation and get settled in before dark. I was taking all the events in stride, although my left leg was noticeably affected and my gait was jerky and awkward. I had no panic about my situation. I encouraged Elaine to feel confident that I would soon be back to normal. I assured her that people recovered from strokes.

My composure in the first 60 hours was grounded on what I remembered from 10 years of writing about stroke. The time I spent in ICU gave me time to recall and reflect on what I had been told about CVA and TIA 25 to 35 years earlier.

I knew what the worst-case scenario was: the lead for one of my February Heart and Stroke campaign news releases read, "If you think of stroke survivors as pitiful creatures—people with eyes filled with terror and anguish, confined to wheelchairs or walkers, perhaps unable to speak or understand what they hear …"

But I was confident that my stroke had not been severe. I focused on the positive and was reassured by some of my memories—many of them were encouraging. There were three stroke-related interviews that were top of mind as I lay in the Venice hospital bed.

One was a 1978 conversation with a retired missionary surgeon, Dr. Walter Strangway.

Nearly 80 years old at the time I interviewed him, he told me had suffered TIAs in middle age before having major strokes later in life. He could have a TIA overnight, wake up in the morning unable to move parts of his body. He would lie in bed waiting for the TIA to live up to the transient part of its name and go away. He could be in his Angola operating room with a scalpel in his hand in the afternoon. He was always confident of surviving these minor brain attacks because his mother had survived five TIAs. So I knew from the get-go that you could survive a brain attack. I hoped my problems were closer to TIAs than a major stroke. That was reassuring. So was my knowledge of rehabilitation of stroke victims.

After returning from Angola to Toronto, Dr. Strangway started an innovative stroke rehabilitation unit. He based rehabilitation on the idea that a brain can be re-trained. Healthy parts of that big, grey organ, if properly encouraged and challenged, would take over functions that had been performed by those parts damaged by stroke. That theory produced results for him—he had rehabilitated himself after two significant strokes. He focused his efforts on things he had difficulty doing, practicing them until he could do them again. This approach was often successful for his Riverdale Hospital patients—so I had faith that whatever deficits I might acquire from a stroke or TIA could be overcome. On December 31, I seemed to be off to a good start in recovery.

Another interviewee I thought about was a television host I wrote up for a publicity campaign in the mid-1980s. Margie Castle was a vivacious and animated TV personality in young middle age who seemed to exhibit no deficits from a severe stroke she suffered in her late 30s. It was only later, when I examined prints of the photos I had taken of her, I could see that one side of her face was drooping, completely expressionless. Her effervescent enthusiasm and practiced body language had blinded me to her obvious problems—another memory that boosted my confidence about a positive outcome from my current difficulties. Having a stroke might be going to change my life but I could have some control over how much I let the changes affect me and how other people perceived me.

I keenly remembered putting my foot in my mouth after a 1986 interview with the young stroke specialist who had become president of the World Neurological Society by 2013. When I began writing for Heart and Stroke, Dr. Vladimir Hachinski was a researcher identified as having a brilliant future. Communications director Kelly Sheard set up a data dump for me—an intense introduction to everything and everybody stroke-related attached to the foundation. I interviewed Dr. Hachinski. I wrote up my backgrounder and turned it in. Kelly immediately picked up on the fact that my report quoted Dr. Hachinski talking about "stopping the event in progress."

He asked me what I thought about that possibility. I was startled by the question. As a feature writer by training, not an opinion columnist, I was careful to keep my opinions to myself in my work. I replied off-handedly, caught off guard by the question and knowing Kelly well enough to be spontaneous. "Probably just pie in the sky," I opined. Fortunately, I would someday eat those words, and gladly.

After my contract with the foundation ended, I moved on to write about other subjects. I wasn't paying close attention to developments in cardiovascular medicine. Within a few years I would hear about people going to ER in bad shape with chest pains and getting a needle that completely halted a heart attack. I had no idea what kind of advances had been made in stopping a stroke in progress. But I was confident that the techniques would have advanced. I had to be optimistic. When I had a second stroke, there was no other choice. My optimism was justified. There are treatments that can stop some strokes in their tracks, provided physicians got to treat the patient in a matter of a few hours.

And, through some amazing luck, Dr. Gordon, who was on call that day, holds several patents in thrombectomy, the science of removing blood clots. In what might be regarded as stroke-halting 2.0, he has the capability to go up to or past a clot in the brain and pull it or vacuum it out. Bottom line: on New Year's morning 2014 I got to eat those "pie in the sky" words. Thanks to the development of Endovascular Treatment (ET), strokes *can* be stopped in progress. Sweet.

My recollection of events on January 1, 2014 begin with feeling well enough to get out of bed, visit the bathroom and sit in the reclining chair in my hospital room. Then, suddenly and painlessly, I was paralyzed on my right hand side and unable to speak. I reached the call button with my left hand and immediately had the attention of nurses and orderlies.

Elaine was jolted out of bed by a call from the hospital at 7 a.m. They urgently needed her permission to do "a procedure" because I had "an event." She gave permission over the phone and drove to the hospital. Elaine recalls me being agitated when I first saw her (a precursor of lack of emotional control to come) but anxious to communicate with my left arm and hand, the only parts of me that would move. When Dr. Gordon arrived at the hospital and the cardiac studio was in an advanced state of readiness, the nurses rolled me onto a gurney and wheeled me to the studio, the fluorescent lights in the corridor lending an eerie brightness to the experience.

My memory is that I remained calm the entire time between the onset of the major stroke that morning until the procedure was complete. I was so composed it surprised me then and still puzzles me now.[78] Mostly I felt frustrated by my inability to establish communication with Elaine. Using my left arm and hand, I tried touching my left eye to mean "no" and my right eye to mean "yes," but in the few minutes we had together, she never caught on.

One of things contributing to my tranquility was that I found myself in familiar surroundings. I had been catheterized before, six years previously, and in the ensuing years had undergone perhaps half a dozen MUGA scans (Multi Gated Acquisition scans) and a dozen echocardiograms. I knew the drill and the cardiac studio environment was not alien

---

78 Dr. Gordon confirms my froideur and told me that he could see in my eyes that I was feeling no panic, although he didn't know at the time whether I was going deeper into a locked-in state or whether it was a reflection of my usual way of handing difficult situations.

or threatening. But I still find it hard to believe that I fell into my usual routine of evaluating the people working on me. Did the doctor seem young and confident? More important: were the nurses cute? My shallowness actually makes me wonder about myself.

There was no sense of impending doom, no surge of fear, even though I knew what was happening and had some inkling of how serious my situation was. That's unnatural for me when I am fully aware that I am in a life-threatening situation. In my career, I was fine sitting at a desk, serenely dealing with other people's problems. But when I figured my own ass was on the line, I could lose my cool. Two such events in my past have caused me to panic, go ballistic. A recent one was triggered by self-diagnosing myself with heart problems six years earlier and the other was a near-accident when working for a geographic magazine 20 years before. On both occasions, apprehension had swept over me and I thought I could actually feel my blood pressure rising.

While flat on my back for an hour in the cardiac studio in Venice, I concentrated on squeaking the rubber toy and paying attention to any warm sensations I might feel in my head. I remember speaking to Dr. Gordon when I regained my ability to use my voice. I recall seeing a red image on a screen as I was being rolled out of the studio. After that things go blank.

For the first couple of days after the clot extraction that brought me back from the dead, un-paralyzed my right hand side and allowed me to speak again, I was physically wiped—unable to get up and not even well enough to be lifted out of bed onto my feet. I had a steady stream of visitors from my croquet club, neighbors and friends. My memory is blurry, but I think I coped well with that, chatting coherently.

Neurologists and other specialists checked my progress. I stuck my tongue out dozens of times as doctors ensured it wasn't drifting to one side or the other. Doctors held up their hands on either side of my face, asking how many fingers were out straight, a preliminary test to determine whether my vision had been affected. I faced dozens of simple questions involving general knowledge and awareness of where I was in time and space—tests of my cognitive resources. Speech, occupational and physical therapists arrived at my bedside, each with their own tasks and tests for me. I seemed to be passing all of the cognitive tests with ease.[79] The most difficult immediate challenge was developing the capability to get out of bed and start walking.

At first, it took two strong men to hoist me onto my feet. After a couple of days, one of the therapists would put a leather belt around me to provide a grip should I fall, then help me out of bed. My mobility soon improved to the point that I could get a few yards down the hall using a walker. By the time I was discharged from the hospital on January 8, I was able to use a walker to get around, pull myself into a car and stand in the shower with my walker. Most of my impediments seemed to be on the left, the side affected by the first, more moderate stroke. My right hand side, which had been completely paralyzed for a few hours on January 1, seemed to be performing relatively normally.

There was no time to dwell on long-term plans for recovery. The first priority was preparing for a medical evacuation from Florida—I was being sent home ASAP with a medical escort. That was an unpleasant experience. I had the best of care and treatment but I resented being in public looking like an invalid. I sat in a wheelchair in the airport, had a seat the first row of the airplane with a medic taking my blood pressure every hour, and had to endure what I considered to be the pitying looks of everyone who passed by me.

Rehabilitation after heart failure and rehabilitation post-stroke appeared to me to be significantly different processes. Healing heart muscle damage is one thing; I had done that and achieved far better results than expected with a muscle that isn't supposed to heal completely. Brain damage? My belief was that healthy parts of the brain would take over the functions once performed by the damaged parts. It was going to be doable.

---

79 The only question I remember not being able to answer was one about the vice-president of the United States, an individual I always regarded as being a non-entity.

*Did regular exercise contribute to my ability to survive heart failure and acute stroke? I was one of the first joggers in Mississauga in the early 1970s, startling people who weren't accustomed to seeing a runner on the sidewalks. This picture, taken in the mid-1990s, shows me running on a treadmill set up in my home office. Some of my friends joked that what was hiding inside me wasn't a little boy who just wanted to be loved—instead there was a mental midget who just loved to pump iron*

# 17.
# Now You Know What It Feels Like to be a Woman

*Dealing with the furies unleashed by stroke*

The after-effects of stroke are multiple, a plague of furies that attack you physically, intellectually, visually and emotionally. Heart failure seems relatively one-dimensional: when your heart isn't pumping enough blood to the rest of your body, you run out of steam instantly and fatigue sets in. Drugs play altered roles. Heart failure survivors get prescriptions that can lead to the strengthening of a damaged muscle, others that allow blood to flow more easily. Stroke survivors take drugs that to me seem mostly preventive—blood thinners and statins designed to avert another stroke.

In the last three weeks in January, I began dealing with rehabilitation in Belleville, depending on a walker to keep me stable whenever I was on my feet. I saw my GP immediately on arriving home. Dr. Paul Weatherall referred me to Dr. Curry Grant, who runs the Stroke Prevention Clinic at Belleville General Hospital. Dr. Grant gave me my first full evaluation. Some of the tests I was familiar with. Some of them were new to me. I was surprised to find that my reflexes were noticeably faster on the damaged side of my body.

Dr. Grant had a number of referrals for me. He sent me to BGH's rehabilitation clinic, had me see a nutritionist and my optometrist. The test in the optometrist's office was long and complex, following moving dots of light in a parabolic dish. I already knew that some stroke victims became blind to things happening on one side of their body; I didn't know that loss of peripheral vision was an obstacle to resuming driving a car. I passed the test and began looking forward to the day when I would get Dr. Grant's okay to drive again. I still had my license but had been told to stay away from the steering wheel for the time being.

In the BGH rehabilitation program I had the attention of various therapists—occupational, recreational, speech and physical. Twice a week I would show up and spend half a day with them. The slurring in my speech disappeared quickly. I was not isolating myself and in need of encouragement to resume socializing, to the limited extent I socialized. Occupational therapy was vital—there were a couple of hours of testing to ensure I still had the mental furniture to drive. Passing that was essential to getting permission to get behind the wheel again, which I got in mid-April, after three and a half months of being a passenger in the car.

My physiotherapist put me through my paces on each visit. I would have spent 10 times as long with her as she had time to devote to me. My balance was bad. I walked with some difficulty. But her records and testing showed that I was making progress. I got sheets of paper with exercises that I could perform at home.

Two incidents in Toronto in January provide clues as to my approach to rehabilitation. On January 10, the day of my medical evacuation from Florida, the vehicle that took me from Pearson airport to home was so large and high it was difficult to get into. The medic accompanying me was startled when I didn't wait to be helped into the back seat. I somehow hurled myself through the back door and managed to clamber onto the seat.

Five days later, in a hastily scheduled visit with Dr. Ross, my wife and I took the subway rather than a cab from Union Station to Toronto General. I wanted to see how I could manage on public transportation. I climbed the long set of stairs at the subway station nearest the hospital, using my right hand on the handrail while dragging and flinging my walker in my left hand. My wife was embarrassed to have to explain to people who offered to help me that I customarily refused all offers of assistance and did everything myself, saying, "That's just the way he is."

I felt I had a three-month window in which my brain would be prime for rewiring. Mobility was my first priority. My walker was always at hand for the first few weeks, sitting beside my bed while I slept, beside my chair when I ate, in front of me in the shower. Walking practice was indoors, in my condo and its long, curving hallway. The walker was lightweight with no wheels. After a few days I began carrying it in front of me, touching it to the floor only when I lost my balance. I progressed from walking down the halls without bumping into the walls to walking under the ceiling lights in the curving hall, attempting to smoothly negotiate a distinctly elliptical path.

Once my physiotherapist said I could switch from a walker to a cane, I bought an ice-gripper for the cane tip and began walking a waterfront trail. Soon I was walking up to two miles a day on the ice and snow. That led to the only time I really needed help to get to my feet. I dropped my cell phone and lost my balance while trying to pick it up. With no benches nearby to use to help me to my feet, I had to accept an offer from a young woman to help me stand up. An embarrassing episode. I didn't let the mild incontinence that was another annoying effect of the strokes interfere with my walking program. I would simply wear heavy navy blue track pants, just in case.

As the year warmed up, I would walk a little more than two miles to the library and back, using my GPS-equipped watch to monitor my progress in walking faster. Eventually, worried that using a cane would lead to problems with my gait, I purchased Nordic walking poles, which gave me two-handed support. I didn't like to go any longer distances without a cane or poles until November, when our Florida accommodation was near a long, elevated boardwalk with handrails on both sides. I practiced walking—striding as rapidly as I could—down that boardwalk. A little over a year after a massive stroke left me paralyzed and bedridden, I was fairly confident about tackling longer distances on level surfaces without walking aids.

After my initial rehabilitation program in Belleville, I began pushing myself, too fast and too hard. I resumed croquet in June, playing in two Canadian championships that month. (And got my ass handed to me on a platter in both tournaments.) The mallet served as a cane when I needed it. I was delighted when I won the first game I played and came out on top in my first two games in the second tournament. But I learned I had lost my stamina. While I could play reasonably well on the first day, by the third day, I was missing the ball and dropping my mallet. The overall effect of rushing into competition was discouraging. I have since decided that in the foreseeable future I will play croquet just for fun.

As I write this, more than a year and a half after the CVAs, most people can't see any problems with my walking or croquet playing. Many are surprised to find out that I am a stroke survivor. The left leg that I once had to grab and lift into the car with my hands is fully functional. I don't like uneven ground and I'm not happy on stairs if a handrail is not available. Nor do I like walking down a set of stairs while carrying a box that requires two hands. When I am fatigued, as in leaving the gym, l am even more dependent on handrails on stairs and will cling to them rather than just keeping them in easy reach.

*Crooked smile is post-stroke. A year after I had a stroke that almost ended my life, people would comment on my recovery. There was nothing in my appearance that immediately gave away the fact that I had suffered a stroke. I believed the same until I noticed in pictures that my smile had become unusual, sometimes showing more bottom teeth than top ones.*

Balance issues proved more intractable and I am still dealing with them. At first I would lurch unexpectedly and uncontrollably. I needed a walker in the shower, a grab bar to get in and out of the enclosure. When I looked up or to the side, I would be in danger of falling over. Balance is trainable and mine gradually improved as I became more mobile. Rehabilitation helped, with the physiotherapist working with me on balance exercises. But the time with the physiotherapist was far too short and came to an end after a few weeks.

The exercise program outlined for me in rehabilitation soon fell apart. At the YMCA gym I had access to the wobble boards, the Bosu balls, the cable machines and other equipment I needed for the program. What I lacked included metrics—some way of evaluating my progress—as well as an evolving program that would provide me with variety and adjust to my changing capabilities.

A personal trainer came to my rescue. Realizing that I needed coaching to stick to a program that involved more than my customary aerobic exercise and weight training, I began shopping for a trainer who would ensure I was doing various other exercises properly and motivate me to continue doing them. I found a young woman with advanced degrees in kinesiology, previous experience with stroke survivors and an upbeat personality that made every session pleasurable. It was a lucky break to encounter Sarah Ditmars, who was launching her career as a private fitness consultant in a tiny gym called "Living Energy" less than a quarter mile from my condo.

*Sarah Ditmars is my personal trainer. I found her by sheer luck. With a Master's degree in kinesiology, experience working with stroke survivors and patience working with people who are struggling with disability, she is an excellent resource. My weekly sessions with her are an essential component of my recovery efforts. I get evaluation on my progress and guidance to exercises I should begin doing. – Photo taken on Sarah's tablet Oct 2015*

With her profound knowledge of how people should move their bodies and the exercises required to get muscles to perform better, Sarah evaluated my walking and balance. She led me through the routines that would help me to improve. More important, she kept records and evaluated me with a stopwatch, timing how long I could balance on one leg. She counted the number of slight lurches as I walked down a hallway. Some of her evaluation was subjective—based on practiced observation rather than measurement. I instinctively trusted her judgement. Sarah became my metric for stroke recovery; every once in a while, she would test me and let me know if I was making progress.

I found out how important her contribution to my recovery was when I left for Florida. For the first three months away I stuck to my program with daily visits to the gym and a weekly balance class. Then as the gym got crowded, my participation diminished and my tentative efforts at riding a bicycle petered out. In the spring, when I returned to my condo in Canada, I set up a program with Sarah ensuring each week starts with a Monday morning session with her. It's a great motivator in keeping up an effective exercise and balance program.

Seventeen months after the massive CVA, I was not only back on my bicycle but confident enough to ride it five miles to the gym and back several times a week. I keep my wobble boards in the living room and try daily to spend time balancing while watching television. Standing on one foot is another matter; progress is slower than I like. But I'm not giving up.

The psychological and emotional aftermath of the strokes diminished more slowly than the physical deficits. My slight difficulty in walking soon went away; I learned to manage my penchant for incontinence; only my wife noticed that I drooled constantly. But I didn't like writing about stroke or stroke-related topics—I got writer's block. And emotional lability struck me with a vengeance.

Labile means changeable and stroke survivors can lose control of their emotions as a result of brain damage. Some will laugh for no reason at all. Others will break down in tears. I would choke up when trying to speak, sounding like I was overcome by emotion when I was mostly annoyed by the inability to express myself in a clear, emotionless voice. I was at my absolute worst in February when I submitted my application for a disabled parking permit—I could barely choke out the information required by the clerk. I'm sure I sounded like I was on the verge of tears.

My choking up elicited all kinds of pity from people who supported me. They would wait for me to be able to speak clearly and say something like "That's okay." But it wasn't okay. The best response I ever got was from my massage therapist. I was getting one of my regular treatments from Christine Bennett and chatting away, when I choked up. Christine asked me what was the matter. I explained about emotional lability and losing control. She said, "Now you know what it feels like to be a woman."

That was empathy without a surfeit of sympathy, exactly what the situation called for as far as I was concerned.

Despite the fact that my emotional lability was mild, I complained about it to every doctor I saw. I had always been known for my ability to appear calm—when I was acting as Director of Emergency Information for Ontario, I was sometimes referred to as "The Iceman" for my apparent unflappability. The doctors' answer, whenever I got one, seemed to be treatment with Selective Serotonin Reuptake Inhibitors (SSRIs). It was always presented as optional and I refused it. I had never taken drugs in that class and had heard unpleasant stories about them.

Instead, I chose to confront the problem in a different way. Because the trigger for most of the emotional swings was talking about my strokes, I decided that being upfront about my rehabilitation problems would be therapeutic. That didn't work very well. More than a year after having strokes, talking about my CVA could still affect my emotions and my voice.

There were psychological effects as well as emotional ones. There was no dramatic change in personality. I seem to have remained the same contrarian curmudgeon but my ability to write was affected. For the first time in my life I had writer's block. It got progressively worse but it was selective. It affected my ability to do my newsletter for Croquet Canada—I would sit at my computer for hours on that small project and accomplish absolutely nothing. Eventually I had to resign all my positions with the Canadian branch of the sport. Yet I could write for the club in Florida, where a large number of club members had visited me in hospital and my problems were widely known.

Writers' block affected this book, which originated when Audrey Bradshaw, the Belleville stroke rehabilitation nurse, suggested that since I had written so much on stroke, I should write up my own experience. I couldn't start writing with stroke so I transformed the book into memoirs and left the stroke chapters to last, hoping I would be able to write about it as a logical continuation of the story of my career. It's still not easy to find the words I want to use.

My inability to comprehend all the information provided to me by stroke specialists in Belleville and Toronto was also a psychological effect. I can understand most medical terminology and much of what doctors tell me, but when I was shown MRIs of the inside of my head, my mind seemed to slip into neutral. I did not comprehend. There are none so blind as those who will not see. I felt I was not processing information properly when Dr. Curry Grant or Dr. Frank Silver showed me what particular brain damage was causing specific problems I was having. Back in 1978, when I first started writing on CVA, I had been shown human brains in jars, brains cut open to expose the damage done by stroke. I really didn't like looking at images of the inside of my head showing similar injuries.

I remembered all the encouraging things the doctors had to say. I have a refined technique of hearing what I want to hear and blocking out other information. Dr. Grant and Dr. Silver have taken time with me to show me where blood flow has re-established itself around arterial blockages and other relevant information based on a state-of-the art MRI that I had done at Toronto Western. I think my mind refused to process that data; it's more than I wanted to know. I have dumped my MRI information on a flash drive that I carry on a chain with my MedicAlert token. If I am ever hospitalized again, any doctor who treats me will have information on what is old brain damage.

Both my stroke doctors encouraged me to return to my routine of wintering in Florida. Dr. Silver referred me to the anticoagulation clinic at Toronto General, where I learned to test my own INR (international normalized ratio) that is a guide to how long it takes my blood to clot. Stroke survivors often set a goal of an INR of 2.5, taking carefully adjusted amounts of warfarin to control clotting. I now take my INR regularly and report the results by email to a nurse at TGH, who responds quickly telling me when to test again and if I need to adjust warfarin dosage.

In mid-October 2014, I gathered up my medical needs for a winter in the south. I had a cooler chest full of prescription drugs—beta blockers and ACE inhibitors that I was still taking in continuing heart failure treatment, statins and surprising quantities of warfarin for blood thinning.

Just before I left I had a consultation with Dr. Silver. He evaluated my strength, my left-right differences, my reflexes and my walking ability. In that consultation I raised the possibility that I had been traumatized by the near-death experience I had endured 10 months earlier. In my mind, that would help explain my sudden writer's block, my odd reactions to events relating to croquet and the fact that my emotional lability seemed to be specific to stroke-related items. He didn't seem to put much credence in that line of thought.

So I headed south with my memoirs about a third written, knowing that I had a big event awaiting me. The Venice doctor who had performed the life-saving procedure on me was a friend of a croquet-playing acquaintance. Dr. Gordon would talk to me about what happened on New Year's Day. I had the report he had dictated. I needed to chat with him because the language and concepts in his report were hard for me to understand.

I dragged my feet in setting up the interview, a clear indication to me that there were psychological factors at play. I frittered away five months without getting up the nerve to face the music. I was actually running out of time in Florida and had only a couple of weeks left when I finally gave our mutual acquaintance the go-ahead to set up a meeting.

In a phone conversation with Dr. Gordon establishing the time and place of our meeting, he asked me how I was. His tone of voice made me think he didn't expect me to have recovered to something near normality. And he gave me a heads up. "You've probably been told this already," he said, "But you died on the table during the procedure. We all thought you were gone." I had not been told. Dr. Ross had once referred obliquely to my near-death experience as one that would take a long time to get over, but no one led me to believe I was actually dead for a time.

My wife was worried that I would not be able to control my emotions when I met Dr. Gordon. As things turned out, I seemed to revert to my old, super-calm approach. I wanted to thank Dr. Gordon again for saving my life, something I had done before I was wheeled out of the cardiac studio. But my overriding purpose was to gather information for the hardest chapter to write in my memoirs.

The meeting took place in a pizza party at our mutual friend's house. Dr. Gordon arrived on a motorcycle. While the other people in the room ignored us as best they could, Dr. Gordon and I quietly discussed in plain language the things his report said in medical code words. He regarded the whole episode as next to miraculous. Something out of the ordinary had happened that morning. I absorbed as much information as I could, resolving to write it up, then have another meeting with Dr. Gordon the next week to make sure I had the story reasonably straight.

Dr. Gordon turned out to be one of a kind. In his late 40s and known to his neighbors as "Dr. Chuck," he is outgoing and popular. I thought he would be a cardiologist, neurologist or brain surgeon. He was none of the above, with a specialty I had never heard of—interventional radiologist. He had started training to be a surgeon but changed direction to specialize in radiology, then narrowed down his interest to interventional radiology. Instead of depending on a scalpel to do his surgery, he worked through catheters inserted into patient's arteries. Thrombectomy, the removal of problematic blood clots, is one of his primary interests.

His email address reflects the fact that he sees himself as a raptor—an outside agent that swoops in and carries something off. He invents "snares" that can be inserted in an artery though a catheter and pull blood clots out of an artery. He patents his medical inventions under the name Charles Samuel Squire Gordon. He told me that after doing the procedure on me, he patented a new snare, one that is permeable and will take solid material out while leaving the liquid behind.

He has worldwide patents on another medical device, a clamp that stops the femoral artery from bleeding after a catheter is removed. I brought home the literature on his patents and intend to do more writing on the subject. So far, all I have noticed is that he gets some of his mechanical inspiration from the way motorcycle designers have solved their unique challenges.

I expect he will still be in Venice when I return next winter. He explained that he prefers to practice in a smaller community. If he moved to Tampa or Miami, he would find a large medical bureaucracy that might cramp his style. Sometimes he does things that are out of the ordinary. In my case, for example, he heated the catheter with live steam to make it more flexible and allow it to reach further into my brain.

I intend to find out more about his work and inventions when I return to Venice this winter. It could bring my writing on stroke full circle—from the early days when all that could be done was help people with rehabilitation to the present when medicine can actually bring the event to a complete, if shuddering, stop.

In the late spring of 2015, back in Belleville, I began to learn more about contemporary treatment of stroke. But I had to take drugs to allow the learning to begin.

# 18.
# SSRIs—Serenity Now!

*Crying on the outside*

Whenever I discussed my strokes, I would choke up. My worst experience was applying for a disabled parking permit—I was barely able to speak. It sounded to me as if I was about to burst into tears. I believed it was simply a psychological-emotional reaction to the near-death experience of acute stroke –paralysis, inability to speak (aphasia) and brief unconsciousness. I knew it was called emotional lability (changeability), that it was common in stroke survivors and that I had only a mild case.

My emotional lability was both annoying and embarrassing. I have always prided myself in projecting an aura of calmness and self-control. Much of the work I had in crisis communications came my way because of my apparent unflappability. Then, after I had strokes, I began to resemble the people who couldn't cope when stress levels soared.

At first, I thought the lability would diminish with time. When it didn't, I faced it head-on. Instead of avoiding discussion of stroke and its repercussions, I would talk about the stroke, struggling to control my emotional lability during the conversation. I figured that I might be able to talk it out. Eventually, time and distance from the event would diminish its emotional impact. Talking would help speed up the process.

Results were mixed. I made some progress in self-control, but I knew the problem was far from solved. When fighting to control vocal indications of emotionality, I knew my capabilities were limited—full emotional lability could return with a vengeance at any time.

After about a year and a half, I threw in the towel and gave up on trying to cure myself. I had complained to all my doctors, even my urologist, about the problem. Dr. Curry Grant of the Stroke Prevention Unit at Belleville General Hospital suggested that I could treat the annoying symptoms with prescription drugs.

There was a major obstacle to my taking his advice. The drugs were SSRIS—Selective Serotonin Reuptake Inhibitors. SSRIS, in my opinion, are anti-psychotics, not anti-depressants. From the time in the 1980s that I first heard of them, I considered them to be a crutch, taken by people who couldn't deal head-on with their problems and needed medication to cope with stress. People spoke of appalling SSRI side effects, including encouraging violence and suicide.

Dr. Grant said the SSRI he recommended could not only reduce the lability but might also dry my mouth as a side effect, helping to control the drooling that bothered my wife.

I reluctantly began taking half the minimum dosage of Escitalopram the first of May 2015. After a few weeks on half-doses, I wasn't having any intolerable side-effects—bad dreams, suicidal thoughts, sleeping all the time, etcetera, etcetera. The positive effects were noticeable. I could deal with stroke-related matters without getting upset, without a quaver in my voice. So I bit the bullet and began taking full doses. That worked even better. Since I began taking the full minimum prescribed dose, the emotional lability seems to be well under control.

I still refer to my SSRIS as "anti-psychotics." I have been corrected by MDS who said they were really anti-depressants. I preferred my nomenclature because I was convinced my problems were psychological. Stroke, in my opinion, had made me crazy—as good an excuse as any for being legitimately somewhat mentally disturbed.

I was presented with an alternative explanation—a physical one—when Dr. Grant guided me to a medical text on the limbic system. It talked about stroke-damaged brain cells in the part of the brain between the stem and the neocortex. I read it and my understanding was that when some limbic cells were damaged (infarcted), you lose some control over emotions. When enough cells are damaged by a stroke, the survivor may have crying jags accompanied by a quivering jaw. I have never seen this pseudobulbar effect, but I imagined it was something similar to a three-year old child's tantrum.

Intrigued by the idea that my lability might be a result of a few fried brain cells rather than psychological or emotional trauma, I discussed it with a retired medical friend whom I visit for a couple hours every week and who has been an invaluable help in reviewing this memoir and keeping it on track.

He has been retired for decades, having finished medical school in 1952. He said in his day they did not use the phrase "limbic system" but used to refer to the reptilian brain and the "fight or flight" response it controls. A light went on for me—I realized that for the first time in my life I had been regularly experiencing the "flight" response.

That could explain why my emotional lability always seemed to be triggered by something to do with stroke. It also gave me a clue as to why I developed selective writer's block (I could write about anything, except some subjects that were stroke-related), and why I can still occasionally feel some twinges of deep-rooted emotionality when I am writing on the subject of my stroke. The lability does not affect my writing or thinking about other serious health matters—dealing with my heart failure experience is strictly ho-hum.

How the SSRIs dampen lability is a mystery to me. I am simply delighted that it is almost gone. Sarah Ditmars, my personal trainer who spends a lot of time dealing directly with my stroke-related problems (balance, the ability to turn my head while walking and look up while standing) agrees that my choking up was noticeable on many occasions. Now it has almost vanished.

I take a lot of prescription medicine. My current daily consumption of pills is 14. The crazy pill has become my favorite—the others keep me alive; the SSRI brings me serenity, enhancing my joy in being alive.

There are unexpected benefits of my SSRIs as well. Suddenly I developed an interest in what had happened to me. I thought I had been listening to my doctors but not focusing on understanding the detailed information they were giving me. I suspect I didn't internalize half of what I had been told, not because I was incapable of comprehending it, but because stroke information could trigger my fight/flight reaction. I took flight by shutting down.

By nature, I am an inveterate researcher. I normally use two computers at the same time. I type text or surf the web on one and use the other as a dictionary/encyclopedia. Any word or phrase that puzzles or intrigues me gets put into a search engine.

I had known since January 8, 2014 that Dr. Gordon had used a penumbra device to remove the clot from my brainstem. Dr. Gordon had told me in our all-too-brief interviews in March 2015 that it was a miniscule vacuum cleaner used through a catheter. It was 19 months after my acute stroke that I got around to typing "penumbra" into BING.[80]

Why the delay? Normally, I could be expected to research that word as soon as I read it in the radiology report in Venice FL. Yet for more than a year and a half, I procrastinated. I avoided taking my normal course of action. I attribute it to the same phenomenon that caused my emotional lability and writer's block—a damaged portion of my brain that affected my behavior. It was steering me away from dealing with that particular problem. The flight-fight response had gotten stuck on flight when dealing with stroke.

When I finally did BING the word "penumbra," a treasure trove of information poured onto my computer screen.

I discovered the life-saving thrombectomy I had undergone was a part of a broader medical field called Endovascular Treatment (ET). Two major studies of ET's effectiveness in treating stroke victims had been completed within the past year. The North American study, called ESCAPE,[81] came to some remarkable conclusions:

> (A) controlled trial show(ed) that a clot retrieval procedure, known as endovascular treatment (ET), can dramatically improve patient outcomes after an acute ischemic stroke. The study, led by researchers at the University of Calgary's Hotchkiss Brain Institute (HBI), shows a dramatic improvement in outcomes and a reduction in deaths from stroke.

---

80 BING is a popular search engine sponsored by Microsoft. Wags say the acronym means "Because It's Not Google." I prefer it for precisely that reason, so I never google things.

81 This is an acronym used for the trial named Randomized Assessment of Rapid Endovascular Treatment of Ischemic Stroke.

> Overall, positive outcomes for patients increased from 30 per cent to 55 per cent. In many cases, instead of suffering major neurological disability, patients went home to resume their lives. The overall mortality rate was reduced from two in 10 patients for standard treatment of care to one in 10 patients—a 50 per cent reduction with ET.

That described my experience exactly. I suffered an acute ischemic stroke. Instead of dying, I had ET and went home to resume a normal life. Knowing that stroke is one of the leading causes of death and disability and that at least half a million people have strokes every year, I assumed this was big news that I had somehow failed to notice.

I searched the web for news stories. Nothing from North America. There was one story from Australia. Astounded that such a major development in treatment of a devastating syndrome could go unnoticed, I contacted the research team. The researchers seemed to agree with me that the story had been under-reported. One researcher told me a national publication in Canada had taken a pass, turning down a major story with a Calgary connection.

I pitched it to *The Globe and Mail*, using a contact I thought might remember me from decades ago to contact the health editor. I talked to the health section and made a formal pitch by email, but I have yet to hear back from the paper. I also approached Maclean's. At a lunch with Peter C. Newman, I outlined the development in ET and revealed to him that I had survived an acute stroke. We agreed that it was too important a story to ignore. He offered to put me in contact with health editors at Maclean's or to write the story up himself in his regular column. I suggested he put it in a column.

The ESCAPE researchers have recommended that clot removal with removable stents become standard procedure for treating stroke in patients who meet the criteria for the procedure. The existing standard procedure involves tPA [82] for suitable candidates. Only about 15 hospitals in Canada have the trained interventional radiologists and sophisticated imaging capability required for thrombectomies. It will be an expensive process gearing up to make ET fully available.

---

82 Tissue plasminogen activator, a pharmacological agent which can dissolve some clots.

A few weeks after I decided to write a news story on ET developments, my retired doctor friend presented me with the September 8 issue of the *Canadian Medical Association Journal*.[83] The cover story was on acute ischemic stroke, with an appalling picture of a stroke-affected brain on the front cover. The comprehensive account came to the conclusion that "acute stroke care is rapidly catching up to acute coronary care."

We are all familiar with people living normal lives after heart attacks. If you are middle-aged or older, you probably know people who have had bypasses or stents or even replacement valves. It's become a normal part of everyday life. Stroke may soon be the same.

In the late 1970s, when I first started writing about stroke, people unfortunate enough to suffer an acute stroke often ended up disabled or dead. Now, only about 40 years later, those victims have a good chance for normal life. The developments in treatment of stroke have to be one of the great stories in medical progress. I am one of the first beneficiaries.

---

[83] http://www.cmaj.ca/content/187/12/887.full?sid=6c415b37-a1d4-4021-9404-b11821007f09 Subscription required.

# EPILOGUE

# 19.
# There are Lives That are Erring and Aimless, and Deaths That Just Hang by a Hair

Robert W. Service's "The spell of the Yukon" was one of my favorite poems from high school days. The work is often considered doggerel dashed off by a bank clerk who tallied columns of numbers while others around him boldly sought their fortunes in an early 20$^{th}$ century gold rush. The literary oeuvre of a Walter Mitty type if ever there was one.

A memorable line from the poem is, "Yet it isn't the gold that I'm wanting, so much as just finding the gold." In my youth, that seemed to address my wish for a life full of novelty and discovery. Whether I would end up wealthy wasn't a high priority. My life had to be adventurous and innovative.

Service also wrote, "There are lives that are erring and aimless, and deaths that just hang by a hair." That was prophecy for me.

Until I was 30, almost every choice I made was erring. In university from the time I was 16 until I was 24, I started off in engineering, switched to pure science, to history, to political science and back to history. Five universities. Six majors. When the cushy academic job I thought I wanted didn't materialize, I ended up in an unsuitable occupation. Unhappy at not being able to use my talents the way I wanted. But with a family to support.

Sorting out the results of youthful erring aimlessness led to a prolonged life crisis. One dimension—finding adventure, excitement and novelty in my 30s—was easy. My talent for writing and aptitude for photography made it a cakewalk. Extricating myself from the complicated life I had created was slow and messy.

In my 40s I was finally free of the obligations and burdens that were wrong for me, keeping only my children. I was still aimless. I sought new projects that seemed interesting, always willing to drop them for something novel or more exciting. The destination wasn't all that important, but the journey had to be stimulating and challenging. I wanted to enjoy the ride.

Many acquaintances called me crazy for refusal to settle on a career, for the risks I seemed to take and for the objective hazards I was apparently willing to face. My stories and pictures—polar bears, avalanches, ice climbing, back country expeditions, rock climbing—seemed to require risk-taking that had my death just hanging by a hair. The operative word is *seemed*.

My battle scar from the adventurous years is evidence of how safe I was. It's above my left eye and very small, concealed in a wrinkle. I got it taking a photo of a domestic chicken. A captive golden eagle—a raptor with a six-foot wingspread—attacked me. In her demented mind, I was molesting her trans-species adopted chick. That blemish is a souvenir of my efforts to soar with the eagles. And of my aversion to working with another species of avifauna.

My death actually was hanging by a hair several times. By then I was in my 60s, with no interest in taking chances. Radiology reveals horrific scars left by close encounters with the Grim Reaper. My heart is enlarged, a result of its efforts to cope with catastrophic failure of its left ventricle. My brainstem is an obscene mess, thanks to two strokes. Magnetic resonance images of the grey matter between my ears look like Rorschach inkblots. Those scars are evidence that no matter what chances you take in life, there's a good chance that a cardiovascular misfortune will get you in the end.

*Invictus*, a poem by William Ernest Henley, also appealed to me in my youth. It seemed to speak to my life situation. The opening lines resonated with me:

> Out of the night that covers me,
> Black as the Pit from pole to pole,
> I thank whatever gods may be
> For my unconquerable soul.

I felt alone in the world. With dysfunctional, alcoholic relatives, family support was nil, often negative. Two or three years ahead of myself in school, I had no peer group support. I was always the youngest—and usually the biggest—kid in my class in elementary and high school. Always feeling like a square peg in a round hole and resented or ignored by others for being immature, too large or overly bright. I concluded I could rely only on myself.

Fortunately, the last half of the 20th century was an environment that fostered success. If my story has a moral, it is: *be born at the right time.*

Had I been born later, demographics would have been my adversary rather than my friend. A little older than the baby boomers, I surfed their wave. As society prepared itself for the tsunami of those born after World War II, I got first choice in many areas—notably education, housing and employment. When I was single in my 40s, demographic and social trends made large numbers of slightly younger boomers available for entertainment, for pleasure, and for finding the right partner to have a "happy wife, happy life" retirement and old age.

Had I been born earlier, the results would have been catastrophic. I would have been blind from cataracts in my 60s, dead from heart failure or strokes before I was 70.

Living through dramatic technological change favored my career. In my working years, the world transformed from a mechanical, analog planet to a computerized, digital one. The implications of that change are enormous for a communicator.

I built my original credentials in a national paper with a mass audience before the Internet fragmented audiences. Thirty years ago, only a select few got to write for *The Globe and Mail* on a regular basis and their articles were widely read. Lots of people got to know who I was and what I represented. Even in 2015, some people who get an out-of-the-blue email from me will reply because they remember my byline from newspaper days.

My four decades of writing and communications career took place in the best half-century in modern times for those who like to work for themselves, go their own way and deal with exciting things. It's been a slice.

*Ron and Elaine Truman – photo by Roy Grandy*

*Index*

# A

acid rain, 86n20
AIDS research, 93
alcohol, and interviews, 133
Algonquin Park Residents Association, 120
Algonquin Provincial Park
    leaseholders and cottagers, 118–121
    moose management, 124, 124n37
    Native hunting, 141–142
Algonquin Wildlands League (AWL), 119, 121
*Angler and Hunter* magazine, 88
angling, 27–28, 79
animal rights activism, 89–93, 126, 127
animal users and user groups, 90–93, 124
archaeology, *Globe and Mail* stories, 41–43
archives, 8, 9, 55
arenas and ice, 160–161
arts, and tourism, 102–103
Association of Major Power Consumers of Ontario (AMPCO), 115
Association of Municipalities of Ontario (AMO), 104, 156–159
avalanches, and skiing, 24–26

# B

Baker, Dr. Brian, 193
BC Tourism, 23

Belleville General Hospital (BGH), 208–209
Bennett, Christine, 214
beta blockers, 187–188, 190
Bradshaw, Audrey, 215
Brewer, Carl, 83–84
British Columbia, downhill skiing, 23–26
bush plane museum, 69–70
Buss, Mike, 124

# C

Canadian Ski Marathon (CSM), 21, 41
CANDU reactors, 95–96
cardiomyopathy, 183, 187, 189
cardiovascular accident (CVA). *See* stroke
cardiovascular problems
    beta blockers, 187–188, 190
    in family of RT, 183–184
    indications and diagnosis, 184–186, 187–188, 189–190
    overview, 4–5, 182
    recovery and rehabilitation, 182, 190–196
    severity of, 186–188
    and sleeping problems, 193
    surgery for defibrillator, 188–189, 190
    VO2 max testing, 193–194
Castle, Margie, 202–203
Catholicism in Truman relatives, 85n19
Chief Provincial Firearms Officer (CPFO) of Ontario, 32–33
children
    education about wildlife, 122–123
    *Globe and Mail* stories, 40
China, and fire-fighting story, 59–60
Christian, Terry, 40
Coburn, Brian, 103
comic book on energy, 153–154
communications consulting. *See* crisis communications

compass from whaling ship, 42–43
conservation authorities (CAs), 104
consultant career, overview, 72
Convention on International Trade in Endangered Species (CITES) meeting, 91–93
Cree women, crafts and traditional ways, 135–138
crisis communications
    beginnings, 83–84
    definition and "first rule," 86, 98
    on emergency preparedness, 93–95, 96–97
    and environmentalism, 86–89
    fur industry and animal users, 88–93
    in hunting and recreation, 87–88
    municipal sector and CAs, 104
    nuclear issues and reactors, 95–96, 97
    with Ontario government, 83, 97, 98–99
    overview, 3, 71–72
    partnership venture, 104–105
    RT's character and skills for, 71–72, 84–86, 94
    and SARS, 98–99, 100
    and 9/11, 100, 101–102
    in tourism industry, 98–103
    training in Ottawa, 94–95
croquet, 5, 55, 196, 200, 205, 210, 211, 214, 216
cross-country skiing, *Globe and Mail* stories, 20–21, 41
culture, and tourism, 102–103

# D

Darlington 89 and Darlington 91 exercises, 95, 96, 97
Day, Dennis, 201
death, RT's return from, 198–200, 216–217
deer, 29–30, 135–137
Deerhurst Inn review, 37–38, 38n10
digital technology, introduction, 147–151, 159
dilated cardiomyopathy (DCM), 183, 187, 189

director of emergency information, 83, 94, 95, 97
    *See also* crisis communications
Displayphones, 148
Ditmars, Sarah, 212–213, 212f, 221
downhill skiing, *Globe and Mail* stories, 19–20, 22–26
Doyle, Richard, 38n10
drinking water issues, Native community, 143–144

# E

Eagleson, Alan, 83–84
electricity
    politics and policies of, 145, 156, 166–168, 170–171
    supply in Ontario, 115–116, 154–156, 159, 166–167
    use reduction, 156–162
Elliptigo, 196
emergency preparedness, 93–95, 96–97
emotions
    lability issues due to stroke, 213–214, 219–221
    and logic, 127–128
endangered species, 115n34, 123
Endovascular Treatment (ET), 222–224
energy and industry
    charetting approach to change, 161–162
    comic book for kids, 153–154
    efficiency in use, 156–162
    non-conventional energy, 152, 166
    speech writing, 115–117, 154–155
    *See also* Ministry of Energy (MoE); specific type of energy
Energy Choices Conferences, 116, 155
environmentalism
    and crisis communications, 86–89
    energy and electricity, 152, 167–168
    impact and goals, 87, 88–89, 121–122
    phonies and urbanites in, 119, 121
    and speech writing in water resources issues, 110–111

*See also* wilderness conservation
ESCAPE study, 222–223
Evans, Cliff, 11f
Eves, Ernie, 103
Exercises Darlington 89 and Darlington 91, 95, 96, 97

# F

F-1 cameras, 50
Federal-Provincial-Territorial Tourism Ministers' conference on SARS, 98–99, 103
Ferguson, Will, 116–117
Firearms Acquisition Certificates (FACs), 31–32
fishing, 27–28, 79
Fort Severn, ON, 134–135, 138–139
freelance writing. *See* writing career of RT
Fulford, Robert, 102
fur industry, 88–92, 93, 124, 125
Fur Institute of Canada (FIC), 89–92, 125

# G

Gibson, Dan, 121
Gill, Earle, 87
*Globe and Mail*
    on Algonquin Provincial Park, 119
    archaeology stories, 41–43
    children stories, 40
    digitization claims, 46
    Eagleson story, 84
    end of work at, 43, 78
    environmental reporting, 87
    fishing stories, 27–28
    guns and shooting stories, 30–34
    hunting stories, 28–30
    killing of stories, 38–39

  last article, 44–46
  merger of sections and expansion of writing, 34–37
  NDP insert, 53–55
  overview of work at, 2, 17
  photography and photo department, 48–49, 51, 52–54
  Recreation section work, 19–35, 37
  RT's views on, 35, 46
  sailing stories, 28
  skiing stories, 19–26, 41
  stroke story, 223
  Thursday section work, 34, 36–46
  Travel section, 22
  women's section stories, 38–40
Gordon, Dr. Charles, 197–199, 198f, 203–204, 216–218, 222
Grant, Dr. Curry, 208–209, 215, 220
Greenpeace, 88–89
guns and shooting stories, 30–34
  laws and licensing, 31–34
Gupta, Dr. Anup, 187

# H

Hachinski, Dr. Vladimir, 203
Harris, Mike, and government, 54, 104, 114, 115, 117
health problems of RT. *See* cardiovascular problems; stroke
Heart and Stroke Foundation, work for, 181, 183, 202
heart failure. *See* cardiovascular problems
Henley, William Ernest, 228
Herscovici, Alan, 90
Holden, Alfred, 121
Hollett, Dr. Peter, 190
Hudak, Tim and 100-event tour, 100–101, 106–110
Hunter, Mike, 134
hunting
  and crisis communications, 87–88
  education about, 125–126

*Globe and Mail* stories, 28–30
and hides for crafts, 135–137
*Landmarks* story, 60
Natives in Algonquin Provincial Park, 141–142
RT as hunter, 29f, 30–31

# I

ice in arenas, 160–161
implantable cardiac defibrillator (ICD), 188–189, 190
Internet, and speech writing, 107
*Invictus* (Henley), 228
ischemic stroke, 223–224

# J

Jackson, Cam, 103, 112
Johannsen, Jackrabbit, 21–22

# K

Keating, Michael, 87
Kerrio, Vince, 114, 115
Killington, VT, downhill skiing, 23
Kolonoski, George, 56f

# L

lability issues of stroke, 213–214, 219–221
Lam, Jean, 98, 99
*Landmarks* work
    adventures at, 18
    fire-fighting story, 59–60
    mission of magazine, 59
    moose hunt story, 60
    photography, 53, 58

polar bear tagging story, 56–58, 62–70
snapping turtles story, 61–62
sturgeons story, 60–61
language, and children, 40
Left Ventricle Ejection Fraction (LVEF), 189–190
Lei, Dr. Calvin, 187
Liberal Party (Ontario), and energy/electricity, 166, 167, 169, 169n60, 170

# M

Mace, Edward, 76, 77
magazine work, overview, 18
Mamiya C330 camera, 50
Manitoulin Island, wilderness tour for VOP, 76–77
*Mary and John* ship, 11n2
McConkey, Diamond Jim, 23–24
McCormack, George, 132
McLuhan, Marshall, 126–127
Mike, from Winisk, ON, 134
Ministry of Energy (MoE)
    comic book for kids, 153–154
    speech writing, 114–117, 154–155
    and wind power, 151–152
    writing work, 151–154
Ministry of Natural Resources (MNR), 59, 114–115, 136–137
Ministry of Tourism (Ontario), wilderness tours, 73, 80
Minnesota heritage and archives, 8–9
Mitty, Walter, 1–2, 13
moose, 60, 124–125, 135–137
Moose and Deer Hide program, 135–137
*The Moose in Ontario* booklet, 124
"More to Discover" tour, 107
Mt. Kirkup, BC, downhill skiing, 24–25
Municipal Electric Association (MEA), 117
Municipal Energy Conservation Program (MECP), 156–158
municipalities

crisis communications, 104
electricity use, 156–162

# N

National Archives of USA, 9
*National Post*, stories for, 43
Native issues
    drinking water, 143–144
    Fort Severn, ON, 134–135, 138–139
    hunting in Algonquin Park, 141–142
    interviews with locals, 133, 135
    Mike's story, 134
    other writings, 143–144
    Polar Bear Provincial Park, 132–134
    RT's views on, 141
    traditional way of life, 138–139
    Winisk and Peawanuck villages, 129–132
    women and hides, 135–138, 136f
NDP government (Ontario)
    energy policy, 116–117
    insert for newspapers, 53–55
    park policy and hunting, 141
    RT's views on, 54, 116
Neillands, Robin Hunter, 73, 74–78
9/11, and crisis communications, 100, 101–102
Non-Utility Generation (NUG), 166–167
Northern Telecom (Nortel), work at, 147–151
nuclear issues and CANDU reactors, 157n46
    crisis communications, 95–96, 97
    opposition to, 155–156
    speech writing, 115–116

# O

obituary for D. Roseborough, 44–46

O'Dette, Jack, 120
ODU Otter plane, 63–65, 67–68, 69–70, 70f
100-event tour, 100–101, 106–110
Ontario Energy Corporation (OEC), 167
*Ontario Energy Network,* 151, 156–157, 162
Ontario Federation of Anglers and Hunters (OFAH), 87–88, 120, 125–126
Ontario Hydro, 95, 96, 116, 117, 166
Ontario Municipal Board (OMB), 174, 174n66, 175
Ontario Native Affairs Secretariat (ONAS), 141, 143
Ontario Power Authority (OPA), 175–177
Ontario Provincial Police, 33, 82, 95
Ontario Recreation Facilities Association (ORFA), 160–161, 162
Ontario Ski Resorts Association, 23
Ontario Tourism, wilderness tours, 73, 80
Ontario Wilderness Guides Association (OWGA), 36
OptiSolar, 165f, 168–178
*Outdoor Canada,* 119

# P

paintball, 75
parks, and wilderness conservation, 118–119
Peawanuck, ON, 129–132
penumbra device, 222–223
Peter Munk Cardiac Clinic, 187–188, 192
Peterson, John, 49–50
photography
    in archives, 55
    b/w and color, 53
    digital technology, 55
    and *Globe and Mail,* 48–49, 51, 52–54
    *Landmarks* work, 53, 58
    learning, 17, 47–48, 49–50
    NDP insert, 53–55
    1970s technology, 50–51
    of ODU Otter plane, 70, 70f

and risk taking, 51–52
of women, 52
Piper Museum, 10
Piper PA-12, 7–8, 10, 10f
poachers, 60, 61
Polar Bear Provincial Park, 132–134
*Polar Bears and Other Scares* (Truman), writing of, 215, 216–217
polar bear tagging story, 56–58, 62–70
    air travel to and from, 62–65, 67–68
Pope, Alan, 114, 115
Provincial Archives (Ontario), RT's photos in, 55
ptarmigan shooting incident, 139–140

# R

Rae, Bob, and government, 55, 116–117
Recreation section of *Globe and Mail*, 19–35, 37
Red Bay site story, 41–42
Renewable Energy Standard Offer Program (RESOP) legislation, 168
retirement life, overview, 5
Rife, Bob, 29, 30, 31, 33, 34, 37n9
*Robertson v Thomson* class action lawsuit, 46
Roseborough, Doug
    and conservation, 120, 122–124, 127
    and fur industry, 89
    moose management, 124–125
    obituary, 44–46
    partnership with, 123–124
    in RT's career, 30, 124
Ross, Dr. Heather, 187–188, 192, 195, 216
Royal Canadian Air Force (RCAF) base, at Winisk, 133
Royal York hotel, 73–74
RT. *See* Truman, Ron (RT)

# S

sailing, 28, 38–39, 76–77
Salway, Tony, 25
Sarnia, ON, solar energy, 165f, 170–174
SARS (Severe Acute Respiratory Syndrome), 98–99, 100
Sault Ste. Marie, bush plane museum, 69–70
schools
    comic book on energy, 153–154
    wildlife education, 122–123, 125–126
seal hunt, 88–89
*The Secret Life of Walter Mitty* (Thurber), 1–2
9/11, and crisis communications, 100, 101–102
Service, Robert W., 226
Sheard, Kelly, 203
Silver, Dr. Frank, 215–216
sleeping problems, 193
Smith, Kirk, 89, 93–94
Smith, Vivian, 39
Smithsonian Museum, 7–8, 10, 16
solar energy
    career overview, 4
    politics and policies of, 175–178
    public reaction to, 173–175
    RT's fit in and views on, 163–166, 177–178
    solar farms in Ontario, 163, 165, 168–178
    work at OptiSolar, 165f, 168–178
speech writing
    bad news in, 113–114
    as career, 110, 113
    energy and nuclear issues, 115–117, 154–155
    and Internet, 107
    and jokes, 109
    for ministers, 115–117
    at MNR and MoE, 114–117, 154–155
    overview, 72

    tourism industry, 100–101, 103, 106–110, 111–113, 114
    water resources issues, 110–111
    wildlife management, 114–115
"The Spell of the Yukon" (Service), 226
Sportsmen's Show (Toronto), 26–27, 32
SSRIs (Selective Serotonin Reuptake Inhibitors), 220–223
Strangway, Dr. Walter, 202
stroke
    after-effects, 208–209, 213–216
    description, 199–202, 204–205
    lability issues, 213–214, 219–221
    procedure on blood clot, 197–199, 203–205, 222–224
    recovery and exercising, 5, 202–204, 205–206, 208–213, 211f
    research and articles on, 222–224
    return from death, 198–200, 216–217
    and return to routine, 215–216
    RT's, overview, 5, 182, 197
    and SSRIs, 220–223
    writing work and interviews by RT, 181–182, 201–203, 223
Styles, Toby, 91
sunken ships stories, in *Globe and Mail*, 41–43
SuperBuild program, 102–103
Suzuki, David, 127, 168n58
Sweet, Linda, 38

# T

Tampa, FL, 185–186
Teasdale, Shirley, 78, 80
technology, change in, 147–151, 159
technology writing, overview, 145–146
telephones, change in, 147–151
television, 127–128
terrorist attack, simulation, 81–83, 94
thrombectomy, 203–204, 222–223
Thursday section of *Globe and Mail*, 34, 36–46

Toronto, cultural tourism, 102–103
Toronto Humane Society, 90
Toronto International Film Festival (TIFF), 101
*Toronto Star,* 111, 121
tourism industry writing
    crisis communications, 98–103
    overview, 4, 80
    and SARS, 98, 100
    speech writing, 100–101, 103, 106–110, 111–113, 114
    and water resources issues, 110–111
TransBord III exercise, 81–83, 94
trapping, 30, 89–90, 125
Travel section of *Globe and Mail,* 22
Truman, Charles (great-great grandfather), 8–9, 13, 14
Truman, Elaine (wife), 184f, 229f
    and heart problems of RT, 190, 193
    and stroke of RT, 200–201, 204, 209
Truman, George (uncle), 11f
    book about by RT, 8, 9, 10–11, 12, 15–16
    family adventures, 13
    around-the-world flight, 7–8, 9–12, 15–16
    living family, 15
Truman, Grandpa, 14–15
Truman, Harry S, 11, 11f
Truman, Ron (RT)
    dislike for bears, 69
    father's work, 85
    future at 30 years old, 1–2, 226–228
    reputation at newspapers, 43–44
    return from death, 198–200, 216–217
    shooting incidents, 139–140
    writer's block, 213, 214–215
    writing career (*See* writing career of RT)
    writing of *Polar Bears and Other Scares,* 215, 216–217
Truman family
    archives, 8, 9

Canadian branch, 14–15
cardiovascular problems, 183–184
Catholicism in, 85n19
character of members, 3, 13–14, 16, 85
in early North America, 11n2, 12–13
heritage and ancestry, 7–15
US branch, 9–14
wives and women, 13

# U

underwater archaeology, in *Globe and Mail,* 41–43
United States, tourism to Canada and 9/11, 100, 101, 102

# V

Venice, FL, 197, 200–202, 216
video production, 125
Visit Ontario Program (VOP), stories, 75–80
VO$_2$ max testing, 193–194

# W

Walton, Lloyd, 64
water resources issues, 110–111
Watson, Paul, 90
Western Hemisphere Travel Initiative (WHTI), 100, 103
Whistler, BC, downhill skiing, 23–24
Whitewater, BC, downhill skiing, 25–26
white water tours, 79
wilderness conservation
    Algonquin Park, 118–121
    education in, 122–123
    writing about, 119, 125
wilderness tours in Ontario, 73–80
wildlife management

consulting career, 30, 118–126
deer and moose, 29–30, 124–125
education in, 122–123, 125–126
end of work in, 126–127
influence of D. Roseborough, 123–124
*Landmarks* stories, 60–62
RT's interest in, 59
speech writing, 114–115
windmills, 152n43
wind power, 152n43
photo collection, 152, 153f
writing about, 151–152
Winisk, ON, 65, 129–130, 132–134
women
Cree crafts, 135–138
*Globe and Mail* stories, 38–40
photos by RT, 52
in Truman family, 13
and yachting, 38–39
wood burning, 152
worms in the office, 54–55
Worthington, Peter, 127
Wright, Orville, 7, 11
writer's block, 213, 214–215
writing career of RT
adventurous assignments, 2–3, 16–17, 52, 69, 70, 140, 227
beginnings and inspiration, 2
overview, 2–5, 17–18, 226–229
skill as writer, 71
*See also* crisis communications; *Globe and Mail*; *Landmarks* work; speech writing

# Y

yachting. *See* sailing

CPSIA information can be obtained
at www.ICGtesting.com
Printed in the USA
LVOW01s1408230416
484938LV00023B/155/P